THE MESSY SELF

THE MESSY SELF

EDITED BY

JENNIFER ROSNER

PARADIGM PUBLISHERS
Boulder & London

Copyright © 2007 by Paradigm Publishers

Published in the United States by Paradigm Publishers,
3360 Mitchell Lane Suite E, Boulder, CO 80301 USA.

Paradigm Publishers is the trade name of Birkenkamp & Company, LLC,
Dean Birkenkamp, President and Publisher.

Library of Congress Cataloging-in-Publication Data
The messy self/edited by Jennifer Rosner.
p. cm.
ISBN: 978-1-59451-291-9 (hc)
ISBN: 978-1-59451-292-6 (pbk)
1. Self (Philosophy) 2. Self. 3. Orderliness. I. Rosner, Jennifer. II. Title.
BD450.M4585 2006
126—dc22

2006022346

Printed and bound in the United States of America on acid-free paper
that meets the standards of the American National Standard for
Permanence of Paper for Printed Library Materials.

Designed & Typeset by Straight Creek Bookmakers in Adobe Caslon.

11 10 09 08 07   2 3 4 5

For my parents

CONTENTS

Foreword, *Arthur C. Danto*   ix

Introduction, *Jennifer Rosner*   xv

Acknowledgments   xix

Part I. Love and the Messy Self   1

A Strange Disorder, *Diane Ackerman*   2
My Tourette's, *Gayle Pemberton*   2
Conservation, *Debra Spark*   10
The Mommy at the Zoo, *Beth Ann Fennelly*   28
Prologue to *Psyche, Jane F. Crosthwaite*   30
Psyche in Love, *Wendy Wasserstein*   32
Since You Came, *John O'Donohue*   62

Part II. Self-Understanding and the Messy Self   63

The Clause, *C. K. Williams*   64
The Last Place on Earth, *Patricia Foster*   65
Facing North, *Mary Kinzie*   71
The Fiction of the Self and the Self of Fiction, *Rebecca Goldstein*   75
The Real Story, *Liv Pertzoff*   86
The Envoy, *Jane Hirshfield*   88

Part III. Self-Deception and the Messy Self   89

The Superficial Unity of the Mind, *Sarah Buss*   90
Kidding Ourselves, *Steven Pinker*   97
Man Alone, *Louise Bogan*   101

Part IV. Identification and the Messy Self   103

The Disappearance, *Ilan Stavans*   104
With Solomon Ibn Gabirol, *Richard Chess*   114

Gifts, *Faith Adiele* 115
Song of the Red Earth, *Meena Alexander* 120
We're All Colored, *Huston Diehl* 121

Part V. Well-Being and the Messy Self 131

Winnicott on the Surprises of the Self, *Martha C. Nussbaum* 132
Buried, *Carol Edelstein* 145
Legal Selves, *Robin West* 146

Part VI. Creativity and the Messy Self 163

Unimaginative, *Corwin Ericson* 164
The Man Who Mistook His Wife for a Hat, *Oliver Sacks* 167
"You..., there..., listening...," *Donald Morrill* 175

About the Contributors 176

About the Editor 180

≈ *Arthur C. Danto* ≈

Foreword: Beginning with Love— The Messes of Selfhood

"**I** THINK I KNOW PHAEDRUS ABOUT AS WELL AS I KNOW MYSELF,**"** Socrates says to his amiable companion in Plato's dialogue, *Phaedrus*. But a moment later, he leaves the reader wondering just how well Socrates really knows his friend, since he says, by way of deflecting an idle question put to him by Phaedrus, that "I can't as yet 'know myself,' as the inscription at Delphi enjoins. And so long as that ignorance remains, it seems to me ridiculous to inquire into extraneous matters." Accordingly, Socrates continues, "I direct my inquiries to myself, to discover whether I really am a monster, more complex and swollen with pride than the man-serpent Typhon, or a simpler, gentler being whom heaven has blessed with a quiet un-Typhonic nature." "You strike me as the oddest of men," Phaedrus observes, pointing out that though Socrates is a native to the countryside they are walking through, he is unable to answer questions about the landscape. To which Socrates responds, "I am a lover of learning, and trees and open country won't teach me anything, whereas men in town do." The implication is that in regard to the question of what he is, a main source of knowledge is what others think he is. Like Jean-Paul Sartre, of whom his lover, Simone de Beauvoir, once said that he was "allergic to chlorophyll," Socrates knew enough about himself to realize that he deeply belonged to the city. He only followed Phaedrus outside the city walls because he believed the latter possessed a text on love, which was, Socrates is made to say in Plato's other dialogue on love, the *Symposium*, the one subject on which he actually knew something.

What is the self, as an object of knowledge that even someone as clever as Socrates feels he lacks? It certainly must not be entirely transparent to itself if it cannot tell whether it is a monster. How will it ever find out? Probably Socrates will find out in the same way in which he might come to learn that Phaedrus is not a monster—by seeing how he acts in various situations. In that respect, the self lacks what philosophers call "privileged access" to itself. We find out what we are in the course of observing ourselves, in just the way we observe others. So Socrates really does know himself about as well as he knows Phaedrus—not very well at all. We are closed books, so to speak, as much to ourselves as to one another, and have to discover through inference what the books contain. A book is the evolving story of our life, which is disclosed to oneself as it is to others in the course of living that life and seeing how we respond to the various situations life throws our way. We know that Socrates was brave from the way he conducted himself in battle as a middle-aged man, and how, as an old man, he accepted the death penalty with grace. We know that he was hardy because he seemed indifferent to cold and hunger. But how much did he know before he found out how he behaved under the extreme conditions in which he found himself in the historical reality of his times? "I direct my inquiries to myself," Socrates told Phaedrus. But what exactly does that mean? It certainly cannot mean, as philosophers have come to see it, some extraordinary feat of introspection. Self-knowledge is not obtained by gazing into an internal mirror. It is acquired by seeing what we do, and for that we are in no better position than anyone else. Perhaps we are in a worse position, because we may have certain illusions about ourselves, which others see through before we do. What we are for ourselves is not necessarily what we are for others. That is why Jean-Paul Sartre famously said that hell is other people. We are always hostage to *their* knowledge—or at least to their opinions.

Sartre's picture of the self is of a fiendish apparatus of interfacing mirrors. There is a mirror in which we see our own image, which Sartre calls our self *for* itself.

There is always something that we are for ourselves, and Sartre went so far as to build that "for" into his analysis of the self: the "for itself" is indissolubly subject and object at once. But there is another dimension to the self, which he spoke of as *pour autrui*—our "being for others." The sad truth is that what we are for ourselves and what we are for others do not always coincide. We are each hostage to what others take us to be. That is why being with others is indispensable if we are to know what we really are. "I'll be your mirror," the Velvet Underground sang. If you want to know what you are, ask me. Without others to tell me what I am, I am lost—even if I don't especially like what they tell me I am. In the end what we are is a set of superimposed double exposures, a hall of broken mirrors at various angles to one another—a cubist composition, constantly revised.

That's as true of Socrates as it is of anyone. Xenophon's Socrates barely overlapped Plato's Socrates, and neither of their Socrates quite coincided with the Socrates of Aristophanes, who portrays him as something of a con man, something of a windbag, who could not easily be distinguished from the thinkers that Plato's Socrates thought most ill of—the so-called Sophists, who claimed the power to teach virtue to others and to win tough cases in the law courts. In fact the Socrates that Aristophanes portrayed in his savage comedy, *The Clouds*, directs a school that bilks those who come to acquire wisdom in exchange for their tuition. Most Athenians who saw the comedy would not have known Socrates personally, and could not tell caricature from truth—supposing that Plato's portrait of him is not itself a benign exaggeration. In Plato's *The Symposium*, the sexiest man in Athens, Alcibiades, declares in front of Aristophanes—as an admittedly drunk witness—that the legendarily ugly Socrates, contrary to appearance, is really the most beautiful man in Athens. What are we to believe? What is Socrates to believe if others are unable to agree on what he is? How is he to know himself when the mirrors won't agree with one another? No wonder Jennifer Rosner speaks of the self as messy. The mess in part is epistemological. If the self is subject and object at once, what exactly is it of which, as subjects, we are aware? Who can tell us if those who know us best are unable to? And what are the consequences if we cannot find out—if every man and every woman is a walking quandary of ineradicable ignorance of that which happens to matter most to him or her?

What we know is that the self is embodied, that our selves and our bodies are one—or nearly one. *Nearly* one, in the sense that there are parts and properties of our bodies that we know at best externally to be part of what we are, and that we know abstractly, affect our destinies, our powers, and our well-being. As a general rule we count as ours those parts and properties of our bodies that others who are part of our world are aware of as us. Socrates had a snub nose and protruding eyes, as well as a bald head and a pot belly. He is probably the only individual in the ancient world whose image we can identify without difficulty. Since others are our mirrors, Socrates certainly would have known what he looked like, even if he never saw himself in an actual looking glass. An important part or set of parts of our bodies is our sexual characteristics, which deeply define our destinies in life, and which the world does not easily let us overlook. Almost at the outset of our life, what we are and are to be is determined by the body's sexual configurations.

I once set out to distinguish philosophically between two intricately interconnected bodies, of which every human being is made—the body that is the self and the body that is merely ours. One difference is that the body that is the self lives in history and in culture—it *has* a history and *has* a life—while the body on which our life depends merely exists in time and space, like a tree. I called this "the body/body problem." At the time, I thought about how much is known about the body on which our life depends, in comparison with what was known about bodies at the time when Socrates lived. Anatomical knowledge has a history, and no one even knew that blood circulates until the sixteenth century. Today, we know how little is known about the brain; Aristotle believed the seat of the soul was the diaphragm. But of embodied selves, the Greeks knew pretty much what there was to know—knew about love and courage and pride and anger and the will and its weaknesses—even though each of us, as I said, must learn whether we are brave, or morally weak, or capable of love. That kind of knowledge, in contrast with medical knowledge, defines what we call human nature, and until recently, it has changed hardly at all through the centuries. It is as embodied selves that men and women were written about by the poets and the playwrights of ancient Greece, and when we read them, it is like seeing ourselves in an antique mirror. When Paris talks to Helen in their marriage chamber in Troy, everyone today understands exactly what they feel:

"Come, then, rather let us go to bed and turn to love-making.
Never before as now has passion enmeshed my senses, not when I took you the first time from Lakedaimon the lovely and caught you up and carried you away

in seafaring vessels, and lay with you in love on the island Kranae, not even then did I love you and sweet desire seize me." Speaking, he led the way to the bed; and his wife went with him.

It is still true that the way we get self-knowledge other than by living our lives is by reading the poets, who speak on this topic, as it were, in close harmony on the subject we as humans know most about. Our doctors can tell us about the body, but their knowledge, vastly more adequate than anything Aristotle or Hippocrates dreamt of, tells us little about the body that is the self. For that kind of knowledge Homer still can hardly be bettered.

Sexual identity is public and defined by the body, but it means different things to embodied selves at different times in history and in culture, and though the bodily difference between male and female is largely the same, everywhere and always, the topography of the sexed self varies depending upon where and into which culture we are "thrown," to employ a deep and useful concept of Heidegger's. What it means to be a man or woman from the perspective of the self has to be learned the way Greek or Latin is learned, as a system of meanings. Others tell us that we are boys and girls and what that means in terms of our own lives. And others try to test us to make sure that these lessons in self-identity are mastered. As the bodies that are ours develop and differentiate along sexual lines, the differences are not merely inscribed in the configuration of the protuberances and openings with which we find that we are endowed. The body that is the self and the body that is the self's are, as Descartes said in the great *Sixth Meditation,* "so intimately conjoined and as it were intermixed that my mind and body compose a certain unity." A *certain* unity, a kind of knot of language, thought, and flesh, of some of which the self is aware and of some of which it is not. How, considering its constant companion and their involuted relationship, could the self *not* be messy?

Jennifer Rosner is an analytical philosopher and a modern—or even, in certain dimensions, a postmodern self. As a young woman her self has been formed in a world whose defining question was: What is a woman? She came to her current situation in life by living through, with others, one of the tremendous changes in the history of self-consciousness, in which that question had no settled answer, and everyone—but especially every woman—was a pioneer. Men and women alike had to unlearn nearly everything and begin all over, and nothing has been the same ever since, nor will it ever be the same again. As it was for Socrates, the question of self-knowledge marginalized all other questions, however pressing those other questions were. Socrates lived through a war, for example, like and unlike the wars Americans have lived through in recent decades, and that experience certainly reshaped the persons whom Socrates taught to ask what they were—monsters like Typhon or creatures equally grotesque, or something simpler and gentler. No American of my generation could imagine, looking at how we have treated prisoners, that they as Americans were capable of such actions. But we see ourselves in the mirrors of the world, which hold truths disagreeable but undeniable.

In any case, Jennifer Rosner has wisely decided, acting for her generation and for those who have faced and will continue to face the prospect of having to come to terms with their identity, to follow the poets and to read stories. And again like Socrates, she recognizes that there is no better place to begin than with the subject of love. *The Messy Self* is for messy selves, there being, today more than ever, no other kind. The frontiers of the self, like the frontiers of art, are everywhere.

Jennifer Rosner

Introduction

"I am large; I contain multitudes."

—Walt Whitman

*"One must still have chaos in oneself to be able
to give birth to a dancing star."*

—Friedrich Nietzsche

THERE IS NOTHING SIMPLE ABOUT BEING A SELF. Even the drive for simplicity is complicated; the yearning for tidiness, messy. Being a self is messy and we are messy selves. We are ambivalent when we yearn to be resolute, and restless when striving for calm. Our feelings clash, our wills waver, our desires are incompatible. Our minds take leaps that defy logic; our dreams visit us as decodable illogic. We are only partly rational. Our growth is rarely linear. We can think in wishes and deny reality. Even as we doubt and deceive ourselves, we are creative, evaluative, and self-interpreting. And, always, we live with the possibility of falling apart.

The instability in our constitutions is not a modern phenomenon. It is part of human nature; it has been true of us for as long as we have existed. The ancients recognized interior conflict, but it was the moderns who squarely acknowledged the disorder, the irrationality, and the disharmony at humanity's heart. Freud, like Plato, conceived of the self as constituted of parts, ideally reconcilable yet always (and in reality) prone to clashing. But where Plato saw irrationality issuing from clashes among the self's elements, Freud saw irrationality inhering in the elements themselves, thereby locating the roots of our chaos and disorder far deeper than in the incidental clashing of ordered parts. Freud's view of the irrational self was echoed in other modern movements, like cubist painting, atonal music, expressionistic literature, and existentialist theory, each reacting against classical and Enlightenment themes and together eroding confidence in thoroughgoing rationality, order, and contented civilization. The self—and indeed the universe in its entirety—lay largely outside the categories of human understanding.

We manifest a variety of reactions to this modern diagnosis of unreason: reactions of struggle, of acceptance, of denial, and alternations between. Denial is a favored strategy when our messiness gets too uncomfortable. We tidy our work desks and our houses, and find ourselves buoyed by the promise that we *ourselves* might thereby be tidied. We saturate ourselves with antidotes to ambiguity and uncertainty, and grope for methods to reduce tension and ambivalence. We read magazines like *Real Simple*. We respond to the chaos that lurks beneath the thin veneer of civilization by rubbing another coat of polish on the veneer.

Our discomfort obscures the fact that breaks in reason enable creativity, that doubts lead to richer analysis and evaluation, that discordances bring texture to relationships that would otherwise be flat. The image of a tidy self is reassuring, yet falsely so. To tidy up our messes, or to deny them, can lead to an impoverished life: a narrowing of our aspirations, a stunting of our creativity, a less robust recovery from our traumas, paler friendships, and muted loves.

A messy self may be disconcertingly easy to relate to, identify with, and describe. But it is by no means easy to define. Indeed, a tidy definition will miss the point. My own field of contemporary analytic philosophy works predominantly with an ideal of the self as resolute, unified, and rational—an ideal I question, as surely as I fail to achieve it. This ideal is, of course, championed by the larger culture, with added emphasis on simplicity and its dangerous relative, oversimplification, exercised in much of public, especially political, discourse. I have felt propelled—by a sense of alienation from this ideal and the reductionism it encourages—to seek out new ideals and conceptions of the self that can accommodate the ambivalence, incoherence, and irrationality that mark our human experience. As a starting point, I have invited thinkers from a variety of disciplines to write of lives, and of selves, that are—in a word—*messy.*

At the risk of appearing orderly, the writings in this collection broadly span six categories: love, self-understanding, self-deception, identification, well-being, and creativity.

Love takes many objects and forms; it pulls us in many directions. In the words of Jonathan Lear, "it establishes an ever-present undertow." Some have thought that love is a longing for beauty or for goodness. Others have speculated that love aims to restore a lost unity with another. In Aristophanes' myth, as depicted in Plato's *Symposium*, love is a pressure to be reunited with our long-lost halves. In Freudian theory, it is a drive to restore our own pasts, a longing to return to an unindividuated, merged state.[1] In some traditions of thought, love ascends toward greater fulfillment, understanding, and flourishing; in others, love descends, with humility, into longing, incompleteness, and passivity.[2]

Certainly, loving is a messy venture in which boundaries blur, dependencies transfer, self-conceptions are lost and traded and reclaimed. Diane Ackerman aptly titles her poem "A Strange Disorder" and in it she deftly hunts out what is haunting both about caution and about passion. Gayle Pemberton celebrates love's power to affirm and heal, even if through tics, in "My Tourette's." In "Conservation," Debra Spark evokes sheer longing in a character's unmet desires for connection and comfort. Beth Ann Fennelly's poem "The Mommy at the Zoo" grapples with the dissolution of memory (and self?) in the throes of mothering. Jane

Crosthwaite's "Prologue to *Psyche*" orients us to the layers of identity contortion and moral challenge we confront in Wendy Wasserstein's heretofore unpublished play *Psyche in Love*. Wasserstein dramatizes love's messiness in a tale of betrayal and regained trust, through a sloughing off of sister-selves and a slathering on of beauty creams. John O'Donohue's "Since You Came" captures what utter transformation can come in the encountering of another.

"This ramshackle, this unwieldy, this jerry-built assemblage/this unfelt always felt disarray; is this the sum of me?" In C. K. Williams's poem "The Clause," we witness a mind reaching to unfold the layers of its own unknowability, and we share in its unease to forge on as it cannot help but do, with longing and with judgment. 64 In "The Last Place on Earth," Patricia Foster exposes an illness-shattered core, as she struggles against a breakdown that neither she nor her doctors understand. In Mary Kinzie's poem "Facing North," the self is out of place, a traveler-pilgrim for whom attempts at self-understanding and repair result in new brokenness. Each of these writings represents a quest for deeper self-understanding, for clues to identity, even legitimacy, and for pathways to wellness. Rebecca Goldstein examines the process of writing itself to show how we become receptive to large truths that transcend our personal experience when we enter into the lives of the fictional selves we write about and read. Knowledge seeps in as the bounds of personhood and time are loosened in our engagement with the selves of fiction. In "The Real Story," Liv Pertzoff artfully questions whether a bounded self, or story, makes any sense at all. In "The Envoy," Jane Hirshfield marvels at the unexpected comings and goings of understanding and feeling, at what mysterious messengers sometimes open, sometimes close, our pathways to self-knowledge.

Of course, our desires to know ourselves and our world are most times tempered by our suspicions and fears of what we might discover. The strategies by which we perpetuate our own ignorance and befuddlement are numerous, and whether we intentionally deceive ourselves or engage in less paradoxical strategies, there is no doubt that we do much to avoid facts about ourselves that would be difficult to confront. Perhaps human flourishing requires judicious doses of self-deception. Certainly, we can tolerate even injudicious doses without apparent loss of integration. In "The Superficial Unity of the Mind," Sarah Buss contends that an integrated sense of self requires only the most superficial unity. Our powers of self-interpretation enable us to accommodate a vastly heterogeneous set of impulses, and to tolerate, even if by glossing over, very deep internal conflict. According to Steven Pinker, what is intolerable to a sense of self is not its disunity, but the idea (and evidence) that one is not as beneficent and effective as one would like people to think. In "Kidding Ourselves," Pinker shows the ingenuity of minds threatened by the appearance (and reality) of a lack of "beneffectance." Louise Bogan's "Man Alone" pinpoints the estrangement from self and other that self-deception breeds.

Conflict among our desires, hopes, dreams, and beliefs may challenge our sense of authenticity, even if it does not challenge our sense of unity. What is it to be authentic? And how do we emerge as individuals, related to others through sameness and through difference, in the larger community? In Ilan Stavans's "The Disappearance," the authenticity of a self is so compromised—the boundaries of reality and fantasy so blurred—as to prompt an interrogation into the very nature of subjectivity, reality, longing, and a sense of belonging. Richard Chess reveals a person in a pained straddle of faith, longing for refuge in this vast universe, in "With Solomon Ibn Gabriol." "Gifts," by Faith Adiele, shines a two-year-old's light on burgeoning authenticity and identification in the face of racial, religious, and economic difference. Meena Alexander's lyric "Song of the Red Earth" carries us to the dust, the dissolution, of an irretrievable childhood identity. In "We're All Colored," Huston Diehl illuminates muddles of color perception as she recalls teaching elementary school in rural Virginia in 1970.

To *flourish* authentically in the larger social world—is it possible with all our messiness? Perhaps it is impossible *without* it. In "Winnicott on the Surprises of the Self," Martha Nussbaum examines the life and work of Donald Winnicott, a psychoanalyst for whom models of love, creativity, and good relationships necessarily presuppose the acceptance of messiness and imperfection in oneself and in others. When applied to society, Winnicott's ideas have rich implications for expression and growth. In "Buried," by Carol Edelstein, we find perfectionism posing a subterranean threat to wellness. Robin West explores the law's relation to messiness and well-being in "Legal Selves," especially with regard to domestic violence and sexual harassment.

Many believe that our well-being is enhanced by creativity.[3] Creativity itself requires a restless mind; imaginative leaps and associations require breaks in rational thought.[4] Corwin Ericson rails against some of his own leaps and associations in "Unimaginative." Oliver Sacks explores a fascinating collusion of pathology and creation in "The Man Who Mistook His Wife for a Hat." Donald Morrill conjures creativity's golden magic and its maddening limits in "You, there, listening …"

Perhaps it is because of our inherent instability, with threats to our integrity coming from inside and out, that it is also in our natures to impose order on our experience whenever possible. We categorize, organize, filter in, and filter out information about ourselves and the world around us. Moreover, we reflect on our desires and beliefs, and guide our actions in accordance with our reflections: we act for reasons. Certainly, we need to structure, in order to comprehend, the data of our experiences, and there is benefit to authorizing our actions through reflection and reasoned deliberation. Just as certainly, our restless minds need to break through the structures of understanding and the dictates of reason to make leaps in growth and creativity. Well-being may require the acceptance of ourselves as much in the ways we are *ir*rational as in the ways we are rational. *The Messy Self* is intended as a forum in which to highlight our self-complexities. Taken together, the writings herein analyze, accept, bemoan, resist, frown upon, and ultimately *celebrate* our essential messiness.

Notes

1. Jonathan Lear, *Love and Its Place in Nature: A Philosophical Interpretation of Freudian Psychoanalysis* (New Haven: Yale University Press, 1998), pp. 148ff.
2. For a fascinating and comprehensive discussion of love and its role in ethical thought, see Martha Nussbaum, *Upheavals of Thought: The Intelligence of Emotions* (Cambridge: Cambridge University Press, 2001).
3. See Mihalyi Czikszentihalyi, "Happiness and Creativity," *The Futurist* 31, no. 5 (September–October 1997) and *Creativity: Flow and the Psychology of Discovery and Invention* (HarperCollins, 1996).
4. For a wonderful discussion of creativity and rational disruption, see Jonathan Lear, *Open Minded: The Working Out of the Logic of the Soul* (Cambridge, MA: Harvard University Press, 1998).

Acknowledgments

I want to thank the contributors to this volume for their thoughtful, provocative, and original writings. I am extremely grateful for the editorial support and advice from Jason Potter at Paradigm Publishers, and David Lenson and Corwin Ericson at *The Massachusetts Review*. Many friends and colleagues gave me valuable advice throughout the production of this book. I want to thank Marilyn Abildskov, Chris Benfey, Lee Bowie, Michael Bratman, John Broglio, Melinda and Andreas Calianos, Christoph Cox, P. J. Ivanhoe, Michelle Joffroy, Sara Just, Keith Lucas, Becky Michaels, Meredith Michaels, Catherine Newman, John Perry, David Rosner, Nina Ryan, Gary Watson, Michelle Wick, Gideon Yaffe, and Lynn Yanis. Harry Frankfurt's wonderful writings inspired me again and again. I am most grateful to Bill Corwin, and to our daughters, Sophia and Juliet, for their boundless love and affection and for their continued tolerance of *my* ever more messy self.

I

Love and the Messy Self

❧ Diane Ackerman ❧

A Strange Disorder

A strange disorder rules the house
where lately slender method scared
papers into files neat as hedgerows
and caution laid its dropcloth everywhere.
Now books lie slaughtered on the rug,
the telephone rings, old letters dune
among bills and maps and coffee spoons
in a room spontaneous as a compost heap
where you work the oracle of my thoughts
and haunt the prison of my sleep.

❧

❧ Gayle Pemberton ❧

My Tourette's

I AM A SUCKER FOR WALTZES, although I have never danced one. Not only am I clumsy, but the slightest spin of my body makes me very dizzy. I have not been to an amusement park in nearly half a century, and were I to go, my movement would consist of going from one popcorn stand to another. It is not the waltz as dance that moves me, but rather its rhythm, which, more than any other time signature, is so expressive about love. Nothing beats a love song in waltz time.

My two favorites are "Lotus Blossom," a wordless beauty composed by Billy Strayhorn, and "They Were You" from *The Fantasticks*, written by Tom Jones and Harvey Schmidt. Strayhorn, who was the writing genius behind so many Duke Ellington classics, knew about love, I'm sure, and "Lotus Blossom" is a serene, yet thrilling waltz. "They Were You" represents all that the creators of *The Fantasticks* in its 42-year run hoped to achieve: simplicity, clarity, beauty—leaving us longing for the illusion that young love triumphs. The other great waltz from the show, "Try to Remember," has disappeared from the repertoires of many singers because it is nostalgic for September, and after 9/11, one does not easily sing of that month.

I suppose many people think of waltzes as old-fashioned, even though savvy songwriters still write love songs in three-four. I think of myself as old-fashioned and trendy, sometimes at the same moment. It can be messy and confusing, too, like love.

My parents were born before World War I. I did not factor the full significance of this until I became an adult, when I realized how great an impact it had on my childhood and adolescence. I feel it still. What was most obvious to me growing up was that my parents were at least ten years older than those of most of my friends. My older sister and I were late children. My mother was well into her thirties before she became pregnant with my sister, and she was thirty-eight, my father forty, when I was born. In fact, my parents were closer in age to some of my friends' grandparents. While there have always been forty-something parents pushing prams—especially fathers—it seemed rare in the middle of the 20th century to see forty-ish mothers doing it. What I knew as a child was that my parents, without articulating to me their hesitation or boredom, participated reluctantly in various parent-child activities at school, if they bothered at all. Neither was a candidate for lining up the cherubs at a Christmas pageant, chaperoning dances, helping the pep squad hang banners, or sitting in a PTA meeting devoted to lunchroom etiquette. I felt the consequences of their age every day as I grew up in the 1950s and 60s, in what they deemed appropriate clothing, recreation, and comportment. They were delightful, wonderful, loving people, and I adored them, but the answer to my entreaties of "may I" frequently was "no" unless they knew the parents sponsoring an event. And they didn't know the parents or the grandparents.

It was only when I began to place my parents' lives in a context wider than the walls of our home that I reached a sound understanding of their values and mores. All of my grandparents had been born in the 1880s in the Midwest, and all of them were intent on maintaining or gaining a place in the growing black middle class. The physical, psychological, political and social fallout from slavery was not just in the South; it was everywhere. My grandparents and parents became part of the racial "uplift" movement that sought to shake it off with every step forward. What this meant, in part, was the desire to live a life in defiance and contrast to degrading and painful racial stereotyping. It meant, in part, being black Victorians, believing that hard work and a secure family life were beneficial to both the public and the private good. My father was fond of saying, "everything in moderation," and he believed it, despite his own immoderate eating and cigarette smoking. And it meant, in part, making sure that they bore no resemblance to the caricature of black people as the quintessence of sexual aggression and licentiousness. I am sure that my parents never saw each other in the nude, and I recall the shock my sister and I experienced when our mother told us, years after the fact, that she had miscarried ten years after I was born. We had been sure that our conceptions were a result of the two times they had engaged in intercourse. We simpering teenagers were wrong, of course, but all of this indicated that in our home, sex was not a topic for discussion and that I had no idea what it was, even after I had been told the "facts of life." My sister and I have repeated the story many times of how serious my mother was when she proclaimed to my sister, "I'd rather see you dead than pregnant." Sarah Bernhardt could not have done it better.

Like any good Victorian, my father had a couple of pulp fiction novels in his room, with cover art promising hot times inside. I remember thumbing through one whose cover had a matador and a woman in a pose, I suppose, of ecstasy. If there were hot times inside, I never found them, the juicy parts making no sense to me. But my father knew that I had read the book, and he asked my mother to tell me that I was not to read such things. That was how communication on the topic of sex occurred in our home. My father would have considered it the height of impropriety to speak to his daughters about anything sexual.

I have inherited from my maternal grandfather a habit of making up silly songs. The first one I can recall I composed when I was ten. I decided that singing "I've got the cutest little bottom in the house" was a satisfying way to spend an afternoon. My father, shocked to hear me, directed my mother to tell me to stop. And I will never forget my mother's face when I ran downstairs after going to bed with a biology book from the library and asked her, "What is masturbation?" She paled and blurted out, fidgeting, "itmeansplayingwithyourself." Thanks, I said, thinking that I had been masturbating for many years with my games of solitaire, jacks, and riding all over hell and gone on my bicycle.

In adulthood, my sister discovered that one reason she had no dates in high school was because my father, who, in his work at the Urban League, helped black people find work, scared off any interested young men with his fierce countenance. Watching Preston Sturges' brilliant 1944 comedy, *Miracle at Morgan's Creek*, together one afternoon quite a few years ago, my sister and I howled at the surname, Kockenlocker, with William Demarest doing anything to ensure the virtue of daughter Trudy, played by Betty Hutton. "It would have been a good surname for us," my sister said. Or, to be even more precise, we both said out loud, Kockenblocken.

I do not mean to suggest that my parents were formal or humorless. On the contrary, we had a lively home, filled with laughter, spiced with silliness and sarcasm. My parents were thoroughly modern people with sophisticated, wry senses of humor. My father was a terrific dancer, light on his feet; he could foxtrot and Lindy Hop with the best of them. My mother, in a silly mood, would wave her index finger in the air and do a little trucking to a jazz record. They both loved music and bridge. My mother loved the movies. Their views of life, however, were informed by the 19th century. They only married when my father had finished college and some graduate school and had a secure job. They planned one child only when they could afford her, and this occurred several years into their marriage. The second child was not planned. And clearly, sex was something people did, but did not discuss. Given 21st-century America, there's something to be said for that.

Ignorance, innocence, repression and confusion about sex combined to create in the adolescent me an enormous sense of guilt and dread. I had a pretty and sexy friend, Gabby, who was starry-eyed in expectation of "doing the do," maybe with Wes Montgomery, as we listened to his incredible jazz guitar work on the little plastic phonograph in her room. The movies had given me some sliver of an education, but sitting in Gabby's room, I didn't know if I wanted to "do the do" with Gregory Peck or Harry Belafonte, with Deborah Kerr—who could fall into a kiss like no one else on screen—or with Gabby. I did fear that given the chance, I would be terrible at it, anyway, despite my sense that I was a passionate type.

My mind was a mess, my body frumpy, my outlook melancholic. I had no clue of how to flirt or to indicate that I was open to flirting. I was a stay-at-home teenager, college student, and graduate student. I also felt responsible not only for my personal failings since birth but also for the woeful state of the world. A friend of my sister had once done my astrological chart, and I was taken by her forecast that I "would never forget a cut or a kindness." I might have been saved an enormous amount of trouble had she made it clear that the cut or kindness had to be directed at me, instead of anything I witnessed, read about in the newspaper or saw on television.

To make matters worse, I suffered from an extraordinary memory. Not only couldn't I forget a cut or a kindness, I couldn't forget anything. Years after the event, out of the blue, without context or reason, I would be paralyzed by my memory of having fleeced, as Gabby would put it, a dime from my mother's coin purse when I was seven years old, or having failed to wash my hands before making salad. Then began the spiral of remembering a whole litany of my failures and sins of omission and commission until I placed my hands over my ears—as if that could help—to stop the noise inside. My exterior was breezy enough, and one had to get on with life. I had been taught, and I concurred, that public displays of just about anything fundamentally private or relating to expressions of love, hate, or insanity were unseemly. I had to uphold not only my self and my family, but also, as my parents put it, "the race." Walking down the street with my hands over my ears would not be fitting.

I am not aware of the existence of "black guilt" as in Catholic or Jewish guilt. Indeed, black guilt is a term reserved for discussions of our penal system and the assumption that black people in, or not in, the vicinity of crimes or charged with them—particularly men—are guilty. I was raised an Episcopalian, and no matter how close its liturgy and some of its high church traditions are to Catholicism, to speak of Episcopalian guilt should elicit giggles. Perhaps Episcopalian guilt is feeling bad about going to the golf course instead of mass. Clearly, the sources of my angst were not religious, or religious as we think of it.

Some years ago, I determined that the foundation of my extreme guilt was in my failure to live up to the standard of being a female in my family. I had not failed in any gender roles; they were not rigid in my family. My father enjoyed cooking and always did holiday meals; he scrubbed the bathroom and kitchen floors every Saturday and cleaned the toilets. My mother was good with money, and she always had a few spare dollars so that we wouldn't starve or wake up to a dark, electricity-less home. No, it had to do with a particular type of uplift in my family that at its core celebrated women who were light-skinned and/or pretty. Almost every woman in my family fit the bill. The only time I ever saw my mother as anything but graceful, kind, and elegant was after I introduced her to a couple I knew where the wife was quite homely and the husband very handsome. My mother seemed quite offended by them and later said words to me to the effect that where she came from, things like that just did not happen. So, I was not prepared, and no one prepared me, for a conventional life. I was prepared to serve the world in some capacity. The rub was that although my parents loved me to death, and I loved them to death back, they never expected me to enter into a romantic liaison with anyone. Such a scenario creates a pile of rubble at the foot of one's self-esteem and makes one likely to respond to the advances of a slug, a jerk, or someone with a similar messy situation.

I might have gone through life with my hands either literally or figuratively over my ears had it not been for a woman, Dana, with a similar mess, in my graduate years who took a shine to me—it was Deborah Kerr or Gabby after all—and gave me the opportunity to fall in love. It makes no difference whether one is thirteen, thirty, or ninety when it comes to first love. It's an unforgettable blush, rush, internal meltdown, and when it's gone, the mark it leaves on the heart is different from those that follow. I was Dana's experiment whom she dumped fairly quickly after her mother discovered what she was doing. I was not much wiser about sex when it ended, about two months after it began, but the experience served to confirm my certainty that regardless of everything, I was a passionate person, and that was good. To my wonderment, I had no rushes of self-deprecating memory during those magic two months. But when Dana was out of the picture, I developed what I call my Tourette's.

I doubt if I have a bona fide case of Tourette's Syndrome. People with the neurological disorder have involuntary verbal tics, rapid movements of their necks, eyes, and a range of other motor spasms. In the popular imagination, people with TS yell obscenities and racial epithets while walking down the street or in theaters or church. But, after Dana, whenever my mind, in leech-like fashion, glommed onto an unpleasant memory, I heard myself say, "Dana" and the memory disappeared. There were variations, like "Oh, Dana" or "Ah, Dana" or "Dana" and her last name—all *sotto voce*, of course. This went on for several years, until I fell in love again, experienced what was to become the usual nanosecond romance, and without my conscious intervention Dana magically became Gwen.

Fear was a powerful motivator for black people of the generations of my grandparents and parents. In their efforts to try to uplift themselves into full political and social citizenship in this country, failure meant succumbing completely to the capricious nature of race relations, which could change from hour to hour, from day to day, from benignity to malignancy in the blink of an eye anywhere in the United States. Success meant carving out a place of some relative security with the knowledge that given the tenaciousness of racism, in all likelihood there would be no full political or social citizenship. That place might be in a good neighborhood, a government job, or a psychological room fashioned in one's head. To create or find such places was difficult enough, but to do so while simultaneously seeking to subvert racial stereotypes was exhausting.

Nonetheless, there was enormous creativity that sprang from black America musically, literarily, in political and social theory, in speech, in walk, in sport, in art. Black people took pride in each other's achievements and in the cultural products fashioned, and sometimes improvised, from cauldrons of despair, stress, and resistance. Yet, the appreciation of public achievement or victory by many blacks did not translate into a private wholesale admiration for, quite literally, the color of blackness. Whatever one chooses to call it—self-hatred or a belief that light skin color, silky, straight hair texture, or Nordic facial features made a person "better"—the appropriation of an anti-black aesthetic by many blacks of all classes effectively destroyed the possibilities of real black solidarity in this country, the Civil Rights Movement notwithstanding. In the very private world of my family, there was solidarity and love that came from parenthood and kinship, as well as the certainty that, as a brown girl with unremarkable looks, I needed to be saved from sex because, in all likelihood, there would be no love. Not once in my life did either of my parents, remonstrating with me about some unattainable desire I had, ever suggest that I would understand them when I was married or had children. Both of my parents were surprised when my brown sister announced that she was going to get married.

I have been unlucky in love and made my peace with it. I am merely one of a band of people who keep things in balance and make it possible for others to find love with great success. My last failed love affair began as an epistolary romance that went on for a year and a half. If I were to count the days Kelly and I actually spent together the magic-to-tragic-to-quits arpeggio lasted eighteen days. I had never fallen so hard. So thoroughly overwhelmed was I that I felt the air leave the room when she was in it. Love like that is chemical, and it carries symptoms of a major disease for which there is no cure. As in other romances, I had been drawn to her by a promise of passion, but her passion turned out to be mostly rage. Whether she might have wanted to return my feelings and couldn't, or would not, could not take the risk that Gabby called "the big love," I'll never know. But for two years after it was over, I could not listen to music of any sort at all, and music keeps my soul alive. For three years, I had the return of a constant dull pain down my left arm that a doctor years before had diagnosed as "heartache" after she could find no physiological basis for the pain. At times in the ten years since the letters began, my Tourette's has been nearly a constant low hum as I spiral from the memory of something I should have said yesterday to a seventh-grade day when I accidentally bumped into a kindergartner on the icy playground, who banged her head and had to go home after recess.

"Kelly."

Poof.

On one level, I understand that my Tourette's helps me cope with my imperfections and mistakes, dashing the memory before it lingers long enough for me to revisit its pain. Saying the name of this decade's lost love cuts another wee slice from the mountain of sadness and regret that became my heart. Yet, I believe there is even more to my Tourette's and it functions as a psychological place I've created to maintain my sanity.

There are few pieces of literature written in English more evocative than Virginia Woolf's *A Room of One's Own*. In the episode of the tailless Manx cat, Woolf writes,

> The sight of that abrupt and truncated animal padding softly across the quadrangle changed by some fluke of the subconscious intelligence the emotional light for me. It was as if some one had let fall a shade. Perhaps the excellent hock was relinquishing its hold. Certainly, as I watched the Manx cat pause in the middle of the lawn as if it too questioned the universe, something seemed lacking, something seemed different. But what was lacking, what was different, I asked myself, listening to the talk. And to answer that question I had to think myself out of the room, back into the past, before the war indeed, and to set before my eyes the model of another luncheon party held in rooms not very far distant from these; but different. Everything was different. Meanwhile the talk went on among the guests, who were many and young, some of this sex, some of that; it went on swimmingly, it went on agreeably, freely, amusingly. And as it went on I set it against the background of that other talk, and as I matched the two together I had no doubt that one was the descendant, the legitimate heir of the other. Nothing was changed; nothing was different save only—here I listened with all my ears not entirely to what was being said, but to the murmur or current behind it. Yes, that was it—the change was there. Before the war at a luncheon party like this people would have said precisely the same things but they would have sounded different, because in those days they were accompanied by a sort of humming noise, not articulate, but musical, exciting, which changed the value of the words themselves.

Before World War I, a sensibility lived in Victorian and Edwardian rooms that the carnage of the war destroyed. The British upper class could not return to a kind of expectation or, dare I say, to a combination of arrogance, innocence and hopefulness, no matter how unreal or contrived. No British class could. My Tourette's is certainly not the hum of expectation, but rather, words spoken over the grave of a different sensibility, the one shared by my grandparents and parents.

There is a famous painting by Eastman Johnson called *Ride for Liberty—the Fugitive Slaves* from 1862. Johnson, who was white and from Maine, established his reputation painting blacks in various antebellum settings. In some paintings, he appears to be endorsing the plantation myth of happy darkies. In others, there is more ambiguity. In *Ride for Liberty—the Fugitive Slaves*, there is unambiguous drama as a husband, wife, and two children, on one horse, gallop across the landscape. The husband guides the horse with a young child braced against his stomach, as the wife—interestingly, of a lighter hue than her husband—holds a baby. The husband is guiding the horse forward, of course, but the wife, holding the baby, is looking over her shoulder to see if they are being chased. It is a motion forward defined by what has been left behind. A possible future, the present, and the past are caught in one single frame of a painting, and more than any other single image I've seen, it captures the sensibility of my parents. For them, everything, public or private, boiled down to a relationship to racial history. Life is Janus-faced. The parents of my friends did not seem to use such a calculus in raising their children. And the only parent who had anything public to say about it all, Satchel Paige, who probably had a few years on my father, offered contrary advice: "Don't look back, something might be gaining on you."

Erasing again and again a memory of my own failure and guilt, real and ersatz, via the name of someone I have loved, is more than a neurological tic. It is an odd affirmation of the success of my loving, no matter how short-lived or sad. It is also a paean to the resolute and fundamental belief in the inextricable link between the public and private that lived in the core of my forebears' hearts. With each "Ah, Kelly" I hold myself to an ideal of behavior and decorum born in the uplift dreams of my family, as I simultaneously deny the power of that ideal to anymore disrupt my self-esteem. The memory of failure, of looking back, is undone by the restorative affirming of love, of celebrating the forward-looking nature of love, even when it has failed.

My mother lived to be ninety-three. She developed dementia in the last year of her life, and long after she had forgotten the fact of my father or a marriage, or failed to make a connection between the faces of two women and some word called "daughters," she could recall an incident from her adolescence. My mother overheard one of her mother's friends, a Mrs. Johnson, prattling on about how my mother wasn't a great beauty. For three-quarters of a century, my mother—who *was* a looker—had held onto this moment, and she was only able to toss it away when all memory had left her. Sometimes sitting in her wheelchair she would begin to weep for no apparent reason. On asking her why, she would just say, "Mrs. Johnson." I may have inherited some propensity from her. I do sometimes worry that should I live to be an old woman, my speech may be reduced to a series of verbal hieroglyphs, in waltz time, of "Dana, Oh, Gwen, Ah Kelly, Ah, Oh, Oh."

Note

1. Virginia Woolf, *A Room of One's Own* (New York: Harcourt Brace and Co., 1981), 11–12.

Conservation

I T'S HIM," DANA SAID from her spot at the window, and Tom rose to join her.

Jerome was not the person Dana remembered: clean-shaved and suited, blond hair cut to a quarter inch of his skull, skin the pink-yellow of raw chicken. Now, in jeans and T-shirt, sparse hair cinched into a scraggly ponytail, mustache drooping over his mouth, he looked like some backwoods math professor, a man who'd traded equations for dope.

"God," Tom whispered. "That's *him*?" A question for Dana though she'd only met Jerome once, back when she and Tom were first dating.

"Well, *you're* the one who would know." Tom saw Jerome only a week ago. How much could he have changed since then?

"Get the door," Tom instructed.

"No, you. He's your friend."

Four years ago, Jerome was a rising star at the network where Tom was a news producer. Then he dropped out, joined an ashram or something. He flipped. That's what Tom said. At the time, Tom took his departure personally. After all, he brought the young man aboard and championed his ideas, which were invariably just cock-eyed enough to work. He argued for Jerome's quick promotion out of booking into news, a trajectory (had Jerome continued on it) that would have resembled Tom's own rise to the top of the network. "The guy's brilliant," Tom used to say. "A real maverick." And he wasn't one to compliment. If you said someone had hidden talents, Tom laughed. He liked his talents right out in the open, thank you.

And now here was Jerome, on a Sunday evening in early September, halfheartedly ambling up the path to Tom and Dana's place, as if this might or might not be a house he cared to call on. Stalks of collapsing daylilies lined the brick walkway, and the windows by the front door featured construction paper frogs that Benjamin, their eldest, made at school.

Dana was in the stairwell at the station, that one other time she met Jerome, Tom having stopped Jerome (in mid-descent to the newsroom) while he was in mid-ascent (to the tape library). This must have been back in Tom's early flush of enthusiasm about Dana, just after the unemployed macrobiotic whom no one liked. What a thrill to be with someone who had her own professional aspirations. "Jerome," Tom said, "this is *Dana*," the stories Tom told about Dana implied in the way he inflected her name. And Jerome did what? Nodded, hurried on?

Whatever it was, Dana felt embarrassed, though (as Tom insisted, or must have insisted, later) it was Jerome, not she, who should have felt odd. He shouldn't have been so impolite.

"Jerome!" Tom cried now at the door, raising his arms for an embrace.

Jerome extended his arm for a handshake, and Tom ignored the formality, stepping back to say, "Well, come in, come in." In sweatshirt and jeans, Tom had the avuncular manner of an old sports hero, welcoming the renegade teammate back into the fold. Dana tried to do the math on Jerome's age. If he came to the station not long after college, and stayed five years, and left for four.... Well, never mind. He was clearly out of his twenties, but perhaps because of his slack posture, or the way he dug two fingers into his T-shirt pocket for something (cigarettes?) that weren't there, or the slide of his pants off his hips, he had the aspect of a younger man.

"Let's sit, and I'll get you something. Can I get you something? Like some tea? We've got mate tea."

After all this time, Tom had discovered Jerome, working in the kitchen at the Lotus Seed, a health food store with a four-table café and a constant, inexpensive buffet of baked tofu, steamed kale, brown rice and the like. Both men had conditions—arthritis and asthma in the case of Tom, severe eczema in the case of Jerome—that they were trying to regulate through diet. They avoided alcohol and foods that made them mucousy. They knew the benefits of bromelain, boron and acidophilus.

"OK," Jerome said to the offer of tea, and Tom disappeared into the kitchen. From upstairs came the sound of the kids, bumping down a slide they had formed out of old sofa cushions.

"So, you're The Wife," Jerome said, joining her on the couch.

"That I am," Dana admitted. Perhaps he didn't remember that they met once before?

"And you do something …" This wasn't quite as rude as it sounded. He was trying to remember.

"I do do something. Sometimes I do."

Jerome grinned. "Sorry."

"I'm a conservator."

Jerome placed his hand behind his right ear and pushed his earlobe forward.

"Conservator," Dana repeated.

"An artist?"

"Sort of halfway between artist and scientist. I patch up old pictures."

Jerome nodded his head while rocking it side to side, as if he found this funny.

Tom came back with mugs.

"Thank you." Jerome took his tea with both hands then held it to his chest as if the mug were a little furnace.

"Well." Dana stood. "You two must have a lot of catching up to do."

Jerome raised his eyes, bemused. "Whose pictures do you patch up?"

"Well, at the moment nobody's. The chemicals were making me sick, so I've had to take a break. But I do have a job, if that's what you're asking. I work part-time at the Museum of the Astonishing Mind."

"The what?"

"It's a …." There was never a quick way to explain the Museum. "It's a workshop for outsider artists. Generally people who are developmentally disabled or in some way mentally ill. I help the artists. And we have a gallery out front."

Jerome reached into the neck of his shirt to scratch his back. She sensed that he didn't want her around. Which didn't surprise her. There was a charge that bordered on the sexual between Tom and the people he employed. They wanted his attention; they wanted their stories on air. The brief exchange about her employment was a digression in the business of the evening, which was … well, who knew? It wasn't about a story.

"So maybe I'll stop by some time," Jerome called, as Dana was leaving. She smiled vaguely. Both her father and her husband were important men within their fields, and Dana had long ago made peace with the attention they received, the way it nudged her just out of most people's consideration. If people paid attention to her, it was normally to get at the men in her life. "Yes, I'll definitely come for a visit. I'll make a day of it. First, your place. Then …" He made a woop-de-doo loop with his forefinger. "The Institute of the Incredible Kneecap!"

"I'm sorry?" Dana said.

"Or maybe the Ankle Atelier. Or the Great Groin Gallery. I've always meant to go there."

"Was it good to see him?" Dana asked, when Tom finally came to bed.

"I guess. He's funny, isn't he?"

"I thought he was rude."

"Nah. He just doesn't see things as other people do."

And yet he saw Dana as a housewife, amusing herself with a part-time job while the kids were at school. That was clear enough.

"He hasn't been in touch with anyone else over at the station. Doesn't want to. 'Greasy socialists,' he said." Tom's own voice twisted into the slight mocking tone she already recognized as Jerome's. "Why—he kept asking me—should he go back?"

"So?"

"So what?" Tom said, a touch of irritation in his voice. He didn't like to chat once he was in bed for the night. He liked to sleep.

"So, how was it? Did you learn anything more about what happened to him?"

"No, why should I?"

For a man in his job, Tom was strikingly uncurious. Dana wondered if his colleagues ever hated him for this, the way he dismissed a line of thought by refusing to pursue it.

"Never mind."

"Don't get angry."

"Well, I *am* angry. It was just a question."

"It was just a question back."

Dana huffed. This could spiral out of control. Someone might drive off in a car in a few minutes.

"Oh," Tom said, conciliatory but also annoyed that he had to offer something else. "I forgot to tell you. When the kids came in…"

"I'm sorry. I tried to keep them away."

"No, it's OK." He began to laugh. "Jerome asked Sarah what she wanted to be when she grew up. And she said…" Tom waited a beat. "'A giraffe.'"

Her marriage, Dana sometimes felt, was an argument about the relative merits of what you did in the world versus how you lived in the world. On the side of the former were Tom's unfailingly interesting colleagues, men (and sometimes women) who'd invariably just returned from Baghdad or Sarajevo. On the side of the latter was Dana's perfect pleasure in her kitchen, where she was now making lentil soup. The kids were down the street at a birthday party, the afternoon light cut through the room, the trash can formed its long, regal shadow, and Dana remembered how, as a girl, she'd study dust motes in a light beam and think she was finally getting a handle on how everything in the world really was, all that was really *there*, if she'd just still herself and *look*.

The doorbell—comically loud—jolted her back into the world. For a time whenever it rang, the kids staggered backward then collapsed on the floor. "These sound waves," Benjamin explained, after his first pratfall, "are really rough."

"Oh, hello." Dana's voice wavered. Such a surprise to find Jerome at the door. She'd assumed it would be a neighbor kid, selling magazine subscriptions.

"Just thought I'd come for a visit."

"Oh." She couldn't remember the last time someone stopped by unannounced. "Tom's gone, I'm afraid. In Canada, on a story, that CEO of Graphic Maps, you know the pedophile." The story was in all the papers.

Jerome peered behind her. Did he think Tom was back there?

"Not that you aren't welcome to come in." She stepped back, making way for Jerome.

"Actually—" Jerome palmed the back of his head, the very caress Dana gave her kids before they went to sleep. He squinted. "I wasn't looking for him. I was looking for you."

"You were?"

"Want to go swimming?"

"Swimming?"

"Tom says you love to swim."

"I do." Under what circumstances might Tom have revealed this? It seemed too minor for even desultory conversation: My wife likes artichokes. My wife swims laps at the Y.

"So … there's this spot I found. On the Gunpowder. If you want to."

She knew the Gunpowder, a river north of her home, had hiked there once.

"Well, I've got to get the kids at four."

Anyone else would have heard this as a no, but Jerome looked at his watch and said, "Great. That gives us plenty of time."

He drove. An ancient Ford Fiesta, so rusty that the passenger side floor offered a dime-sized view of the road, tar lightening into gray and eventually the dusty tan of a dirt road. The strangeness of the outing lifted with the beauty of the day—warm, but not oppressive, a light breeze, pumpkins dotting fields as they turned off the highway. The season would end but here it was: one last chance for a summer pleasure.

"So." She turned to face Jerome fully. He was bleeding just behind his right ear, the skin there chapped and angry. "You have a twin I heard." Tom mentioned this before Jerome's previous visit.

"Yes. That I do."

"Do you look alike? I know twins don't like that question."

"Hmmm?"

"Do you look alike? You and your twin?"

"I wouldn't know. I haven't seen him in years."

His manner warned Dana off asking how come. Her shorts felt tight over her bathing suit bottom. She did not really want to stand in the equivalent of underwear before Jerome. She might have weighed this disinclination a bit more, before she agreed to come. The dirt road grew rocky, but Jerome didn't slow for the change in terrain. "Can I ask about the time you were away; what you were doing?"

"I don't see why not."

It would be matronly, of course, to suggest he slow down.

"So…" Dana said leadingly.

"Let's see. For a while, I traveled in the South Pacific. Later, I was a Buddhist monk."

"Really?"

"Well, I wanted to be a nun, but they wouldn't let me."

Dana laughed.

"And I went to Switzerland after that."

"Why Switzerland?"

Jerome smiled, as if grateful for a question he was willing to answer. "I heard about a choir that sang in a Romanash church there. Boys' voices. The beauty, people said, was beyond compare. I didn't know what such a thing would sound like—beauty beyond compare. Not something you usually trouble yourself with in the news business; there's all that tragedy and scandal to get to first. So I went to hear it. Only I went in the wrong season. The concerts were given in the summer, but I stayed, because I met a shepherd who needed help with his herd." After a moment, he added, "I learned how to make cheese, then I came back here, because I'd left without finishing something."

"What was that?"

"I don't know."

This was a little Zen koan for Dana, or so she supposed. It didn't make her curious. It irritated her. As koans did. There was something swarmy and self-righteous about the impossible puzzle, though what she knew of Buddhism otherwise attracted her. She'd like to practice a little non-attachment right now and not feel so bothered by the conversation. Jerome and she were having a silent tug-of-war, though over what, she couldn't say.

Jerome turned the car into a narrow road, a tunnel of trees ending in a small clearing. There was no beach but a dirt path that cut between the foliage then led steeply through shrubs and down to the river.

"I'm not going back to the network. I do know that. I'm not interested in that sort of probing anymore. And no more news. I don't read papers anymore. No TV." He laughed. "After all those years of being so plugged in, it's a relief, I tell you."

This confession thawed something in him. Or maybe it was stepping out of the car, pulling off his T-shirt for the heat of the sun. She disrobed on her side of the car; he on his, emerging in yellow swim trunks to say, "This way." He started toward the path. Dana took some comfort in the cushion of flesh at his abdomen. Some evidence of…what? Excessive desire? Occasional laxness?

"And you?" he said. "Tell me about this astonishing conservation work."

"Oh," she waved her hand at his back as if to dismiss the topic. The truth was now that Benjamin was five, and Sarah was four, she might not return to work. She had never truly been certain that her reaction to the chemicals in her lab—it started with lacquer thinner and turpentine—wasn't a sign. She was altogether too consumed with the business of knowing and being known in the art world. (She still commuted to her job at the National Gallery, when she first got sick. If she worked in Baltimore, people would forget her, or, worse, confuse her for a mere restorer. At the time, such things mattered to Dana.) "It all turned out to be a little more bureaucratic than I bargained for, though once I got to do a Renoir, which was how I met Tom."

"Is that so?" he turned, cocked his head in the "do tell" posture of a girlfriend.

"He came in to produce a story on the restoration. I was telling the reporter—Harry Terry, do you know him?"

Jerome climbed up on a rock that bordered the river, then said, "Don't think so."

"Well, I was telling Harry about how you're supposed to match the technique of an era, when a cameraman interrupted. 'Ask her if she'd piss on an Andy Warhol. If she had to.' Harry rolled his eyes. 'Andy Warhol's piss paintings. It's a legitimate question,' the cameraman kept saying. Finally, Harry turned off his microphone.

"'Sorry,' he said to me, then handed the microphone to Tom and said, 'you fire that guy, or I'm quitting.'"

"And?"

"Tom fired the guy. On the spot." He was courageous, in his way, had that cowboy-reporter thing that always attracted and intimidated Dana. You got the virtue—if it was a virtue—if you married it. You didn't need to have it yourself.

Jerome dove into the river. "It's deep," he called out, when he emerged, shaking water off his face. "It doesn't look it, but it is."

Dana stepped gingerly in, waiting till she reached her waist to dive under. The water was cool and clear, the river's muddy look just an effect of the riverbed. Something—maybe a trout?—slicked by Dana's leg, and she went under again, began to swim. She did love swimming, almost more than anything, and a river swimming hole was the best: the water's skin against one's own skin, the child-like pleasure of neutralizing sound by floating on one's back, the illusion that the water (because it moved) was fresh. And talk. There was no pressure to talk when you swam. "Oh, God," Jerome said as he dipped in and out of the river. "Oh, God." It made her think of some Chekhov she read in college, some story where men bathe in a pond together, and one old man can't stop saying, "Oh, God," as he splashes water over his face. Or something like that. Jerome looked like an emaciated walrus, water streaming down his hair (still in its ponytail, she wondered if he ever let it down) and through his moustache, over his now slick back. He kicked over to Dana, put his finger to his lips and whispered, "Look." Downriver, a stately blue heron stood motionless by the bank.

They pulled themselves from the water, some 45 minutes later. Dana needed to get home for her children. "I came back to Baltimore," Jerome began, as if he now knew her well enough to answer the question she posed earlier. "Because I need to learn how to be around people. I kind of forgot how."

"Hun."

Tom. They spoke every day, even when he was on assignment. She could picture him running his hand over his high forehead, as if still surprised by the retreat of his hair from his face.

"I fell asleep." She could smell the river on her skin, her pillow slightly damp from her hair. "God it's only eight."

"How are the kids?"

"Fine. Fine. Asleep." She felt groggy and distracted. "They went to Leif's birthday party, came home exhausted."

"Glad you got a break."

"I made soup." Her voice was tight.

Why did Tom always assume she vacationed during her non-parenting time? And yet, hadn't she? Today, at least? She didn't want to tell him about her outing, as if this would contradict a message she never could convey: when *he* was parenting, she was paying bills, cooking, folding laundry, buying food.

"Right. Well, I'll let you go back to sleep. I'll try to get you in the morning. Okay?"

"Okay."

At work the next week, Dana was helping Susan McFlarrety choose colors for a 16-foot-long scarf, when she looked up and saw Jerome, standing next to the loom. Susan—a squat woman, given to butting her head against walls—followed Dana's gaze then turned to Jerome and cried, "I made this!" She held up a scarf, which promptly unrolled, like a medieval scroll, to the floor. Susan protested when workers at the Museum encouraged her to make items of a more practical length. Jerome lifted the scarf's corner, carefully considered the weave without offering the cheerful, high-pitched praise of most visitors to the Museum.

One-armed Kylie approached Jerome and said in her slurred voice, "What's your name?"

"Jerome," Jerome said gamely.

"Jerome." Kylie rested her head on the pillow of his chest. "I love you, Jerome."

"I love you, too," he said automatically, glancing at Dana, "but you understand this can't be an exclusive relationship, right?"

Kylie wandered back to her button collection. She'd spent the morning deciding then re-deciding which buttons she wanted to glue to the frame of an unfinished painting. "I'm too *tired* to paint," she announced theatrically earlier in the day. And the staff let this disinclination to effort stand. At any one time, half of the twenty clients were merely drifting through the Museum's six small rooms.

"I thought I'd come see you," Jerome said to Dana. "Maybe take you to lunch."

The workshops themselves—with their loony, life-sized puppets staring out each window, their lopsided sculptures decorating the minute front lawn—occupied a corner house near a dilapidated shopping district. Nearby, the only place to eat was Jenny's Pub, a dark grotto, even at mid-day, serving things like nachos and potato skins. Jerome—committed to sobriety, denizen of the tofu ether—probably never went into restaurants like this.

"What can I get for you?" a waitress said enthusiastically.

"I'll have some tea," Jerome said.

"A bowl of minestrone soup."

"Did you see the specials? We've got shrimp poppers for $6.95 today."

"I think we're set," Dana said.

"And there's a chocolate mud pie dessert. You won't want to miss that."

"Like I said."

Dana turned from the waitress to Jerome. "Well, this is a treat. Getting to go out and all." He waited. He seemed eager, as if ready for Dana to be quite interesting, the evidence of her conversation so far notwithstanding. She should hazard something about the artists with whom she worked, the curlicue track of their minds, the images they obsessively repeated. "My husband," she began instead, not sure of how she planned to finish her own sentence. "He… He thinks quite a lot of you."

"I suppose I've always wondered what he thought of me."

"He thinks you're brilliant."

Jerome laughed dismissively.

"And now the brilliant man encounters a shrimp popper." She meant this as some frank reference to herself—you got political analysis and a thorough comprehension of world history from Jerome; from Dana, you got a restaurant that offered shrimp poppers. But she saw instantly that it must sound like she was asking him to contradict her with praise.

"In fact," he said slowly, hand rising to the back of his neck, his stare overly direct, "I had some popping in mind."

She flushed. What was *that* supposed to mean? Something crude?

Dana hadn't liked being single, back when she still lived in upstate New York, or in her first years in Baltimore, but she hadn't quite lost the desire to be pleasing to men. She'd developed a mild, flirtatious manner in her twenties and thirties, and she fell into it, even now that she was married and had two kids, and found the whole spectacle of her flirtation humiliating. There was a slight pause while she processed Jerome's words then answered with a campy, mock enthusiastic, "Well, *that's* what we like to hear."

And so began Dana's crush. Which went as crushes do, harmlessly at first, with Dana enjoying her brief encounters with Jerome at the Lotus Seed, her awareness that she dressed more nicely when she went shopping there. And, too, with her trying to gauge his interest. Was it an accident that he visited when Tom was out of town? That hand that brushed hers as he rang up her Lotus Seed purchases? Just a hand, or something else? It was all very high school and dumb, and she could hold her thoughts and the silliness of those thoughts together in her head without much agitation. But then, something… didn't quite change, but her internal narrative heated up. She imagined Jerome kissing her, the slight sag of their bodies into one another, the relief of the kiss, the kiss as confession. Jerome pulling her into a bed, the specific hotel where she would meet him, and the ruse that would get her there, the train of the life she wanted chugging alongside the train of the life she should live.

All of it fantasy. She was as loyal as a rock. Put her somewhere and, barring an avalanche, she stayed.

At night, there was the possibility of switching this longing to Tom, of reversing their current sexual dry spell. "It's not that I'm not interested," Tom said, once home. The kids were asleep, but as Dana began to kiss Tom's neck, he pushed her away. He needed to unwind. He wanted a beer and to watch part of the ball game. Dana couldn't blame him. There had to be a small part of the day when you weren't answering another person's demands. She'd had her own stretch, after the kids were born, of being too tired for sex. And it wasn't like she had lots of energy now. By the time Tom came to bed, Dana was invariably asleep.

The bells of the Lotus Seed's wooden door clanged behind Dana. She grabbed a basket and looked around. No Jerome stocking produce at the front of the store, no Jerome at the cash register, no Jerome stirring a pot of something behind the back counter.

She shopped anyway. She liked this place so much better than the supermarket, the small comfort of the vegetables' claim to be organic, the musty yeast smell, the row of "healthy" cookies. It didn't really bother her that it cost more.

A door at the back of the store banged open and shut. Jerome coming from some basement storeroom. "Hey," he called, "I've just been thinking of you." This admission gave her the requisite thrill. "Can you sit?" He pointed to the café tables, empty now that it was 3:30.

"A little bit. I've got to get the kids at 4:00."

"Mind if I take a break?" Jerome turned to ask a tall, skinny white girl with Rasta hair and a pierced nose and lip.

"No problem-o," the girl said leeringly, giving Dana an appraising glance.

"So," Jerome began, as he sat, "I was just over at the Baltimore Museum of Art looking at paintings and thinking how much I'd have liked to have you with me, explaining things. I was looking at all that Dutch stuff, those still lifes."

"Oh, yeah, they're meant as moral directives. Like fruit, youth is luscious. It too will rot. All things must pass. All that vanitas stuff."

"Thus the skulls next to the grapes. Yes, I think I got that."

Dana felt vaguely deflated. She'd never have guessed how the still lifes were meant to be read if she hadn't been told, back in college. "And contemporaries would have gotten all that symbolism, too."

"Unlike us. We're left to trod through the muck in our fluffy slippers."

"That's us, all right."

"Well, listen. I stepped up to one of the paintings, close, when the guard wasn't looking. There was something reflected in the shine of the apple, a window from behind the viewer, or something. I couldn't quite tell. So I stepped up and touched it." Jerome tapped the air with his finger to illustrate.

Dana jumped at this, as if it were she, and not the painting, he had touched. "You shouldn't..."

Jerome gave her a wry look.

"Well, you *shouldn't*. There are oils in your finger that can really damage—"

"Thanks, Mommy," he said, snide, and Dana felt what she never felt as a mommy—a desire to hit him. "The thing is," he added, hunching forward, "a bit of the paint came off on my finger." He looked down at the pad of his forefinger as if paint still there.

"It's flaking."

"That's it! That's what I wanted to ask you. What do you call that, if the paint comes away. I left a note in the museum's comment box that said the painting was chipping, but I knew that wasn't what I meant. So how do you fix that? Could *you* fix that if you tried?"

"It *used* to be that you removed the painting from a stretcher and put it on a new canvas. But if the damage isn't that extensive, you use adhesive to prevent the painting from flaking more."

"Makes sense. You want to figure out how it can stay together, before you imagine some deception."

"And certain people don't paint the flaking parts. They leave them blank and just try to stabilize what's there." Dana looked at her watch. "Gotta go."

They stood for a farewell, a hug and kiss on the cheek having become standard between them, as it was with most of Dana's friends, but then she bent her head and briefly brushed his shoulder with her lips. She hurried for the door, instantly ashamed. It wasn't really a kiss. Oh, how she hoped he wouldn't register the gesture, that he'd think (but, of course, this was a mother's thought) that she was merely wiping her nose. "I love you," Dana always said to Sarah, "but I am not a tissue."

It started stupid, as their fights always did. Tom and Dana were driving to Philadelphia, a city Tom knew but to which Dana had never been. The occasion was the second wedding of Dana's old college roommate. Hennie—a friend from work—agreed to baby-sit, and she managed to act (bless Hennie) as if Tom and Dana were doing her a favor, giving her time with their wonderful children. Not that Dana was for arguing against her kids' virtues, but really.

"Well, she *is* lucky," Tom said, shortly after they drove off. "She'll never have any herself."

"She still might."

"Not likely."

But that wasn't what started the fight. What started it was a traffic jam. Dana dozed, and when she woke, they were in the middle of it, backed up (from the looks of things) for miles. Tom cursed. There was a cocktail party that night. All of Dana's old friends. The wedding wasn't till lunch tomorrow.

"It's OK," Dana said. "If we miss it, we miss it. We'll still get there for the wedding."

"Just . . . fuck," Tom said, hitting the dashboard. "Fuck, fuck, fuck."

Dana's father had rages over traffic, and she and her sisters used to sit—very good and very cowed—in the back seat, as their mother said, "Your father needs some quiet now." The old bad daddy gets what he wants, no matter what. That was the lesson of Dana's childhood. The famous man rules.

"Your manner isn't moving the traffic." Dana struggled to keep her voice even. "It's just making it a drag for me to sit here. We could talk, or something. This could be an opportunity."

"*You're* the one who's been sleeping."

She was quiet, then said, "So what're you working on at the station?"

"This and that."

"Like what?"

"Well, we're going to do a report on that new drug-resistant staph infection. Maybe as part of the flu coverage. Three babies and a college student have already died of it."

"How horrible."

"It's not horrible. It's a good story."

"I mean the deaths, for Christ's sake. How horrible about the deaths. Losing a child to a stupid infection. I'd never get over it."

"You think I would?"

"No, no, never mind." This was impossible. She could not get engaged in a conversation with her own husband. All they ever managed to do was trade anecdotes about their kids' cute behavior. "I saw Jerome yesterday."

"Yeah?"

"I was getting some stuff at the Lotus Seed. He seems really interested in my conservation work."

"That guy is a lost cause."

"What, may I ask, makes him a lost cause?"

"I think that's obvious."

"That he doesn't work for you anymore?"

"No, no, he doesn't need to work for me, but he gave it up. He gave everything up to live like some college kid, clerking at a store, and reading his philosophy books. He can't possibly be happy doing what he's doing."

Jerome might stop by, it occurred to Dana, while Tom and she were away, and he'd meet Hennie. Dana could picture him, arm above his head, propped against the door frame, his ready-to-talk posture, and Hennie saying something outrageous then laughing her laugh, a beat too long and loud, a shade too antic, but appealing all the same, and Jerome leaning down, cupping her chin, for a kiss.

"There's more than one way to live a life."

"Did I say there wasn't?"

"Yes, yes, you said there wasn't. You say it in everything you do. You…" She broke off, her voice choked with angry tears.

"What's gotten into you?"

"Oh, fuck off, would you? Just fuck, fuck off."

He was silent.

"The happy couple," she said, "off on their romantic weekend."

In the morning, before the wedding, a group of Dana's old college friends met at the Barnes. Dana had seen the prints that were finally released of the museum's collection, but the place itself was a surprise: a big Matisse hung high on the wall of the first gallery, an unfamiliar Seurat nearby, the strange order and symmetry of the paintings—if a picture of an apple graced an entrance to a room, a picture of a pear adorned the exit. House museums were Dana's favorite. She loved the Frick in New York and the Gardner in Boston. The artwork was almost irrelevant to the whole experience of the place, the daydream of Old World wealth and social customs into which the building invited you. *It must have been like this. And this. And this.*

Tom and Dana had gone to bed angry—no sex, of course—and been tensely polite on the drive to the museum. Once there, Tom stomped ten yards ahead of the others. Eventually, Dana lost sight of him altogether; he was moving so quickly through the galleries. In the end, she found him sitting on a bench by the exit.

Under these circumstances, a wedding ceremony would surely be excruciating—all that talk of respect and mutual affection—and it was. Twice, Dana left her lunch table to sniffle in the bathroom. She shouldn't have married Tom. She shouldn't have. She had not a thing in common with him. And yet, he was the bargain she'd made with herself. And why?

But the question was entirely disingenuous. She knew why. She wanted kids. "All those years," she joked to her friends back in Albany, "what I thought I wanted was a guy. What I really wanted was a four-year-old." Benjamin and Sarah's snuggly affection; it was worth everything.

"It's OK," Tom said when she came back to the table the second time. "It's OK. Whatever happened, let's just move on from that now." His voice was placating, somewhat wheedling, and she hated him afresh. He reached over and gave her hand a double squeeze; he did the same before the justice of the peace when they married, the only secret part of the ceremony, and the gesture had become their code for love.

"I don't know what I'm doing with you."

Tears sprang to his eyes, and she felt equal parts shame and satisfaction in seeing she'd hurt him. "Dana," he whispered, but everyone at the lunch table was lost in conversation and wouldn't have heard anyway, "sometimes you really say terrible things."

"Any visitors?"

"Huh? This weekend? No. Were you expecting someone?" Hennie had plaited Sarah's hair into a row of neat braids, each ending in a handmade bead. That had been the project for the weekend: making and painting beads. Benjamin wore a necklace of them, which he refused to take off.

"No, I wasn't expecting anyone."

Tom came downstairs, Benjamin in his arms, wrapped in a towel. Tom was singing, "And then the water drains out of the bath. And then we go downstairs and find pajamas. O where O where O where are the pajamas? In the laundry room. Oh, in the laundry room." He stopped in the kitchen to say to the women: "Our Life. The Musical."

Tom's sweetness made her feel worse. They apologized to each other on the drive home, said they felt sick—physically sick—and they did. They always did after their fights. For at least a week, they'd be careful with one another—and Dana would try to abandon the notion that one should be able to talk easily with one's spouse—but then they'd fight again. None of it would stop the affair—the affair in her head—from growing torrid. Jerome and she would have the ferocious, sweaty sex of her 20s, the pre-Tom sex. And why not? If you took a poll, wouldn't most people admit to surviving this way, through their imaginary lives?

She pictured herself asking Jerome this very question, saw him nod as if in agreement then say, "Sure. Most people who are incarcerated."

"I finally found out what happened to Jerome," Tom said, the next night, as he undressed for bed. "His brother died. That's what happened four years ago. His twin killed himself. Because he thought he was a failure at business. Which, I guess, he was. But Larry"—Larry was one of the morning news anchors—"says that's why Jerome quit. He didn't want to end up like his brother."

"My God."

"And here's another thing. He found out from the TV. A local news broadcast. The brother killed himself out in the woods, and I guess at first police thought there might have been a crime. You know, police have revealed the identity of the man who…"

"Jesus. His brother?"

"His *twin* brother."

"Well, that'd fuck you up. God, that's so sad. What about the rest of the family?"

"What about them?"

"I don't know. Are his parents still around? Other siblings?"

"I just *told* you all Larry *told* me."

There was a potential for their weekend fight to flare up again—and around this tragic news. Why couldn't he just talk like a normal person? If he'd said, "I don't know. I wondered about that myself," Dana wouldn't have an urge to throw the novel in her hand across the room.

It was cold. Dana sat by the window of a fancy coffee bar. She was in a tony neighborhood, near the Walters and lined with townhouses, not far from where Jerome lived. She had called in sick yesterday, her first day back from the wedding. And then again today.

Tom and Dana had been in and out of endless Baltimore row houses, back when Dana was pregnant, and they were looking to buy. Dana didn't want to forsake the city for the Roland Park suburb that Tom favored, but then every place they visited—no matter how handsome on the outside—was a mess inside: full of lead paint, exposed pipes and dangerous wiring. "You can put in a bathroom. You can redo the walls," the realtor would always sing, but they couldn't afford the property in its terrible condition, much less take out an extra loan. And Tom's job paid well.

A man passed by on the sidewalk outside, a thin blond, and her head darted up. The Lotus Seed opened at ten. She guessed she was hoping to see Jerome on his way to work. Though she hadn't pictured past this. What would she do? Rap on the window and smile. He'd smile back and continue on his way. One didn't skip work for such things.

She leafed through the *Baltimore Sun* but couldn't focus on a single article. The hour of the Lotus Seed's opening came and went. The day suddenly seemed without possibility, and the responsibilities left to her (supermarket for dinner, the evening with Benjamin and Sarah) felt onerous.

She cleared her coffee cup, pulled on her coat then stepped outside. The official start of winter was a few days off, though the leaves had long since fallen and been carted away, and everything looked bare and gray, as if the entire city—even the trees—were made of the drab formstone one saw over by Fell's Point.

Dana wasn't ready for her car, so she headed aimlessly up a hill. She'd make a short circuit, her exercise for the day, before driving to the airless Rotunda supermarket. She passed Sawyer Road and Houghton and then saw Bridge Street. 14 Bridge Street. That was Jerome's address.

He wouldn't be there, of course. He didn't get off work till six, and yet she walked down the street anyway. His building was what she expected—a brownstone with four names written in tiny pieces of paper in four different hands and scotch taped under buzzers. Four mailboxes, too. She opened Jerome's. It was too early for a mail delivery, but there was an envelope inside. "Jamie," it read, and inside was a key. And no note. She could feel that.

Jamie was who? A girlfriend, come to visit for the weekend? A friend? Why had she supposed he didn't have someone? And why should it matter to her? For all her thoughts, she'd no more cheat on her husband than levitate through the ceiling of her kitchen. She put the envelope back in the mailbox and headed back down the steps.

The street was empty. She was unreasonably tired. Fear and fidelity could look like the same thing. She knew that. What if she started crying? She turned back for Jerome's building with the idea of going into the foyer to hide her imminent tears. Not that anyone was on the sidewalk. She paused at the row of mailboxes then took the envelope from Jerome's box. She was precisely not the sort of person who would open it and go upstairs. Which was why she placed her finger under the lip of the envelope and began to tear.

Jerome's apartment—the high attic apartment, as she had always supposed—was a one-room affair, with an orange counter separating the living area and kitchen, with its fake wood cabinets, dirty stovetop and sink full of dishes. If Jerome was expecting a girlfriend, he might have washed a few glasses. Tom—in the rooms he kept before they were married—always put a vase of flowers on the kitchen table, if she was coming to stay. Despite the dirty dishes, Jerome's place was tidy. Picked up at least, with few clues to the man's personality. (And what did Dana expect? A lot of yoga mats?) There was a plaid couch—apparently a sleeper, as there was no bed in the room—and a single round table with a computer. A trunk was pulled between two armchairs to make a coffee table. On it, there was an art book—paintings by Marsden Hartley. And more art books on the bookcase. *Persian Paintings*, Albert Pynkham Ryder, *Celestial Charts: Maps of the Heavens.* Also a box of white envelopes. She took one to reseal Jamie's key.

High in the walls, the room's windows let in the same diffuse, cold light that had been darkening Dana's spirits since daybreak. If only the day would wake up. She went into the bathroom, stopped to pee there—the dare of it almost preventing her. But Jerome surely wouldn't notice that his toilet paper roll was a few sheets shorter in the evening than in the morning. Two pairs of jeans, shaped as if an invisible man were still in them, hung behind the bathroom door, and Dana found their forms unaccountably poignant. Men. Their small inadequacies when they lived alone. Briefly, she imagined washing Jerome's dishes, scrubbing the top of the stove, and leaving him wondering at the thief, who broke into his apartment, only to clean it up.

Inside the medicine cabinet: scissors, a razor, a stack of hotel soaps, and *condoms*. But why *wouldn't* there be condoms? He wasn't *still* a Buddhist monk; he could have a sex life.

Coming out of the bathroom, she started. There, on a table next to the couch—it must function as a bed stand at night—was her father's book, *The Male Nude in Modern Art.* Her dad wrote it back when Dana was in high school. She and her sisters had called him Professor Dick, behind his back. "My dad," they joked to friends, "he's got a Ph.D. in penis." Not that they didn't know to value art, even then. Their dad had a reputation in the art world, and there were some family trips to Europe, financed by his university.

Now, though, if one of the book's naked men stepped off the page to greet Dana, she couldn't have been more startled. Was it an accident that Jerome found his way to Dana's father's book? It was no longer in print. For some reason, the cover didn't depict a male nude, but spiraling lines on a light blue background. It might have been a math book, save for its heft and shape. (Dana remembered the consternation over the cover, her father complaining, "You'd think it was a secret. Nobody's wearing anything underneath their clothes." Were the times that prudish, as recently as the 70s, that they wouldn't put a male nude on the cover of a book *about* the male nude? Or maybe her father went too far in the image he picked. It would have been like him to insist his selection was right, no matter how shocking.) And Jerome... could he know... but he must know that Simon Kruger was her father.

She shivered. Was the apartment even heated? She picked up her father's book, brought it to the trunk and stood it up, as if it were a volume at a bookstore. Her ears rattled with something like panic, blood hurrying its way through the tiniest of passages, and she headed for the door. Downstairs, she dropped the key—now snug in its new envelope (though with no "Jamie" scrawled on the front)—back into the mailbox and turned for her car.

The spark of Jerome's smile when she next entered the store, the eager way he waved her to his counter, the heat of his cheek when they kissed hello ... none of it meant he knew where she'd been. Or that he cared for her. He saw her and held up a warning finger. His cell phone (she was surprised he owned such a thing) must have buzzed in his pocket, for suddenly it was at his ear. "Yes." He put his finger in his other ear to hear. "No, no. Let me call you back." There was such a long list of things they never spoke of: she didn't know anyone in his life, had no sense of who might call him in the middle of the day. Today, Jerome wore small wire-rimmed glasses, something she'd never seen him in before.

"Listen," she said, pushing her fingers through her hair. "I hope I'm not out of line here, but I heard about your brother, and I wanted to say how sorry I was."

"My brother? What about my brother?"

"Your twin brother and what happened to him, I mean."

"Oh. What happened to him?"

"I mean, you know, his death."

Jerome pulled his glasses halfway down his nose then looked over them. "My twin brother's not dead," he said, an air of something new in his manner, the door of his perfect attention slamming shut. "Unless you know something I don't know. Where'd you get that idea?"

On Saturday morning, perhaps to put salt in the wound of her own uncertain feelings, Dana told Tom that Jerome had visited while Tom was in Canada.

"Oh, yeah," Tom said tiredly, as if he knew all about it. They were sitting on the kitchen stools, coffee mugs in hand. In the neighboring room, the kids watched a video—"The People of Israel," a *Shalom Sesame* special. Tom and Dana didn't let the kids watch TV, but they fairly begged them to watch videos, knowing how much they might get done during the half an hour of a viewing.

"Do you ever get jealous of me?"

"No," Tom said reassuringly, missing her point entirely. "Of course not." Then: "I know about Jerome."

"You do?"

"Yeah, Jerome told Larry."

"He did?" A rushing feeling came over Dana, not unlike the watery emotion she felt (an acrophobe on the edge of a rooftop) when she propped her father's book on the trunk in Jerome's apartment.

"Yeah, I don't know how it is that Larry knows everything. At least, Jerome wasn't telling the truth when he said he wasn't going to be in touch with anyone at the station."

"Yeah," Dana said. They were silent. Tom's face was impenetrable. Whatever did he think about anything? Why didn't he just *react*? "So, what *did* he say?"

"Jerome?" Tom stood to fill his coffee cup. "Jerome said he made a pass at me."

Dana jerked her head back. "He ..."

"Yeah, right. That's what I said to Larry. 'He what?' 'He made a pass at you,' Larry says. 'Wouldn't I … like … have to *be there*? If he made a pass at me?' I say to Larry. 'Jerome didn't make any pass at me.' Larry just shrugs and tells me that's what Jerome said."

"And…"

"He never made a pass at me. For Christ's sake. A few weeks ago, he took my hand when I was telling him about how sick that stupid pedophilia story was making me. You know how it was the dumbest story, and I was pissed I had to produce the segment, but how it touched something in me in terms of my fears about the kids. Well, if someone said that to me, I wouldn't exactly be like, 'Hey, wanna go to bed?' But he did take my hand and say, 'That's gotta be hard,' and I said, 'It's OK. It's nothing. Don't worry about me.' And it's true, he dropped my hand, and said, 'Well, it's not like I'm making a pass at you or anything,' and of course, I said, 'Sure, yeah, I know that.'"

"Jerome's gay?"

"He's gay. I guess. That's what some people say. *He's* never said it. I don't know *what* he is. "

Neither of them spoke for a moment then Dana began, "But he knew you … I mean he met me…"

"Yeah, but plenty of gay guys are married. Remember that show we did on that? In fact, that was Jerome's pitch, way back when, that story. I think that's why I wanted him to meet you, when we were first dating. Maybe I thought something was up. That he wasn't just another guy trying to get attention for his stories."

Dana didn't know what to say.

"He's just a guy who likes to unsettle, who likes to play with what people do and don't know about him. I'm sure he has some Buddhist justification for it all, for playing with our idea of reality. I bet if you even knew for sure he was gay, he'd drop you as a friend. He seems to have some idea that he can't be known. He's too…" Tom searched for the word, but didn't find it. "He's too 'something' to be known."

"Too brilliant?"

"Maybe so. And maybe I put him onto that idea about himself. I did think he was special. For a long time, I did." When she didn't respond, he said, "What's the matter?"

"Nothing."

"Really?"

"Yeah," she said, turning to face him fully, thinking he'd just spoken to her, that they'd just had a conversation, the way people do. He was forty-four years old. His father had been the headmaster of a private day school in Washington DC. He'd spent his entire childhood around privilege, but he'd joined the Peace Corps and gone to Yugoslavia, just before it fell apart. He'd been to Poland and Africa and the Middle East. He'd had coffee with Ariel Sharon and Bruce Springsteen. Bill Clinton and then George Bush waved hi, when they saw him at news conferences. He never had a close female friend. He never wrote a love letter. He'd cried three times in his life, once at his father's death, once when he almost backed his car into a child, and once last week at the wedding, when she said that harsh thing to him.

He was defined in a way that she was not. He had what he wanted and was working with it. He had agreed to live his life, and Dana, on some level, hadn't; she still thought something needed to change. And why was that? The waning of her professional life? A poor choice of partner? A reluctance to grow up?

"The problem with relationships," Hennie once said, "is that we expect our partners to have all their own virtues and all our virtues, as well." How smart that seemed to Dana at the time, even though Hennie was dating a man whose name she wouldn't reveal. She just called him "The Dog Man," because he'd found her missing dog. That's how they met. Things were never good between Hennie and The Dog Man. But then Hennie added, entirely earnestly, "We really should do things on the kibbutz-system: go to this one for sex, this one for conversation, this one for financial support."

"This one for Orioles' tickets," Dana put in. The Dog Man sold beer at Camden Yards.

"Yes! Isn't it a great idea?" Hennie asked in her too bright way.

"Sure," Dana said and laughed, as if she had the emotional flexibility—and plain nerves—for such a thing, as if she understood how to step out of a marriage. And back in.

Beth Ann Fennelly

The Mommy at the Zoo

I used to sleep better I used to
be smarter remember for example words
and remember when I learned them

there was a word for example
for the way a snake loves
a tight place a crevice a chink in rocks

now the word won't answer
though my daughter knocks
the python sleeps tight in his glass hut

the word has slipped
my mind between a rock
and a hard place

Mr. Snake you
you are a ...
a something-o-phile

O you sneaky ...
something-o-phile ...
I rummage

but the word
is nowhere no
where in my diaper bag

among the handiwipes and gummibears
sippiecups of Juicyjuice
crayons slinky and cow-that-goes-moo

before I was a Mommy
say 4 or 5 years or
decades ago I could think in complete

sentences remember all
my favorite words like the one
about loving the tight fit which I did

in the French Quarter
where the hot rain rained down
in the alley beside the bar

where I was bolted against the iron gate
by Tommy's hard cock
hot rain falling on my upswung face

each vertebra fenced
in the tic-tac-toe grid
each vertebra X-ed

on a treasure map
bezel set what a night
for a girl forged of carbon

all bone and saxophone
notes bouncing to her
through the hot drops of rain

who was she
that fresh squeezed girl
just temporarily out of her mind

if it's true as they say
that I am now
that same she

the word I seek
would come slithering
find a chink and wriggle in

like my child up ahead
darting through scissors
of grown up legs

her silhouette
in red exit light
slow down I'm coming wait

wait up

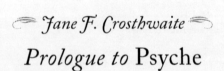

Jane F. Crosthwaite

Prologue to Psyche

I F LOVE IS A METAPHOR FOR INTEGRITY, if we betray ourselves as
readily as we betray others, and if a Rabbi named Zeus can represent
the wisdom of the ages ("I'm also the President of the Soviet Union and
the United States, not to mention the Coach of the Norwegian Luge Team"), then
Wendy Wasserstein can relocate a Greek myth, quote popular music lyrics, and
remind her readers that common, folk knowledge is the substance of moral life.

Hard work along the arduous journeys of our lives, enriched by the possibility of love, could help all of us become mature adults.

Wasserstein honors the serious dimension of these journeys with the humility and grace of humor or, as Huston Smith once said of Zen wisdom, with "transolympian horseplay."[1] As Wasserstein sets her dramatic retelling of Psyche and Cupid's love in a smoked-fish shop in Flatbush, she asks her readers to navigate within a mess of mixed identities (Greek, Jewish, Norwegian, Freudian) and to consider whether she is a hopelessly confused playwright or an insightful voice for the cross-cultural and interrelated nature of human desires and options. The beauty which so distinguishes the mythical—and the Flatbush—Psyche is inevitably reflected in, and challenged by, the multi-layered and ambiguous beauty of her future mother-in-law, Venus. Wasserstein's wit wheedles the reader into recognizing Venus as a beauty from Wisconsin, a former luge contestant, the owner of a Beauty and Spa Salon called Venus di Norway, and still the eternal meddling, jealous, vain, and insecure mother of Cupid.

Leading us into deeper contortions of identity, Wasserstein would have Psyche's sisters, themselves meddling characters in the original myth, now play siblings named Ego and Id.[2] Three daughters of a father, once a psychiatrist and now a shop owner, are at once parts of a family and parts of a single self; they embody the options of settling for superficial success, of using boredom to fuel jealousy and distrust, and of encouraging Psyche to stab her loving husband with a fish fork. The core of Wasserstein's depiction of the difficulties of the moral life, of course, lies within the desires and doubts of Psyche herself. Hounded by beauty which is at once her greatest gift and her curse, she is unable to trust the lover/husband whom she has not seen with her eyes but in whose attentions she revels. She betrays him by looking, only to see the beauty which she—of all people—should have already known by other means. She moves on to betray Venus by opening a bottle of anti-aging cream for herself, again forgetting far more potent sources of beauty than skin or youth.

Cupid who shot himself and then shoots Psyche with love's arrow is the straight-arrow hero of this tale, a paragon of good (mostly) son and faithful lover. Psyche it is who must learn the lessons of identity, persistence, struggle, responsibility, and common sense. Order in this messy universe is represented by maturely chosen marriage ("… never to marry the first Ear, Nose and Throat man you meet"). Although surely a piece of stereotypically Jewish advice, we are also reminded that love and marriage are, in fact, the order-seeking devices employed by almost all religious traditions against personal and social chaos. In this light, the Rabbi is the religious high priest of order and wisdom, blessed with the common sense and good humor to know that he is mostly just pointing a "finger at the moon," yet another Huston Smith analogy, this one again acknowledging human inability to get it all neatly tied up.[3]

Knowledge, which the Rabbi promises in a framing Bat Mitzvah lesson, comes through accepting responsibility for our given circumstances—even beauty—and from the common sense of our multiple traditions. The Greek chorus of this adapted, but largely intact, myth of love and order in the universe comes in the several pop musical refrains which intone commonsense clichés. But the clichés have mostly been hard-won, and they echo in our memories, especially the finale of "I Say a Little Prayer for You."

The Rabbi Zeus summarizes the knowledge we should have gained: only G-d is holy, our messy lives are mysterious to us, our best response is to know our place and to seek the hand of our neighbor and sing together. Should Psyche's beauty and Cupid's love find each other within our conflicted selves, then life will be even more bountiful, however scarred.

Notes

1. Huston Smith, *The Religions of Man* (New York: Harper, 1958), 141.
2. Wasserstein has been remarkably true to the capsule account of the story of Psyche and Cupid made available by Edith Hamilton's classic book, *Mythology* (New York: Mentor Book from New American Library, 1940, 1969), 92–100.
3. Smith, 144.

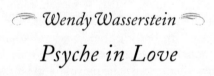

Wendy Wasserstein

Psyche in Love

SCENE ONE

(A synagogue in Flatbush, Brooklyn. The Rabbi Zeus, decked out in full rabbi regalia, approaches the habema. *He speaks to the audience.)*

RABBI

Welcome, friends and family of the Bat Mitzvah. Everyone here at Congregation Bet Cedar Sinai wants to congratulate our Bat Mitzah, Flora Berman, on her beautiful reading from the Torah today. It's especially meaningful because, as many of you know, tonight is the beginning of the *Whitefish Nacht* Celebration, the annual Viking-Jewish holiday of smoked fish.

Flora, today you are a woman and you can thank God every morning you were not born a man. Every Bat Mitzvah girl who has stood on this *habema* has asked me, "Rabbi Zeus, can you explain to me the meaning of my Torah portion?" And my answer is, "Of course I can. I'm your Rabbi!" But today, Flora, I'm not going to. Instead, I would like to address something else. Something even bigger than the Torah. But what could be bigger than the Torah? I'll tell you.

What you must grapple with, Flora, now that you are a woman, and what every single one of us must grapple with here today, through sickness and through health, is knowledge: intellectual knowledge, emotional knowledge, and physical knowledge. What you need to seek in your life's journey. How to open your perspective. How much, how little, and when.

And that's why I have decided to share with you today, dear congregation and Bat Mitzvah girl, one of my favorite stories: the myth of Cupid and Psyche, both of whom I happen to have known very well. Psyche's father, a well-known psychiatrist, was a member of this very congregation. I know you're thinking, "How was a girl with a name like 'Psyche' Jewish?" Don't ask. I'm a Rabbi named Zeus.

So why Cupid and Psyche? They're not in the Torah. So what? Neither are you. Am I? Is Golda Meir? No. But we're all still worth talking about. Psyche was the most beautiful girl under twenty who ever lived. Trust me, that was some *punim*. She was a real *shayna madela*. She was so drop-dead gorgeous, she was known even to the most beautiful woman in the mid-life category, Venus.

Oy, Venus. She was stunning. A ten plus plus. But it was time for a lift. Venus was aging and, to tell you the truth, she wasn't doing it gracefully. So she sent her son Cupid to spy on the beauty and get a little gossip, and instead he fell madly in love with her. And you would think this all ends happily ever after. But it took the kind of knowledge that comes out of adversity to bring these two hearts together.

Dear Bat Mitzvah girl, I give you this story as a gift, to mark the beginning of your own womanhood on this very important day. It's a very special girl or Viking who gets Bat Mitzvahed on Whitefish Nacht.

The story begins in a smoked-fish store in Flatbush. Psyche's sisters, Ego and Id, are working behind the counter. What kind of names are Ego and Id? I told you the father was a psychiatrist.

END OF SCENE

※

SCENE TWO

(Early morning, a small appetizer shop on Coney Island Avenue in Brooklyn. There are signs in the window for specials on whitefish, lox, and nova. Lying in the cases are various smoked fish and chopped salads. On the counter are apricot rolls, halvah, and dried fruits. Behind the counter two girls, Ego, 18, and Id, 19, with beehive hairdos and skintight pedal pushers, are slicing fish. They are listening to Ruby and the Romantics *singing* "Our Day Will Come." *They are preparing to open the shop and singing along: "Our day will come if we just wait a while we'll share the joy falling in love can bring.")*

EGO

My day will never come. I'll never get a husband. My name is too weird and my hands smell of fish.

ID

You're wrong, Ego. Joey Brillstein says he loves that my hands smell like whitefish. He says they smell better than Arpège or Canoe.

EGO

Joey Brillstein's a moron.

ID

He gave me this I.D. bracelet. I don't see anybody's name around your wrist, Ego.

EGO

I don't accept jewelry from morons, Id. I'm waiting for a respectable professional.

(From outside, we hear the line of men who have been waiting for the store to open. They begin banging on the window and calling, "Open up! Open up!" Ego walks over to the window and bangs back.)

EGO

Cool your jets! *(To Id.)* My luck! Every day five hundred goddamn men show up here, and I can't even meet one decent Ear, Nose, and Throat Man. At this point I'd settle for a radiologist.

ID

We better let them in.

EGO *(Calls out.)*

Hey, Beauty! Your fan club is here. Psyche, get out here!

(Psyche walks into the store from the backroom. She is 20, stunningly beautiful, and softer than her two sisters. She carries a tray of freshly cooked bagels.)

PSYCHE
Ego, you know they come to see all of us.

EGO
You don't have to be nice! I'm not a charity case. Although Daddy says we're not making any money 'cause nobody comes to shop. They just want to look at you and your beauty. We're running a goddamn peep show.

PSYCHE
I wish you both knew how much I envy you.

EGO
And you know what? Elizabeth Taylor envies me, too. And so does Audrey Hepburn! Her I make especially nuts. Id, open the door.

(Id opens the door.)

ID
Good morning. Can I help you?

PSYCHE
We have a special on Nova today.

RABBI *(To us)*
Every morning, a man would come in and stare at Psyche.

ID
Mister, you get sixty seconds to look at my sister and then if you're not buying, get moving.

EGO
I believe you were asked to move, mister.

RABBI
Doctor.

EGO
Really! Can I help you with anything, *Doctor?*

RABBI *(To us)*
Just looking, the man would say, as he continued staring at Psyche's beauty.

PSYCHE
How 'bout our apricot roll? Or a little Halvah?

EGO
What kind of a Doctor are you?

RABBI
Brain surgery and cardiology.

EGO
Would you like to marry my sister and then find someone decent for me?

RABBI
No thanks. Your sister is too beautiful. I'd never get any work done. Besides, I'd be afraid to touch her. I wouldn't want to ruin such perfection.

EGO
Well who would?

RABBI
But I'll consider marrying you. You have all the basic features of your sister, but it's much less overwhelming. I could cope with you. You're a solid "B plus."

EGO
I don't like jokes, Doctor.

RABBI
I'm completely serious.

ID
What about me? I'm a solid "B minus."

MAN TWO
I have a brother named Eddie. Marry him. He's a root canal man.

ID
He is? Fine! We'll have a double wedding!

EGO
What about Joey?

ID
Joey Brillstein's a moron.

(Id discards her I.D. bracelet.)

EGO
We'd better go get blood tests before you change your mind.

RABBI *(To us)*
And so Ego took her future husband's hand and left the store, with Id close behind.

PSYCHE
Please don't leave without buying anything. (*Holds up a fish.*) How about a Chubb?

EGO
Tell Daddy he can cater our weddings.

(They leave the shop.)

PSYCHE
Next?

RABBI *(To us)*
And at that very moment, a young man walked into the store. There was something odd about him, besides the bow and arrows he was wearing with a Brooklyn College sweatshirt.

(A young man enters the store. No one would suspect he is Cupid.)

PSYCHE
You in a Robin Hood play or something?

CUPID
No. I'm on the archery team. Brooklyn College.

PSYCHE
Well, I'm afraid we're about to take a break.

(Cupid leans forward against the counter. One of his arrows pierces his coat.)

CUPID
You are the most beautiful woman I have ever seen!

(Psyche suddenly bursts out crying.)

PSYCHE
Don't say that! I hate my beauty! I hate it! Why couldn't I be perky or cute or even adorable? That would be tolerable! Even interesting would be fine! Interesting girls with bumps on their noses and crooked teeth are sensitive! Men look into their souls. But I had to be born goddamn beautiful!

CUPID
There is no one in the world more beautiful inside and out than you.

PSYCHE
Well, I wouldn't know. I've never been out of Flatbush.

CUPID
Trust me, Psyche, there is no one.

PSYCHE
How did you know my name?

CUPID
   Everyone knows you. You are a legendary mortal.

PSYCHE
   Where are you from?

CUPID
   Just up the Beach and under the boardwalk.

(Sings.)
   Under the boardwalk, people walking above.
   Under the Boardwalk, we'll be falling in love.
(He takes Psyche by the hand and begins to dance with her as the song continues. He kisses her hands and finally their lips meet. He jumps onto the counter.)

CUPID
   Psyche, fill my arms with porgies, smelts and sturgeon. I want to bathe in onion bialys, poppy, pumpernickel and rye. I love you Psyche. And I swear on my life that one day you will be my bride.
(Psyche fills his arms with fish. He kisses her again before he runs unto the street.)

END OF SCENE

SCENE THREE

(Cupid, in a phone booth, is talking to his mother, Venus di Norway, who sits on a throne surrounded by mirrors, in the Venus di Norway Beauty Salon and Spa.)

VENUS
   I should've never sent you there to spy for me.

CUPID
   Yes mother.

VENUS
   What does she look like?

CUPID
   For a mortal, she's attractive. I'd say a six.

VENUS
   A six? All that commotion in Flatbush just for a six?

CUPID

Mother, I promise she doesn't hold a candle to you.

VENUS

Then why are all those men coming there every day to worship her? They should be worshipping me. I am Venus di Norway the most famous beauty in the world! Who will buy my night cream and moisturizer if this girl becomes more famous? She could become terrible trouble for us. Like Helena Rubinstein or, God forbid, Elizabeth Arden!

CUPID

Mother, she is a mortal. She can't compete with you. You're a goddess. Besides, she's miserable.

VENUS

I hope you didn't fall for that "I'm so miserable" routine. That's how they always rope you in.

CUPID

I liked her smoked fish. That's all. It's very fresh and not too salty.

VENUS

Just remember: the herring is always better in Norway.

CUPID

Mother, I promise. Everything's better in Norway.

RABBI *(To us)*

So Cupid came to see me. At the time, I had just become the rabbi at the local synagogue.

END OF SCENE

SCENE FOUR

(Inside the Coney Island Avenue Synagogue. A receptionist sits at a desk. Past the receptionist's desk, we can also see Rabbi Zeus's office. Cupid walks up to the receptionist.)

CUPID

I need to speak to one of the Gods.

RECEPTIONIST
I'm sorry; we only worship one God here.

CUPID
I am desperate! I am hopelessly in love with the wrong person.

RECEPTIONIST
A shiksa! You better to talk to Rabbi Zeus. (*Into intercom.*) Rabbi Zeus, we're got an emergency out here!

RABBI (*Through the intercom.*)
Send it in.

(*Cupid walks into the Rabbi's office.*)

How can I help you, son?

CUPID
I'm in love with the wrong woman.

RABBI
Is she a shiksha?

CUPID
I'm not sure. I don't know what that means.

RABBI
Assimilation. Doesn't matter. You can never tell these days.

CUPID
My mother sent me to spy on her. She despises her. She wants to eliminate her from the universe.

RABBI
Mothers! They never stop. What's your girl's name?

CUPID
Psyche.

RABBI
I know the entire family. Their father is the shrink who became the sturgeon king. He decided it was easier to treat fish than depression. Gave all the daughters those screwball names. She's a gorgeous girl your Psyche. Even I can hardly look at her.

CUPID
Please help me. I beg you. My mother sent me to spy on her, and I accidentally pierced myself with my own arrow and now I'm desperately in love. My heart is breaking. I must be with her. But I can't disobey my mother.

RABBI

I tell you, all Jewish mothers are the same!

CUPID

My mother's Norwegian.

RABBI

Oh, so you're a Viking!

CUPID

I'm not a Viking. My mother's Venus di Norway.

RABBI

Oy! I had such a crush on her when she was in those ice skating movies.

CUPID

She runs a cosmetics empire now. She has tentacles and moisturizers all over the world. Look, what am I going to do?

(The Receptionist beeps in on the intercom.)

RECEPTIONIST *(On the intercom.)*

Rabbi, the Sturgeon Sisters are here.

RABBI *(Into the intercom.)*

I'll be with them in a minute.

(To Cupid.)

Cupid, this will be tricky. You deceived your mother, and therefore you must make some sacrifices. You may marry your Psyche, but she must never look at you or know your true identity. I'll send you the rest of the plan after I've come up with it. Now go and I will speak to your future sisters-in-law, Ego and Id. Oy, such names.

CUPID

Thank you, wise Rabbi. Thank you.

RABBI *(To us)*

And so the fish girls, Ego and Id, came into my office.

EGO

Rabbi, there's good news and there's bad news.

RABBI

So what else is new?

ID

The good news is Ego and I are both engaged to doctors and today we sold more fish than we have in weeks. The bad news is Psyche. Who knew beauty could destroy you? We promised our dying mother that we wouldn't marry until we found Psyche's soul mate.

RABBI

I have a plan, girls. You must dress your Psyche in rags and leave her on Brighton Beach. There will come a lonely Viking with a herring in his mouth to be her husband.

EGO

You want us to leave our sister to marry a Viking?

RABBI

Big deal. You're getting doctors. Just do it.

ID

Is this Viking Jewish?

RABBI

I know he was a bronze luge medallist.

EGO

Then he's not Jewish.

RABBI

Girls, it's what your mother and God would've wanted. Trust me.

RABBI *(To us)*

And so every Israelite took their first-born…

(The Rabbi looks somewhat befuddled.)

Sorry—wrong story.

END OF SCENE

SCENE FIVE

(Coney Island Beach. The Sturgeon family arrives at the beach, with Psyche wearing rags. Her sisters are weeping. The sounds of seagulls circling above.)

RABBI *(To us)*

And so the Sturgeon family arrived at Brighton Beach, with Psyche dressed in rags. Her sisters kissed her good-bye and started crying.

PSYCHE
Don't weep for me, dearest sisters. You will have happy lives married to secure professional men. Know that I am glad for your happiness and thrilled that our mother can finally rest in peace.

(The family begins to exit.)

PSYCHE
Oh God, why the hell didn't you call me Judy?

(Psyche sits alone on the beach as it turns to dusk. We hear seagulls flying above.)

RABBI *(To us)*
So Psyche sat alone on the beach and began to cry as seagulls surrounded her.

PSYCHE
Go away! Shoo! I hate birds.

RABBI *(To us)*
And suddenly, out of the mist, a Viking appeared with a herring in his mouth and whisked Psyche away.

(Suddenly, out of the mist, a Viking appears. His helmet conceals his face and he has a herring in his mouth. Psyche faints as the Viking lifts her up and carries her toward the sea.)

END OF SCENE

SCENE SIX

(The living room of a very well decorated, fancy Manhattan Beach house. Psyche lies sleeping on a Lazy Boy recliner. Sumptuous bowls of fruit and wine are placed throughout the room. Psyche awakes. A few ethereal voices speak to her.)

VOICE
Psyche, this is your home. We are your servants. We are ready to do whatever you desire. You've learned your lesson. You can't hurry love.

(The voices begin to sing "You Can't Hurry Love.")

PSYCHE
Thank you. Thank you so much. No one has ever been so kind to me.

(Suddenly Cupid appears behind her. His voice and demeanor are completely changed since their first encounter. He is the image of a romantic hero. He puts his hands on Psyche's shoulders.)

CUPID
Psyche, you will only have love and kindness from now on.

PSYCHE
Are you my husband?

CUPID
I am your husband, your lover, your best friend. Your bad times are over, Psyche.

PSYCHE
Oh, my love.

(She begins to turn around. He stops her.)

CUPID
But you must never look at me.

PSYCHE
I want to bask in your eyes and touch your smile.

CUPID
You will only hear my love. That will have to be enough.

RABBI *(To us)*
And so Cupid gently placed a blindfold over Psyche's eyes.

(He places a blindfold over her eyes.)

PSYCHE
Why do I know I am finally home?

CUPID
Psyche, you more than anyone must know there is so much more to see in life than ephemeral beauty.

PSYCHE
I love you.

(He begins to kiss her. The voices continue to sing "You Can't Hurry Love.")

RABBI *(To us)*
Meanwhile, back at the appetizer shop...

END OF SCENE

SCENE SEVEN

(The Coney Island appetizer shop. Ego and Id at work.)

EGO
  Who knew being doctors' wives would be so boring? He's never home.

ID
  The brother is worse. He's always home. Well, at least we're both happier now than poor Psyche.

EGO
  Oh, we definitely are. We should go visit her in Manhattan Beach.

ID
  That would be too depressing.

EGO
  We'll cheer her up. Tell her how our lives have worked out perfectly.

ID
  Good. I'll send a bird messenger to tell her we're on our way.

END OF SCENE

SCENE EIGHT

(The porch of the Manhattan Beach house. Psyche sits in a chair, blindfolded, while Cupid rubs her feet.)

PSYCHE
  I never knew such happiness could be mine.

(The sound of a bird flying overhead.)

PSYCHE
  Is that a bird? Make it go away!

CUPID
  Darling, it's a messenger. Your sisters are on their way.

PSYCHE
Can't be! How could they ever find me?

CUPID
They've been asking every bird on Brighton Beach for your address.

(Psyche begins weeping.)

PSYCHE
My sisters! How wonderful! I can't wait to show them our home. They'll be so happy for me! You don't know how worried they were when they left me.

CUPID
Darling, I know how much you must miss your precious sisters. But remember they are women. When they see how happy you are, they might envy you. Being a Doctor's wife isn't everything it's cracked up to be. Promise me if your sisters say anything against me you mustn't believe them. The truth is I would rest easier if you didn't see them.

PSYCHE
But dearest, I can't live my life never seeing my husband or my sisters. And you won't even let me look at a picture of your mother.

(We hear the horn of a giant Cadillac pulling up to the house.)

PSYCHE
That must be them. Please, I beg you. Let me see them. I promise nothing will ever take my heart from you.

(Psyche pulls off her blindfold and Cupid walks into the house. A flock of birds appear as the sisters run up the steps of the house to embrace Psyche.)

EGO & ID
Psyche!

PSYCHE
My sweet sisters!

EGO
This is some place! Beachfront property! Very nice.

PSYCHE
Isn't it wonderful! And I'm so happy Ego. Finally, I'm home.

(Ego starts pawing the furniture.)

EGO
What is this? Formica?

PSYCHE
It's actually Italian marble.

(Id lifts up a bowl.)

ID
Ego, this is a genuine Steuben bowl!

PSYCHE
Wedding gift. How are your husbands?

EGO
Wonderful.

ID
Fabulous.

EGO
This is a beautiful gown. Who made it?

PSYCHE
I think it's Dior.

ID
Ego, did you see the shoes? I'd walk to Europe for those shoes.

EGO
You know, Psyche, Daddy really misses you. The entire old neighborhood
misses you. Why haven't you come to visit with your husband?

PSYCHE
He doesn't really travel much.

ID
But he's a Viking.

PSYCHE
His Viking days are over.

EGO
So he's home now? Can we meet him?

PSYCHE
I don't think he's home actually.

ID
You don't think? Why don't you know? What does he look like?

PSYCHE
He's the most handsome man in the world.

EGO
Is he tall, dark, blond, short, wide?

PSYCHE
He's perfect.

ID
Blue eyes? Brown? A twinkle?

PSYCHE
He's gentle and kind.

EGO
Psyche have you heard what happened to Rabbi Zeus?

PSYCHE
No.

EGO
Turns out he wasn't a rabbi at all.

ID
He was a communist infiltrator working for a Viking spy ring out of Norway. Headed an international plot to control the smoked-fish business and tamper with the judging of the Luge Competition at the Olympics!

PSYCHE
Really!

EGO
You know what I think? This fabulous house, this husband you've never seen, these drop-dead jewels, are all a front.

ID
Absolutely. A communist front.

EGO
I believe your life is in danger, Psyche.

ID
It certainly is.

EGO
The man you've married isn't handsome, kind, or gentle at all. He's a Viking Commie spy!

(Psyche begins to cry.)

PSYCHE
He's not a Commie spy.

EGO

But you can't say he isn't a Viking! Why do you think you've never seen him?

ID

Listen to your Ego. She's telling you the truth.

EGO

Tonight you must destroy him. For the sake of the free world and your family's smoked-fish business, not to mention Eli Zabar and Russ and his daughters, you must bury him.

PSYCHE

But…

EGO

Here, take the fish fork mother gave me before she died. She would want you to use it. Trust us. We're your only sisters.

ID

If you like, we'll take some of your jewelry now so that the Commies don't confiscate it later.

(Psyche begins to give her jewelry to her sisters.)

EGO

Maybe we should take some things from your closet too.

RABBI *(To us)*

Later that evening, after the house had been thoroughly looted by the well-intentioned sisters, Cupid found his beloved wife sitting in the dark.

(Cupid enters the house. Psyche sits in the dark.)

CUPID

Some herring, darling? Nothing beats Norwegian herring.

PSYCHE

How do you know that?

CUPID

Everybody knows that.

PSYCHE

But you do have a real interest in smoked fish.

CUPID

It's my wife's family business.

PSYCHE
Is that what attracted you to me?

CUPID
Yes, my love. I'm in it for the Gravlax. *(Laughs.)* Did you have a nice visit with your sisters?

PSYCHE
Yes.

CUPID
I'm sorry I was so suspicious. You must miss them terribly.

PSYCHE
Yes. Dearest, would you sing something for me? If I can't see your love at least let me hear it in your voice.

CUPID
Of course.

(He begins to sing "Cupid Draw Back Your Bow." As he sings Psyche lifts her mother's fork to eat a herring. She begins weeping.)

PSYCHE
Your voice is so beautiful.

RABBI *(To us)*
Suddenly, Psyche picked up her candle and turned around to look at her husband.

(Psyche does so.)

PSYCHE
My darling forgive me! How could I ever have doubted you?

CUPID
Love can't exist where there is no trust.

(He immediately runs from the table outside the house. Psyche follows him.)

PSYCHE
My love, come back! Come back! Please! I beg you. Try to understand. I had to see you for myself. Please forgive me!

(She falls down and begins weeping.)

END OF SCENE

✳

SCENE NINE

(The Venus di Norway Beauty Salon and Spa. Venus sitting on her mirror throne, Cupid with his head in her lap.)

VENUS
That's what you get for marrying a fishmonger.

CUPID
Mother, I love her.

VENUS
You don't know what love is. You were infatuated. She cast a spell on you. You sat on one of your own goddamn arrows.

CUPID
But I'm in pain!

VENUS
Why don't you just get into bed and watch television? I think *I Dream of Jeannie* is on.

CUPID
I want a normal life.

VENUS
You'll never have that, dear. You've had a far too narcissistic and difficult mother.

RABBI *(To us)*
And so, the bewildered and bereaved Psyche came to see me.

END OF SCENE

SCENE TEN

(Psyche sits in the Rabbi's office while he is eating whitefish salad from a container.)

PSYCHE
They told me you were a communist.

RABBI
They'll say anyone's a communist. I went to a few meetings when I worked in Hollywood. That's all.

PSYCHE
You worked in Hollywood?

RABBI
Sure. Ever see *The Ten Commandments?* I was the stuntman for the Pharaoh. That's how I know your mother-in-law.

PSYCHE
I never met my mother-in-law. Who is she?

RABBI
Greatest beauty of her time. Then she left the business, married a God, and made a fortune in cosmetics. She has salons all over the world. You must have heard of Venus di Norway.

PSYCHE
Sure. I use her mascara.

RABBI
Well, let me give you some advice. The last thing Venus wants is a mortal daughter-in-law who outshines her. Why do you think Cupid came to your shop to begin with? She had heard about you. That boy went through absolute hell to be with you.

PSYCHE
Wait a minute. Wait a minute. My brain can't hold this. I may be beautiful, but I'm lacking in my perceptions. The Viking with the herring in his mouth is the same boy as the *feygele* from Brooklyn College with the wings and the arrows?

RABBI
I don't like that word, *feygele*.

PSYCHE
He had fairy wings, for God's sake.

RABBI
The Viking with the herring in his mouth and the boy from Brooklyn College with the arrows and wings is your husband, Cupid.

PSYCHE
Oh Rabbi, I've made a mess of everything! What should I do?

RABBI
That's simple, my child. *(Sings.)*
You gotta tell him that
You're never gonna leave him
Tell him that you're always gonna love him,
Tell him, tell him, tell him right now.

PSYCHE

Thank you Rabbi. You're a wise man.

RABBI

And Psyche, remember, always take a little whitefish salad when you travel.

(He covers up his container of salad and gives it to her.)

RABBI *(To us)*

Armed with her whitefish salad and the wisdom of a great Rabbi, Psyche looked for her husband at his mother's Spa and Ice Skating Salon. Upon arrival, Psyche caught Venus in the midst of her triple Lutz.

END OF SCENE

SCENE ELEVEN

("Venus In Blue Jeans" plays as Venus ice skates. Psyche watches her.)

PSYCHE

It's a pleasure to meet you.

(Venus continues to skate.)

PSYCHE *(Louder.)*

It's an honor to meet you. I'm a very big fan. I wear your mascara.

(Venus skates over to Psyche.)

VENUS

You're surprisingly plain. You'll never get my son back.

PSYCHE

I will follow him always. He is my destiny.

VENUS

My son almost died from your deceiving ways.

PSYCHE

I was wrong. I am sorry. I will do anything to win his trust again.

VENUS

The only way you can get your lover back is to steal for me Persephone of the Underworld's secret anti-aging formula.

PSYCHE
> I can't steal.

VENUS
> You said you'd do anything.

PSYCHE
> But it's the underworld.

VENUS
> You'll never get my son back until you prove to him how deeply you care.

PSYCHE
> But this could take years.

VENUS
> I've got time. Better take along some water, dear. The underworld can dry your skin. And by the way, that dress you're wearing is my son's property. *(Throws Psyche some rags.)* But you can have these.

(Psyche begins walking. To try and keep her spirits up, she sings to herself, "Cupid Draw Back Your Bow and Let Your Arrow Flow." After walking six hundred miles, she comes to a sign on a door: "Persephone of the Underworld—Admission by Invitation Only." She opens the door and enters.)

RABBI *(To us)*
> So Psyche set out, in rags, to the entrance to the Underworld, on the Broadway IRT. After getting off at the final stop and walking six hundred miles, underground she came to a door with a sign on it that read: "Persephone of the Underworld: Admission by Invitation Only." With much trepidation, Psyche walked in.

END OF SCENE

SCENE TWELVE

(Persephone sits on an all-black throne, in an all-black underground office. Psyche sits across the desk. They have been chatting a while.)

PSYCHE
> Persphone, trust me, my mother-in-law is impossible!

PERSEPHONE
> She's a real piece of work! Talk about narcissistic personality disorder. Why the hell do you want to be related to her anyway?

PSYCHE
I love her son.

PERSEPHONE
He's a real mama's boy. She says shoot, and he's ready with the bow and arrow. And you know what the strategy is? Nobody falls in love with a woman as beautiful as Venus. So in her mind there isn't a husband alive who isn't secretly in love with her. You must really piss her off.

PSYCHE
But she has everything. She's a goddess.

PERSEPHONE
First of all she married into the deity. She was just an ice skating queen. Second of all she has no soul. And that's what you've got. A heart and soul.

PSYCHE
But they've made me so unhappy.

PERSEPHONE
It's your Psyche and welcome to it.

PSYCHE
I want to die.

PERSEPHONE
Good. You can come live here. I'd like some company. Did you happen to bring any fish with you?

PSYCHE
Just a little whitefish salad.

(Psyche gives Persephone the whitefish salad container. Persephone begins eating it. She is thrilled.)

PERSEPHONE
I haven't had fresh whitefish salad in two thousand years. This is delicious! Do you have any cream cheese?

PSYCHE
No. But we could ship it to you. My father ships all over the world.

PERSEPHONE
He would be the most brilliant man alive if he could manage to ship it here.

PSYCHE
He was a psychiatrist. Now he's the Sturgeon King. I think he can manage to do anything.

(Persephone takes a jar out of her pocket.)

PERSEPHONE
Psyche, this is my anti-aging formula. Bring it to your mother-in-law, and I promise she will let you and Cupid live happily ever after. In exchange you must ship me monthly two pounds sliced extra thin whitefish, sable, nova, and sturgeon. *(Hands the jar to Psyche.)* But remember. You must never open this. It is for Venus only. For anyone else using it, the consequences would be dire. Some medical treatments can't be explained. But if you use this treatment, I promise you there will be complications.

PSYCHE
How can I thank you?

PERSEPHONE
Send a little extra low-fat cream cheese with scallions.

RABBI *(To us)*
So Psyche obtained Persephone's anti-aging formula, and began her ascent out of the Underworld.

END OF SCENE

SCENE THIRTEEN

(Psyche is walking back to the world of the living. She is exhausted. She tries to sing but can't.)

RABBI *(To us)*
She walked. And she walked. And she walked. And she walked some more, until she passed a sign that read: "Now Leaving The Underworld. Your Weight For A Quarter."

(Finally, she comes across a border sign: "Now Leaving The Underworld. Your Weight For A Quarter.")

RABBI *(To us)*
You tell me a woman who can resist getting on a scale. My wife weighs 250 pounds, and she still weighs herself.

(She steps on the scale and sees her reflection in the mirror. She screams in horror when she sees what she now looks like.)

PSYCHE
I am ancient and hideous! I've lost him! I've lost my love and my looks! Nothing matters anymore!

(She opens the jar of anti-aging cream. She puts it all over her face and immediately passes out into a deep slumber.)

RABBI *(To us)*
And after that, Psyche opened the jar of anti-aging cream and rubbed it all over her hands and face and throat and feet, like it was Coppertone. Immediately, she fell into a deep slumber. I took it upon myself to escort Cupid to where she lay, outside the Door of the Living.

RABBI *(To Cupid)*
She's dying, sir. She's lying on the tracks of her tears.
You must forgive her. You must help her.

CUPID
But my mother forbids it.

RABBI
How much longer are you gonna keep doing what your mother tells you to do? Look what that did to Portnoy. Look what that did to Hamlet. Look what that did to Oedipus. Look what that did to me.

(Cupid takes out one of his arrows and shoots Psyche with it, reviving her.)

PSYCHE
Am I dreaming? Is it actually you?

CUPID
I'm here, darling. We'll never be parted again.

PSYCHE
What happened?

CUPID
Persephone's anti-aging cream is a personalized formula. If anyone but the intended uses it they fall asleep forever. Only true love can revive them.

PSYCHE
What will we tell your mother?

RABBI
The mighty God of Power and Wisdom will speak to your mother.

CUPID
You have proven yourself to me, my dearest one.

(He leans in to kiss her.)

PSYCHE
   Could you take off your wings and arrows first?

(He does so, then kisses her.)

END OF SCENE

SCENE FOURTEEN

(Venus adoring herself in the mirror at her spa. Rabbi Zeus enters.)

RABBI
   Venus, you're looking more beautiful than ever.

VENUS
   How are you, Zeus? It's been years.

RABBI
   Remember that night at the Brown Derby?

VENUS
   We landed up under the Santa Monica Pier.

RABBI
   I cherish that memory.

VENUS
   Are you really a rabbi in Flatbush now?

RABBI
   I'm also the President of the Soviet Union and the United States, not to
   mention the Coach of the Norwegian Luge Team. And next month I'll be
   flying to Mars inside Sputnik.

VENUS
   The most powerful God of them all, yet you still have time for me? I'm
   flattered!

RABBI
   I also have something for you: Persephone's anti-aging cream.

(He hands her the jar of Persephone's anti-aging cream.)

VENUS
   Where did you get that? Don't tell me Psyche has seduced you too! Oh Zeus,
   what have I done to deserve that girl in my life? I'm a simple, good woman.

RABBI

Venus, as your old friend can I give you some advice? If Psyche and Cupid raise a family, she will no longer be competition for you. According to the law of the Gods, if they marry she will become a deity and be forever subordinate to her mother-in-law.

VENUS

But she's from Flatbush!

RABBI

Some very nice people came from Flatbush. You came from Wisconsin.

VENUS

Shh! No one in the world knows that except for you.

RABBI

Your secret is safe with me. As far as I am concerned I met your parents on a fjord in Norway.

VENUS

You're a very wise man.

RABBI

And you're the most beautiful woman I've ever met. Venus, you'll never need Persephone's anti-aging cream. You are forever…

(Sings.)

Venus in blue jeans
Mona Lisa with a ponytail
She's a walkin' talkin' work of art
She's the girl who stole my heart.

VENUS
(Sings.)
I'm Venus in blue jeans
I'm ev'rything I hoped I'd be
A teenage goddess from above
A fairy tale come true

END OF SCENE

SCENE FIFTEEN

(The rabbi presides at the end of Cupid's and Psyche's marriage ceremony. Everyone stands in attendance.)

RABBI

And so in the names of the gods, Venus, Zeus and John F. Kennedy president, I pronounce you man and wife.

(Cupid and Psyche kiss. The rabbi turns to the audience.)

RABBI

And so, dear congregation, what can you and the Bat Mitzvah take away from this myth, and what kind of shrink becomes the sturgeon king?

Frankly, the story of Psyche and Cupid is, in this case, a particularly useful one especially for our Bat Mitzvah girl, Flora Berman. First of all, we learn from Psyche's desperate sisters never to marry the first Ear, Nose, and Throat man you meet. From Venus, we learn that beauty's only skin deep and anti-aging creams are a hoax. A wiser beauty would turn to liposuction and cosmetic surgery just as a wiser shrink would have gone into talk radio. Finally, the love of Psyche and Cupid proves that physical attraction plays a tremendous part in any relationship. But so does smoked fish.

Cupid and Psyche lived happily ever after and opened branches of her father's fish shop in airports and malls across Europe and the Far East. They had three daughters who formed their own Luge team, winning silver, bronze, and gold medals at the Lillehammer Olympics. It reminds us all that beauty may only be skin deep but it counts a lot. It reconfirms my belief that boys should be wary of narcissistic mothers, and girls shouldn't always rely on their sisters.

But most of all, dear congregation and Bat Mitzvah girl, the message of today's sermon is get married even if it takes shooting yourself with an arrow. Those of us who refuse to connect in this life, especially those of you who are women over forty, will be prey to plagues like locusts, vermin, and indecipherable rashes. If we don't share our lives, we will lose all sense of self-respect and order. Chaos and mid-life crisis will ensue.

I knew a judge in Beverly Hills named Vicky who quit the bench to join the circus. You ask why? Her loneliness was overwhelming. She yearned for a community. Like Psyche's immortal beauty, Vicky only had her perfect mind for company.

Dear congregation, there is a thin line these days between complexity and ambiguity. Maybe the answer is to look into our soul and simplify. People ask me why do bad things happen to good people. Well, it has to happen to somebody. Why not you? Why not me? Psyche was a good girl. It's not her fault that she was so pretty. It's not her fault she became a victim of her own beauty. It just worked out that way. We need to learn to take responsibility, the way that Psyche ultimately did. If I am beautiful, yes, it is my fault. If I am ill, yes, it is my fault. If there are random acts of violence, yes, it is my fault. If bad things happen to me, then I'm the one who has to deal with them, whether I deserve it or not. Because I cannot blame it on a good and caring God. And I don't care if it's the God of Moses or one of the gods of ancient Greece. God is holy, and we are not. And once we accept that we can learn to truly love one another because we know our place in the universe. There is no reason for anyone, even those of us not as young and beautiful as Psyche or Cupid, to be bitter and alone. Bitterness is a cancer of the soul, wearing away at the human heart and imagination. Connect, dear congregation! Start right now by taking each other's hands and singing "I Say A Little Prayer For You," just like Rupert Everett did in my favorite Julia Roberts movie, *My Best Friend's Wedding.*

(He sings.)

Forever. Forever, you'll stay in my heart
And I will love you

(The rest of the congregation joins in.)

ALL
Forever, forever, we never will part
Oh how I love you
Together, together that's how it must be
To live without you
Would only be heartbreak for me.

Peace be with you. Dear congregation, good night.

END OF PLAY

Since You Came

It is not water.
I cannot lie in it.
Nor can my hands
Reach forward for any rhythm
To draw me near
To where a shore might be.

It is not ground either.
No place for a foothold.
Nor can my eyes find mountains
Where fields might serve the stay
Of stones that harbour only hunger
For the here and now.

It is not completely fire
Though the burning has begun
To singe the cords
That tie the heart's basket
To the one tree
I thought I knew.

It is more the air
That has lost its nerve
To hold the vase of thought,
The word-scratched air
That lets the white rain in
To wash the red font of memory.

II

Self-Understanding
and the Messy Self

C. K. Williams

The Clause

This entity I call my mind, this hive of restlessness,
this wedge of want my mind calls self,
this self which doubts so much and which keeps reaching,
keeps referring, keeps aspiring, longing, towards some state
from which ambiguity would be banished and uncertainty expunged;

this implement my mind and self imagine they might make together,
which would have everything accessible to it,
all our doings and undoings all at once before it,
so it would have at last the right to bless, or blame,
for without everything before you, all at once, how bless, how blame?

this capacity imagination, self and mind conceive might be the "soul,"
which would be able to regard such matters as creation and destruction,
origin and extinction, of species, peoples, even families—even mine—
of equal consequence, and might finally solve the quandary
of this thing of being, and this other thing of not;

these layers, these divisions, these meanings or the lack thereof,
these fissures and abysses beside which I stumble, over which I reel:
is the place, the space, they constitute,
which I never satisfactorily experience but from which the fear
I might be torn away appalls me, me, or what might most be me?

Even mine, I say, as if I might ever believe such a thing;
bless and blame, I say, as though I could ever not.
This ramshackle, this unwieldy, this jerry-built assemblage,
this unfelt always felt disarray; is this the sum of me, if so,
is it where I'm meant to end, just where I started out?

∼ *Patricia Foster* ∼

The Last Place on Earth

PENINSULA OF GREEN JUTS OUT INTO THE CLEAR BLUE of Lake Superior. Pines and fir and the sudden beauty of birch trees shelter the highway from a hot, summer sun. Yesterday it had been cool and rainy but today the sun cleanses the sky, shines down on us as my husband and I park the rental car in a hooded turn-out, then walk into forty acres of Michigan woods with our friend Jon and his Uncle Joe who live nearby. They've brought their dog Leo, a seven-year-old black cocker spaniel known for his slumbers on the couch, though now he's excited, frisky, worrying his nose. He sniffs at the trees, at lilac bushes, licks at pale green lichen coating a stump.

"C'mon, boy," Uncle Joe calls as we walk deeper into the woods. Leo growls at a root that humps up from the damp forest floor. Beyond me a tree bends like the bottom half of a pretzel, the trunk thick and twisted, leaves reaching up to the blue shiver of sky. The men talk politics, heaping scorn on the Bushies, the Christian Right, the arrogance of the Neo-cons, topics so familiar I tune them out, letting myself drift into a little tap dance of symptoms that, to doctors, don't often sound like symptoms because they're as much of the mind as the body: the slow emptying of words and the crash of memory rather than the white heat of pain. It's words I lose, words that dissolve like tissue paper in water, words that drip, collide and splash across my consciousness like frothing waves and then, as suddenly, slip back into uncharted waters. I'm constantly swimming towards them, hoping to catch them before they dissolve.

Even thinking about this, my arms droop, my wrists ache. I'm suddenly, impossibly exhausted.

Another symptom.

As we walk toward a clearing, I notice that Leo's run off into the woods. "Ah, don't worry about him," I hear Uncle Joe say to my husband, patting him on the shoulder. "He knows these woods." My husband loves dogs, particularly big dogs that fetch sticks and run impulsively through his legs. I imagine he's slightly disappointed in Leo. He's always talking about his favorite golden retriever or the black lab that was too smart for his own good, a wandering Romeo with a fickle harem. We can't have dogs in the house because of my allergies (more symptoms), and my husband has had to content himself with the neighbor's three dogs, big, raucous, rescued dogs who unleash a feast of noise next door.

By the time we hike into the clearing—a small meadow of wild ferns and what looks like purple yarrow—Jon says, "Really, it's a scandal the way those bastards are weaving this web of fantasy while the press sits on its—" but before he can finish that sentence, there's a frenzy of yelps, a strangled shriek from deeper in the woods.

We all rush toward the sounds, certain that Leo is in the jaws of a bobcat or a bear, his squeals a high, sharp yip of terror. Even as I'm running, I remember the three bears I saw yesterday, clumsy cubs crossing the road as if they were out for a Sunday stroll or to check on Goldilocks' bed. How will we defend ourselves?

When we break through the bushes, we don't see Leo in the jaws of another animal, but Leo with his teeth sunk in the shank of a fawn lying curled in the brush, her velvet eyes glazed with terror. Leo's ears and snout bloom rosy with blood and he clenches his hold as we rush towards him, shouting "Stop that! Bad dog! Bad Leo!"

"Don't *hurt* him," Uncle Joe yells. Slick with blood, Leo slips through our hands, running in circles, his thick curly fur blood dark and slimy. Blood spurts from the fawn's middle, red poppies bursting on tawny skin. Leo bounds toward the trees, barking joyfully until Uncle Joe catches him and he howls in fury.

With Leo restrained, we turn quickly to the fawn as she half rises—a mangled heap of sticks and skin—then collapses back to the ground. Her legs won't hold. Emboldened, Leo escapes Uncle Joe's grasp and rushes at the fawn, clamping his teeth into skin so quickly that, for a moment, no one moves.

"Bad dog!" Uncle Joe yells, coming at Leo with a stick. To our relief, the swat of the stick sends Leo running.

Again the fawn tries to rise, blood dripping, a high, feeble bleating.

"I can't watch this," my husband says, turning away, following Jon and Uncle Joe and Leo back toward the car. But I squat low between bushes, staring, my hands clenched at my side, knowing the fawn is too weak to survive. "*Let go*," I whisper. I stare at the fawn's eyes, watching as she tries again and again to rise; when she collapses, her eyes go walleyed with fear. Blood the color of dried cherries trickles steadily into the grass. "*Let go!*" I repeat as if speaking to myself, as if this fawn is my animal twin, but to my surprise, she's up, her legs holding. Before I can stand, she leaps into the forest.

After we drop Jon and Uncle Joe and Leo at their summer house, my husband and I wind up the narrow road that bisects Keweenaw Peninsula towards Copper Harbor, the very tip of the peninsula. We're visitors here, voyeurs from land-locked Iowa. I'm teaching a two-week class at Northern Michigan University in Marquette, and my husband's just flown in for a long weekend. Even as we pass through miles of forests, delighted when we see a rush of water, an inlet of Lake

THE LAST PLACE ON EARTH

Superior as clear and blue as the morning sky, we're still preoccupied with what just happened.

"What's ironic is that Uncle Joe was just telling me they need to get rid of the deer," my husband says, "because they're eating up the new growth of trees."

"Not that way. That was an *attack*," I say, slowing down as the road narrows. "I mean, who wants to see prey and predator during a walk in the woods?"

My husband looks amused. "It's the oldest game in town."

But I'm no longer thinking about the deer and Leo, about irony and deflection. I'm thinking about the struggle that took place inside me Wednesday night, a struggle that sent me running, panicked, out into the apartment parking lot in the middle of the night.

As we pass through Osceola, Calumet, Allouez, and Ahmeet, small interior towns with faded yellow houses and deserted downtowns sandwiched between hills, I can't find the words to explain what happened that night and I'm too tired to blurt out the raw images that linger in my mind: the fierce wind, the empty parking lot, the uncomprehending face of the young girl in a silver Toyota. And me: mouth trembling, asking for help. Plagued with Chronic Fatigue and Environmental Allergies—modern illnesses that resist a dramatic plot—I feel doubly silenced because these syndromes lack a linguistic concreteness as if all I can say is that I'm slowly slipping away from myself.

"Running on empty," I complain to my husband on such days.

He nods, calls me Dreamy. "It's okay," he says.

And that's what I want to believe as the fatigue travels ravenously through my body. *Lie down immediately*, I think. *Stop!* Instead, I push the fatigue away. *Back off!* I give it a shove because that's the legacy of my family: to be fierce, relentless, to use the will like a whip. "You've got to be driven if you want anything in this world!" I remember my mother telling me as a teenager. Even as I rolled my eyes, I took in the message. Down with lily-livered loafers! Down with the deserters!

But what happens to the will during illness? What happens if the will begins to balk and meets its match?

We're just outside one of the larger towns of the Keweenaw Peninsula, winding our way over an old-fashioned trellis bridge, the architecture above us like a metal umbrella, stiff and stern, politely rusting. The road curves and suddenly we're climbing up a hill where, to our surprise, we see a small white-washed church, a one-room box with a steeple, perched on a grassy yard beside a dirt road.

We pull over to the side of the road so my husband and I can change places. Now he drives and I sightsee, though today I snuggle down in the passenger seat and close my eyes. I arrange my legs on the dash, grab a blanket to roll up in my lap and rest my arms on. "Sleepy," I say. "But wake me if you see a Beef-a roo."

"Right."

Sometimes we play a game when I'm not feeling well, the premise of which is that one of us gets to be the sickest. "My hair hurts," my husband says now. "I've got this white gunk on my tongue and a back ache. You never have a back ache."

"Do too."

"Not like mine. Mine feels like somebody threw a cue ball and hit me right here." I know, even though I'm not opening my eyes, that he's reaching for a place in the middle of his back. "Driving just kills me."

"Driving will take your mind off your hair."

"Oh, I got the misery," he says, trying to tickle my ankle. "You've got nothing on me."

As we pass a deserted copper mine, I think again about last Wednesday, my fourth day of teaching in Marquette. I woke early to raw blue skies, a light breeze. Once out of bed, I decided a brisk walk would work wonders for my flagging immune system. I started down a wooded path, listening as the sounds changed from car noises and kitchen tasks to the chatter of insects, the scurry of lizards and chipmunks and animals I didn't want to know about. When I stopped to pick some kind of wild daisy trapped behind a tree stump, I saw a beaded earring on the ground, all shades of red, that seemed destined for me. Elated, I picked it up and told myself to "be positive," to imagine myself alert and clear-headed and optimistic for the rest of the week.

But two hours after my walk, I dropped my head on my desk. Did I have the flu? A cold? No. This was merely the condition of my illness. Inexplicably groggy, I jumped back in the shower, letting the hot water pound my body and bring me back to the living. After I walked to class, the earring in my pocket—*be positive, be positive*—I taught for two hours, then met with students in my unair-conditioned office, the heat as thick and tight as a wool blanket. "My mother thinks I'm going to hell," the first student whispered, bent towards me, staring intently at the floor. And then she looked at me with dark, solemn eyes. "And I think so too!" Students told me about the pull of fundamentalist religions, how the Finns grabbed hold of the evangelical church and held on for dear life. They told me about living far back in the woods, getting their hair cut once a year, about losing babies, losing jobs, about going to jail.

"I can't write about what I really want to write about," the fifth student said, leaning near, her breath smelling of pizza and coffee. "It's too … scary." I knew she wanted me to probe, to be her confessional ear, but I could feel my mind closing down, words dissolving, the fatigue leaching all energy as if it were a predator attacking prey. "I have to go," I said suddenly as if I'd just smelled smoke.

As I walked back to the apartment past the library and the dorms, what I felt was no longer exhaustion but something larger, more threatening, a thickening of fear that I'd never heal myself, that rest and showers and herbs and medication would not do the trick. Was it possible this leaking of energy and words was to be my life? Frightened, I wanted to hear the voice of my husband in Iowa, to let him bring me back soft to myself. "The grasshopper that cannot jump well," he'd say shyly, "all the more charming."

Maybe then I'd smile.

Once inside my apartment, I rushed to the phone, hoping for connection. When I'd arrived in Marquette on Sunday, I discovered my cell phone was out of range, the apartment phone disconnected, the office phone restricted to local calls. "It will be fixed," I was assured daily by the administration, but each night when I lifted the receiver I heard nothing but the surge of my own breath. I was alone in small-town Michigan without a phone, a car, a radio, a TV, or even a coffee pot. This ugly apartment facing an empty parking lot seemed suddenly symbolic of how vulnerable I was. Ill. Alone.

Let go!

On Sunday, Monday and Tuesday, I'd tried to talk myself into gratitude as if I'd just arrived in a Third World country. Look, you have a flush toilet. Look, you have cereal and milk and cheese in the refrigerator. Look, you have a table and four chairs where you can sit and drink green tea and read books and jot down ideas.

It didn't work.

Instead, I sucked it up and walked twelve blocks to a pay phone outside a Quick Trip to call my husband, inhaling gas fumes from the pumps and yelling over the gunning of engines. But this Wednesday night I knew I couldn't make that walk. I'd been losing words all day—"cesspool" came out of my mouth when I meant community, "boundary" when I meant horizon, "desperate" when I intended demonic. I didn't know why the words came unstuck, why I couldn't remember names, why Isak Dinesen, Charlotte Brontë or Andre Dubus—all familiar names—had fallen into some mental cellar. "That's 'deary' not 'dreary,'" one of my students corrected me, and I nodded, embarrassed.

That night I went nowhere. The most I could do was make dinner and lie down. After stripping off my class clothes and putting on a pajama top and jeans, I ate an apple by the window, staring out at the five cars parked in the parking lot for thirty, telling myself it was just another sultry night, another ten hours of solitude where I could read and relax and then, yes, then, the words and energy might come back. As I lay down on the couch, the wind came up, fierce and uneasy in the trees. Something eased in me, and I grew quiet and still.

When I woke, it was dark, my mouth dry, my limbs heavy. Blasts of air rattled the windows, making the screens quiver and my papers flutter on the table. The bathroom door slammed shut, and I heard the creak of branches against the roof. I don't know why I was frightened, but I got up and stood absolutely still in the darkness, staring at the window, straining to hear someone's voice, any voice: a girlish giggle, a man calling out a curse, a shout. There was nothing but the wind. And me. And the sudden realization that I'd run away again, had come to Michigan to shake loose the familiar weight of illness as if each new place might be a fresh start, a revision.

On impulse I grabbed the phone, punched in numbers and put the phone to my ear as if magically I could will it to work. There was not even a twitch of sound, and I jammed the phone back into its cradle. *What if I can't finish teaching this class?* I looked at the cut lemons on the counter, the bottled water, the bag of herbs. I'd never been a deserter. I'd always managed. Now I watched the wind catch the blinds. They arced out in a parabola and hung dizzily in suspension, but when they crashed back against the window, something snapped in me: I raced out the door into the parking lot, the wind lifting and twisting my pajama top, swirling my hair as I collided with all that empty space.

I circled that empty parking lot for twenty minutes, the cool air chilling my face and arms as I paced back and forth, watching the street for cars that might turn in. When an old silver Toyota finally did, I had to breathe gulps of air to keep from running toward it as it pulled in next to one of the apartment buildings. I made myself walk—not run—toward the driver's side where I saw a young woman turn to a grocery bag in the passenger's seat. I knew I was hovering, standing too close and when the woman glanced up, she flinched. "What?"

I stepped back. I was quite sure I looked loony in my pajama top, my hair uncombed, a dangle of keys bulging from my waistband.

When she opened the door, her face looked so flushed and young, so open in its uncertainty, I felt both awkward and bemused as I asked if she could help me.

She looked confused, frightened. "What?" she said again.

And then I knew I had made no sense. What, after all, did help mean? How could anyone help with a disease that had so few remedies? How could she know to tell me that the poor little grasshopper is charming? I stepped back, closed my eyes and said quietly, "Could I please just rent your cell phone for one night to call my husband?"

"Oh, I don't have a cell phone."

It seemed so little to ask that tears wet my cheeks and I hunched over like someone about to vomit.

She shifted the grocery sack and watched me dispassionately, then said briskly, "You can use my apartment phone if you need to call someone."

I followed her into her apartment with its shabby drapes and cheap furniture, the stash of empty pop bottles ready to be redeemed. She stood beside me and pointed to the phone, but suddenly I felt ashamed of myself, ashamed of my exhaustion and my panic and my terrible neediness, ashamed of my illness and all the anger it engendered. Too embarrassed to call my husband long distance in Iowa, I rang the professor in charge of the writing program at the university. I'm sure I said several things, but I only remember this: "I need help. I can't … I can't do this anymore."

And then I went upstairs to my apartment and slept.

As we pass through Phoenix, Michigan, I push the rolled-up blanket against the window and curl up tighter. My husband lets me sleep, mouth open, drool on my shoulder, my neck at some tortured angle that's sure to hurt when I wake up. I sleep with the rhythm of the car, its slow, swinging curves, its steady climb up small, rolling hills. When I wake, the car is stopped by the side of the road and I'm alone in the passenger seat facing a two-story raspberry red building where huge white words slightly smudged with age announce: THE LAST PLACE ON EARTH.

I stare at the words with instant recognition. I think of the fawn, fragile, wounded and yet still trying to rise on unsteady legs. A triumph of will. I think of myself walking back to my apartment that night, feeling shattered, my will broken. I didn't know how to "fix" myself, didn't know the next step to take except to ask for a phone line to my husband, to home and comfort. And I think about this: that Wednesday I'd told my students about a term in nonfiction called 'vertical drop.' Vertical drop is not quite the same as an epiphany in the short story, an explosive recognition, but a moment in the essay where the narrator drops down to a deeper level of intimacy, inviting the reader to enter more fully into the dark face of vulnerability. What I didn't tell them is that there's another kind of vertical drop, a release into uncertainty, a psychic limbo where you are present but diminished, where, instead of becoming clear, things become fuzzy and dim and words slip eerily through the cracks. This is the place I live now. Not home. Not comfort. The place I'm trying to crawl out of.

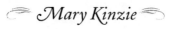

Mary Kinzie

Facing North
Late householder, early pilgrim phase

The self is not an object but an act,
an old friend wrote with a sense of the border loosened
into fear, and time that staggers
with its arm about his shoulder in the leaf drift
yet the thought became so clear, it grew a written
thought, a thought for writing down, drawn out
across the frame of close antithesis
our tongue at once permits and, well, enjoys
while making thought so modestly *more* clear
than it needs to be that truth is piqued
instead of broadened—as the frame we use,
the not wholly mindless now but all too natural

medium of the blank-verse line makes thought
that wanted to be aimless, full of aim,
and the tight shoulders of the slacks and stresses,
although they may shiver a little when intuition
traces out a line as through humid woods,
which stones emerging along the way like faces
make sharper and more conscious as the words flex
and limber up iambically (*not x but y*
fits well here, too), their shift a kind of
anemone whose tissue flutters in the steady current,
combing water of its nutrients.

> Not thing but will, not with but toward,
> not chair but ledge, not sum but subtrahend:
> how easily the grammar bosses us to the wall,
> not me but you, not surge but drag,
> I'd wish to surge but always feel the drag
> that kept myself from jumping off the ledge
> into a circle whose circumference
> you couldn't stand in the center of
> and I'd wish I liked
> the shifting view from nowhere, more.

*

Here I am with the cat on my lap in a room that faces north,
a thin loaf of rooms with a feeling of long shadow in bright day.
Here
in the murk
above the desk where several brand-new strands
of a half-hearted trace of spider web keep reappearing,
there are those volumes
of the furnished-rental world, novels too dull or strange to steal:
Arrowsmith, Studs Lonigan,
The Late George Apley, flotsam by Dos Passos,
all the faded froth of the fifties book clubs,
Will Durant alongside Hardy's *Tess*
the latter in a fine hand-tooled edition
with watered silk endpapers—but why *Tess*,
with her harsh fate, in pretty leather? These oddments mount up
like a rattling cage
shaped to an absence.

*

The only other time I'd tried to write
surrounded by such brokenness,
there were two books:
one, by Samuel Butler, I never finished;
and the novel of the emperor Hadrian's love
for the dead ephebe Antinoüs
in whose name and image he raised up beautiful things
all over Asia Minor,
beautiful places, too, where the emperor
as Yourcenar pictures him
walked on the backs of others
through the architectonic emptiness
of memory: It was something he could do.
It filled the time.

*

That was my leisure reading all one summer
at MacDowell where, when not wandering in the shadow
of Monadnock, I was trying to decode the friendly nervous
        nonsense
of John Ashbery's "Houseboat Days"
in a cottage where for a while each morning
the sun shone directly down a huge stone chimney
on two demonic andirons with carved eyeholes
blankly attentive
to crickets moving
their sandy legs over the spent ash,
                        "... and you
don't see until it's all over how little
there was to learn ..."

>   *Only when smoke*
>   *from their dinners*
>   *has died down*
>   *and the dishes are removed*
>   *may a pilgrim approach the*
>   *human habitations*
>   *to beg her meal*

*

Good heavens . . . there I am the previous winter
north of Chicago, north also
of the little city-center candy blocks
of the eastern seaboard,
in Montreal, doubly adulterous,
my French not very good and perhaps a shade
taller than the man I went there with.
He did not like to give or hear endearments.
His French was excellent. The first night drunkenness
carried us off so quickly
it was as if we had left something behind, in that other life,
and without it
the moment wouldn't come into a shape.
A horrible week-end.
I kept thanking him,
an awful sense of wrong making me abject,
"Thank you for our time together"
(by which I meant
to ask myself,
why had I done this?)
and he made an invisible bow
in French,
"*Mais c'est à moi.*" It made me cringe
to think how obvious
abjection is, to think
how Proust thought of Marcel
thinking of his beloved almost as a doll
he had been molding,
"the docile body which he had pressed
tightly in his arms and explored
with his fingers . . . " (The artist's doll . . .)
In the museums, I leaned forward to the tiny paintings
which he said not to touch.

*

No, the self can't mend, it can only want
and pretend not to want,
aloof, disheartened. Here it is,
breaking things all over again
trying to speak of things all over again,
trying to hull them

the wood asters
the tree with the strange leathery leaves,
the smokebush, the beautyberry

caught at dusk in the crinkled leaf-veil
of the high thin trees
with the few last flecks of day's white
shimmering high above (was I under water?) . . .

all the reality whose exactness
has lost its dignity

and the desk where the words for this
move on a piece of paper
facing north.

Rebecca Goldstein

The Fiction of the Self and the Self of Fiction

WHEN I WAS A CHILD, there were some nights, while waiting for sleep to come, when I would go through a mental ritual that induced a result both thrilling and terrifying. It would begin with my asking how anyone could tell that I was me and not C. C., the girl in my class that I happened to most want to be. Of course I knew that I was me, and C. C. knew who she was. But all that anyone else could see were these two people, me and C. C., and not that *extra* fact, that I was me. For all they knew she was the one kid in that wealthy Wasp neighborhood whose family didn't fit in, and I was the china-doll daughter of a Protestant minister. What could they see that would tell them otherwise? And what, for that matter, could I see? The more I tried to get a fix on what the extra fact was—the word *extra* was of the essence of the exercise—the more it receded from my grasp. The ritual ended with a rush, which was the thrilling and terrifying part and which consisted in the sense that I had lost whatever the tenuous connection was with myself, that the string had been cut and what had been tethered before was now drifting so free as to be almost lost sight of. I'd pull myself abruptly out of the vertiginous heights just at the point when I got too high for comfort.

Who knew that my childish ritual was preparation for my adult occupations as both philosopher and novelist? Both job descriptions involve calling into question what we normally can assume is one's most secure relationship, the one that requires no attending or tending whatsoever, the identity with one's self.

Philosophers have long confronted the confoundedness of self-identity, pounding out the metaphysical consequences of the sense of strangeness that can irradiate our closest relationship. Spinoza goes so far as to channel this sense of strangeness into the very substance of his ethics, working it up into a form of secular salvation, one which offers us some of the benefits of traditional religion, including escape not from death—there is no escape from that—but from its terror. To view things as they truly are, not from within some particular point of view but from the stance of radical objectivity, is to view things *sub specie aeternitatus*—under the guise of the form of eternity. This is the view that Spinoza unequivocally recommends, not only because it offers us the true view of things, but because it also offers us the only solace for our inescapable finitude. Solace consists in the disappearance of the reality of self-identity; that extra fact of who one is in the world gets swallowed up in radical objectivity. The view *sub specie aeternitatus* can't accommodate the extra-ness of that fact I had tried to get a fix on in my childhood ritual. If the true view of things can't accommodate the fact of selfhood, then the self is a fiction of sorts, and Spinoza, no fan of fiction, prescribes permanent untethering. To the extent that we align our point of view with objective truth we lose our connection to ourselves. That rush I experienced in my childhood bed becomes sustained and becalmed, a form of ecstatic rationalism, that delivers to us the ultimate freedom, that of becoming indifferent even to our own demise: "The free man thinks least of all things upon death."

David Hume, a philosopher who is at odds with Spinoza on almost all fundamental questions, agrees with the rationalist on the fictionhood of the self.

> For my part, when I enter most intimately into what I call myself, I always stumble on some particular perception or other, of heat or cold, light or shade, love or hatred, pain or pleasure. I never can catch myself at any time without a perception, and never can observe any thing but the perception. When my perceptions are remov'd for any time, as by sound sleep; so long am I insensible of myself, and may truly be said not to exist. And were all my perceptions remov'd by death, and cou'd I neither think, nor feel, nor see, nor love, nor hate after the dissolution of my body, I shou'd be entirely annihilated, nor do I conceive what is farther requisite to make me a perfect non-entity. If any one, upon serious and unprejudic'd reflection thinks he has a different notion of himself, I must confess I can reason no longer with him. All I can allow him is, that he may be in the right as well as I, and that we are essentially different in this particular. He may, perhaps, perceive something simple and continu'd, which he calls himself; tho' I am certain there is no such principle in me (*Treatise on Human Nature*, Book I, section vi).

Among contemporary philosophers, none has done more justice to the extra-ness of self-identity than Thomas Nagel, who, like Spinoza, claims that the objective point of view can't accommodate the fact that one is who one is, but who, unlike Spinoza, uses this non-accommodation to argue for the limits of the objective point of view. The view from nowhere, which is what Nagel dubs the stance of radical objectivity, is incomplete, unable to accommodate some facts which are, nevertheless, facts. Among these is the fact that I am me and not C. C.

So there is philosophy in which to ponder the problematic nature of the self, its possible fictionhood. And then there is fiction itself.

Literature is a deep and sustained form of enchantment, for both the reader and the writer. It is of the essence of this enchantment that something unusual happens to one's relationship with one's self, as well as with one's sense of sequential time, both of which tetherings are fundamental in shaping a personal sense of reality.

It is not the job of fiction to suggest, as philosophy sometimes does, that these tetherings are mere fictions. But fiction does, just in going about its business of enchantment, tamper with these tetherings. The art of fiction, in both the writing and the reading of it, can be viewed, in fact, as an exercise in controlled and elaborate untethering.

Fiction's metaphysical tampering, most especially with one's sense of self, accounts for one of the most baffling aspects of literary art; Plato himself pondered it: Why are literary artists so much smarter in their texts than in their persons? Authors of immortal texts can come off sounding dull in person, even when asked to explicate their own authored lines, much less anything else. It was not truly these authors then who authored these lines, Plato concluded, and rightly I think, though I would not share his further claim that the dubiety in authorship spreads the stain of doubt on the authored.

Plato was arguably the greatest literary artist among philosophers, a distinction that did not deter him from banishing the epic poets, who were the novelists of his day, from his imagined utopia. He was deeply intimate with the spellbinding aspect of literary art and, being the reality-chauvinist that he was, could not approve of it. In the *Republic*'s stratified scheme of things, the most degraded and irrational form of awareness is *eikrasia*, a state of phantasmagorical confusion, fixed on illusion, deplorably clueless in all matters of what's what. In terms of the Allegory of the Cave, probably the most influential piece of imaginative writing in the history of Western philosophy, *eikrasia* is represented by the prisoners enchained so as to be forcibly facing the back wall on which are cast the passing shadows of an unseen fire (*Republic* 514-5). For Plato, the poets, and those who consume their products, are inhabitants of this lowest realm. This low-end placement earns the poets the philosopher's disapproval and their regrettable expulsion from the rational city.

Toward the end of the *Republic*, Plato permits the bare possibility that someone will persuade him of the redeeming rationality of poetry and then he would lift his ban on poetry "since we ourselves are very conscious of her spell." But the theurgical aspects of literary art clearly made him deeply leery, leading him to fight it out with the extraordinary literary artist inside him. He speaks of poetry in the *Phaedrus* [244-5] as a kind of holy madness or intoxication and goes on in that gloriously conflicted dialogue to link it to Eros, another ambiguous derangement that joins us with the gods even while it undermines our rational take on the world.

It might seem that enchantment, being enchantment, cannot be conducive to truth. This is precisely how it did seem to Plato, at least when he called for the banishment of the poets in the *Republic* and maligned their very sanity in such dialogues as the *Ion*. I would like to respond to Plato not by gainsaying the point that literature is a form of enchantment, for I accept this point without a quibble. Rather the situation seems much stranger to me. The enchantments of fiction are, even though not deliberately truth-*seeking*, nevertheless—deeply and strangely—truth-*attracting*. The writer and reader of fiction puts herself in the way of assaults from truths of the large and impersonal variety, which is, of course, precisely the variety that Plato values.

I do not, by the way, think that one *has* to make fictive enchantment out to be a truth provider in order to justify its pleasures. I am not so much of a Platonic purist as to make such a demand on any art form. Beauty is justification in itself, without the added benefits of truth. Nevertheless I believe it to be an interesting truth that the particular nature of literature's enchantment, which does involve, as Plato charged, being out of one's own head, should sometimes result in a clearer insight into reality than ever the view from within one's own head. Though the narrative artist, unlike the philosopher, is not out on a truth hunt, truth can find her nonetheless. It is, I think, precisely the tamperings with the fact of self that constitutes the essence of fictive enchantment and that puts reader and writer in the way of assaults from large and impersonal truths.

To make out my answer to Plato I am going to draw on my experience both as a reader and, even more so, as a writer. I think that the process of enchantment associated with both is significantly similar but that writing is the far more dramatic form of enchantment, exaggerating, and therefore making clearer, certain elements common to both. Writing fiction is an extraordinarily potent form of self-enchantment, which is, of course, a state distinct from enchantment with self, though the two are not mutually exclusive.

The writer's self-enchantment is, in many respects, simply an intensification of what the actively susceptible reader experiences. To be a susceptible fiction reader requires active powers of imagination, though of course not every deeply susceptible reader will be susceptible to all works, or even to the same works at different times over the course of his life. Probably the most deeply susceptible period of reading in every deeply susceptible reader's life is adolescence, when what one reads gets enlisted in the general all-consuming project of self-construction. Adolescence, with its characteristically blurry outer edges of personal identity, puts one into a particularly vulnerable position in regard to fictive enchantments.

What I want to say, then, as both reader and as writer is something like this: That fictive enchantment puts us into a certain metaphysically compromised situation—the point of Plato's displeasure—which is oddly truth-receptive. The delusions of fictive enchantment induce us to suspend our commitment to certain metaphysical fundamentals without really dislodging them (recalling Plato's charge of induced forgetfulness). Unlike the delusions of madness, this is willed and controlled and fully self-conscious delusion or forgetfulness. Our hold on the given ontological framework is not so much abandoned as slightly loosened, just enough for enchantment to take hold. Fictive enchantment demands a duality of orientation, both around the ordinary first-person facts of who-ness and where-ness and when-ness, but also away from these.

This duality of orientation has its counterpart in the very mechanics of reading and writing. We remain—as writer, as reader—very much tethered to the here and now, where the mechanics of writing and reading require our attention. But we are also—as writer, as reader—transported to the elsewhere, inhabiting the penumbral world that rises up beyond the page. So though we are tethered to the here and now and must attend to it, yet even so our attention lives elsewhere.

This bifurcation of an expanded attention, this sense of being present at two different places, participating in two different worlds, is duplicated on a deeper metaphysical level. We at once maintain our hold on the basic metaphysical matrix, knowing who and where and when we are; and yet, to a certain extent—the extent of our enchantment—we let it go.

It is in this loosening of our metaphysical hold—a loosening which is anathema to a metaphysical purist like Plato—that truth, paradoxically, can slip in, its appearance often taking us, whether as writer or as reader, entirely by surprise. For what this loosening is able to induce is both a form of extra-personal experience, which can be as veridical as it is odd, as well as a re-orientation of events along an axis of significance, both of which states can work singly and, even more forcefully, together to put one in the way of startling truth.

In other words, the phenomenology of fictive enchantment is quite profoundly weird. It is only because it is so familiar and natural to us, at least as readers, that we tend to take it for granted. But it really is a very peculiar business. Fictive enchantment tampers, in a playful and impermanent way, with one's sense of metaphysical fundamentals, facts that hold down our sense of reality, fundamentals which are only systematically questioned in that other weird business, philosophy.

The first of these metaphysical fundamentals is the sense of personal identity—of oneself as impermeably distinct from all others, enclosed within one's own ongoing version of the world, which is semi-opaque (or semi-transparent—an analogue to the half-empty/half-full-glass dichotomy). To enter into fictive enchantment is to feel the walls of the self becoming so porous that the sense of other lives intermingles with one's own. The illusion of inhabiting lives other than one's own, of experiencing, at its most intense, what can feel almost like a discontinuity in personal identity, is delivered to us nowhere else but in

storytelling and madness. Storytelling is the non-pathological analogue to madness, which of course recalls Plato's somewhat less charitable evaluation of the
relation between them.

The other metaphysical fundamental that fiction tampers with is our unenchanted sense of time as merely a succession of moments, the overwhelming
number of which transpire without signifying anything beyond themselves. To
enter into fictive enchantment is also to enter into an alternate, far more dense
and emotive sense of time, quasi-religious in feel because composed only of events
that have an entailed relation to the whole scheme of things, at least as they exist within the particular work. Events *signify* in the world of the novel or short
story or play; experience is presented in units of meaning. The fictive world is
an artificially shaped world, shot through with intentionality. We make our way
through the flickering shadow world of fiction following trails of intentionality,
always seeking the pattern of significance. We live through the internal time of
the plot line, progressing from its beginning to its end, when the story runs out,
a foreshadowing of mortality. The tragic dimension of time—even in a comic
work—is always implicit in fictive enchantment: the story runs out.

It is fiction's power to tamper with our normally tamper-proof senses of personal
identity and sequential time that widens the scope of personal experience for those
who are fictionally engaged and puts them in the way of assaults by truth. The
writer's mind is rendered particularly susceptible to startling discoveries, providing for that semi-paradoxical sense to which many writers have confessed, that
of being so much smarter than themselves when they are writing. This is the very
phenomenon that caused Plato to argue that writers don't have knowledge at all
(*Ion* 533-4). But the highly receptive reader, too, can attain this sense of being
carried to some place beyond herself, open to a different order of insight.

"We might reach a more inclusive understanding of reading (and writing) if we
think in terms of a continuum," writes Sven Birkerts in his essay "The Woman
in the Garden," one in his collection *The Gutenberg Elegies*. "At one end, 'the
writer-the flesh-and-blood individual'; at the other, the flesh-and-blood reader. In
the center the words, the turning pages, the decoding intelligence. Writing is the
monumentally complex operation whereby experience, insight, and imagination
are distilled into language; reading is the equally complex operation that disperses
these distilled elements into another person's life."

There is a certain contrapuntal symmetry between writer and reader that
Birkerts is pointing out here, a counterpoint of complexity and transfiguration,
of moving among language and experience and imagination. There is something
that transpires when we are fictively enchanted, whether as writer or reader, that
makes characters and their extended context live for us, live *vividly*. The Humean
adjective seems particularly apt here, since for Hume vivacity is belief-making.
The vivification that occurs when we are fictively engaged lends the fictions of
literature just enough reality to make us inhabit them almost as if we truly believed
in them: enchantment. Some part of ourselves, whether as writer or as reader,

flows into characters and context, where it is radically transformed, assuming a semi-objectified form that makes it emerge more clearly in its relations and implications. Characters, and their contextual surroundings, must live more vividly for the writer than for the reader, no matter how good, how attentive, how engaged the reader is, but the processes of vivacity-investiture for both writers and readers are, as Birkerts points out, arranged in a counterposing symmetry.

The means by which this happens in a writer is somewhat obscure, not to speak of disorderly. Nonetheless, I think that something along the following lines captures something essential about the creative process, and that it explains how the vivacity of personal experience can get enlarged into something beyond itself. In creating character and context, what happens within the writer is that some aspect of self, some emotion, desire, attitude, fleeting thought or substantive experience or, more likely, a more complicated psychological state compounded of some set of emotion, desire, attitude, etc. gets broken off by virtue of one's attending to it, isolated and objectified in contemplation of its nature, genesis, implications or just plain oddness. I will call this broken-off chunk of inner life a *psycheme*. If a psycheme has the right feel to it, the right degree of implicative complexity and aesthetic malleability, it can become the germ of a character or of a theme or mood or tone, from which all else eventually follows: an entire world wrought. This very private, personal, particular chunk of one's inner life must be turned, in the process of its objectification, into something that will be receptive to reciprocal influxes from the inner lives of readers. This process captures, at least for me, whatever truth there is in the so-called truism that all fiction is autobiographical.

I once, for example, found myself thinking about a certain woman of my acquaintance, who always made me feel profoundly uncomfortable, and these words came to me, quite unbidden: "She's a woman of genius, and a woman of genius is a freak of nature." Of course, I immediately disowned this attitude, shocked—revolted, even—that such benighted words could have formed themselves in me. But they *had* formed themselves; they constituted, in some sense, my own momentary thought. And I have to say that I found the experience, even while I was revolted by it, extraordinarily interesting. It sent my thoughts casting about for the sorts of characters to whom such words would not arrive unbidden and unattached to any other conscious thoughts or attitudes, but for whom these words would be consistent with a general outlook; a character, that is, for whom these words would be characteristic. This stray and disowned piece of me was the drifting spore from which one of my novels, *The Dark Sister*, eventually emerged.

For me, as a writer, I am most taken with psychemes that are already somewhat separate from me, uncharacteristic; they allow me access to characters who really are almost entirely other. Writers all work differently, and what causes a certain imagined context to acquire the requisite vivacity varies from one to the other, of course. Even within the same writer, the conditions of vivacity-investiture vary from project to project. But there is, I think, quite generally something like this process of a chunk of subjectivity coming loose and objectified which then goes on to animate a fictional context. Often there is the context first—you hear some anecdote, say, and think "that could be turned into a story"; but it is only because some psycheme can get injected into it that it takes on the belief-making vivacity. The psycheme is personal enough to make all that derives from it shot through with a liveliness approaching personal experience, which makes for the all-important aesthetic quality of believability; and yet it is general enough so that readers will be able to inject their own emotions, attitudes, etc. into the character, theme, mood that forms itself around it.

As Birkerts indicated, a reciprocal sort of process takes place for a reader of fiction, but with less vivacity. The reader's world is a shadow world of the shadow world of the writer. Something of the reader's own psyche flows out into the character, where it becomes semi-objectified—subjective enough for the liveliness of enchantment to take hold, for personal experience, or something very much like it, to be had through the medium of merging with the characters—and yet maintaining the sense of otherness as well. The trick as a writer is to create characters who will attract such fluxions.

A reader's inner life need not flow into every character in a book, in order for the context at large to become vivified. It can be simply one character, from whose vivified point of view everything else in the book will be perceived. Some books, once enchanting, become dated, go altogether dead; sociological changes have altered readers' inner lives in such a way as to make influxes into the characters blocked and unlikely. There are books that seem to be rather gender-specific. Primarily women will find something in the characters that is receptive to outpourings from their own inner lives, or primarily men will. Other books remain forever accessible to influxes from readers because what has become semi-objectified in them, in character or plot or theme or tone, is universal.

The very process of semi-objectifying a *psycheme* into something that will be intersubjectively meaningful, and the strange tampering with one's sense of personal identity and the expansion of the borders of one's experience that follows, is itself truth-attractive. In being led by a psycheme into experiences not really one's own, even though they have the feel of one's own; in being led out of one's life into lives not one's own, even though they have the feel of one's own; certain structural features of our human experience emerge. Straddling an experience which is both personal and extra-personal coaxes forth a higher-order knowledge of experience, letting us see what is personal and immediate in a more impersonal light and what is impersonal and remote in a more personal and immediate way.

Strangely, the knowledge that emerges is not, it seems to me, entirely propositional in nature. What does this mean? It means that what one learns through the strange experience of fictive enchantment can't be translated into propositions without losing a great deal of the knowledge. This is yet another mysterious aspect of fictive enchantment: to say what one knows from a work of art would require reproducing the work, almost word for word. The attempt to say what it is that one has learned from a novel, in either its writing or its reading, is, at best, a partial affair, for so much of the knowledge is inextricably lodged in the extraordinary experience of *living* the world of the text. And extraordinary experiences can no more (actually rather less) be fully rendered up in propositional knowledge than ordinary ones can be.

The stretching of our experiences outside the bounds of the personal both utilizes and yields truths not encountered as readily, nor as vividly, within the bounds. The deformation in our sense of self, that gives us the illusion of living lives other than our own, both depends upon and conduces toward recognition of both a propositional and non-propositional nature. But the truth-attractiveness of this process is even further intensified when the (impermanent) deformations to our sense of self associated with fiction are joined with another aspect of its enchantment, the alteration in our sense of time, which is intimately linked with a storyteller's insistence on significance.

Stories are told for reasons. Reasons are the loom on which the fabric of the story is shaped. We have no choice but to live out our lives, day by day, hour by hour, in overwhelming pointlessness, the tedium of habitual existence that Proust identified as the sickness for which art alone is the cure (erotic love is a popular snake-oil). We tell stories, at least partly, in order to compensate for and disguise quotidian pointlessness (which does not rule out quotidian pointlessness as the very point of much fiction).

To occupy the novel, then, is to occupy a domain saturated with significance. It is to dwell not in sequential time, the moment-by-moment setting for pointlessness, but in shaped, intentional time, where experience is irradiated with meaning and details are purposefully assembled with an eye to the whole. The enchanted sense of fictive time approaches the fullness of time as experienced by the deeply religious, assured of a grand design emanating from the unseen intelligence behind it all. Where else but in art can we faithless revel in the vision of a unifying meaning bleeding through all of life's scattered modica?

Plunged into dense, intentional time, the surface noise of pointless sequentiality obscured; tethered, but only loosely, to the bounded terms of one's own unitary existence: this heady combination puts one strangely in the way of large and impersonal truth.

What sort of insights does fictive enchantment make us peculiarly receptive to? Except possibly in the case of science fiction (and here it is a question whether it is the thought-experiment imagination and not the storytelling imagination yielding truths), they concern human experience and human existence, often viewed grandly, approaching Spinoza's own view *sub specie aeternitatus*. After all, the vivifying element is a chunk—or chunks—of human psyche objectified into character, plot, and theme, channeled through contexts of meaning, straining toward the connectedness and integration of the story form, shot through with the allusion to mortality implied by the bluntly bounded internal time of a story's shadow life.

The truths coaxed out of that state of metaphysical compromise which is the essence of fictive enchantment can be very large indeed, sometimes approaching the secular analogue to religious revelation, intimations of what makes for a life well-lived (intimations, by the way, which, despite their aura of indubitability, are no more self-validating when they come in the artistic, than in the religious, form).

But there is a less grand and transcendental order of knowledge that emerges from fictive enchantment as well. In order for the "monumentally complex operation" of the psychic interchange between writer and reader to occur, certain structural features of experience must be tapped into, either implicitly or explicitly. And this is why novelists and playwrights, in their out-of-boundedness, often presage insights that come, more systematically and conventionally, from unenchanted theories of psychology and the social sciences. We might even hypothesize, crudely, that the further away from his own personal experience a writer can project, the more profoundly his work will both utilize and yield a recognition of the structural features of human experience. So that, at the very upper reaches of this continuum, in the case of Shakespeare, the insights as to human nature come so fast and furious that Harold Bloom has speculated that Freud derived his seminal ideas from a close and brilliant reading of the playwright (although, acting under the Bloomian principle of "anxiety of influence," Freud suppressed his indebtedness).

It is, in fact, possible, or maybe even unavoidable, to read a great deal of what Freud went on to explicate in semi-scientific terms—certainly, at the very least, the notion of unconscious desires playing themselves out in action—in a great many literary works, not excluding those of Plato himself. Just recall the scenario of the *Phaedrus*, the conditions under which Plato has Socrates suddenly reversing himself on the question of whether a young boy should submit to the entreaties of a useful non-lover or a true (and therefore maddened) lover: Socrates lying there on the grass, discussing philosophy of love in that dreamy setting beside the dreamy young boy.

The existence of the unconscious is unconsciously present throughout works of great literature. To take a fairly random example, an example near at hand for me only because I happen to be currently rereading Dickens' *Great Expectations*, consider Dickens' way of making the eccentric behavior of his characters expressive of buried attitudes.

For instance, the solicitor's clerk Wemmick, who spends his professional life in intimate familiarity with the most sordid, degrading criminal elements of humanity, has, quite hilariously, turned his tiny little bungalow—"I think it was the smallest house I ever saw," Pip says—into a fortified castle, with battlements, a gun fired every night at nine o'clock "Greenwich time," a moat and gangplank, lowered and raised with much ceremony. Dickens catalogues Wemmick's defense mechanisms—the theoretical term may not yet have existed in Dickens' day but the detailed behavior couldn't better exemplify that not yet formulated concept—right down to Wemmick's extraordinarily odd body language: Whenever he is in the depraved world of his professional duties, he transforms his very body into a fortified castle, refusing to shake anyone's hand, that is to let down his corporeal gangplank. Since one of Dickens' ongoing themes is the fate of the spiritually pure in the spiritually contaminated world, and how some learn to maneuver in that world without allowing their fundamental spiritual cleanliness to be touched (one can speculate that this was a significant psycheme for Dickens), it is not so surprising that he would have given us vivid instances of the defense mechanism long before the Freudian notion existed.

But in this essay I am less concerned with enumerating specific truths that have emerged from fictive enchantment, and more with identifying what it is about the state of fictive enchantment that makes such emergence possible. Once one acknowledges literary enchantment as a cognitive faculty, it becomes quite as respectable an epistemological question to inquire as to the grounds of its capacities as to pose the analogous question regarding, for example, theoretical physics. And the answers to both of these questions, the one addressed to fiction, the other to science, share startling similarities. Both faculties for uncovering truths transcending our own direct experience depend upon the isolation within that experience of structural features—in the case of physics structural features that can be given mathematical expression by means of which we gain access into the hidden properties of the material universe, while in the case of fiction structural features that, embedded in plot and character, allow us access into the hidden properties of others' being.

Plato, of course, thought that all artistic self-enchantment is enchantment with the self. This is why he features the artists and art lovers as prisoners of *eikrasia*. Though Plato sometimes mocks the poet for having no idea as to the ultimate source of his truths, no real idea of how he comes to know them, the Platonic mockery is somewhat counterfeit in this case and does not express the crux of his argument with artistic enchantment. After all, Plato's theory of anamnesis, that learning is recollection deriving from our soul's pre-bodily existence, is a profound acknowledgment of the mystery of large truth's ultimate source and the means whereby we, who are so very unlarge, collide with it. Plato's real argument with the epic poets and others is that they offer a kind of invidious caricature of anamnesis, deriving their thoughts not from the universal objectivity delivered up to reason's disciplined activity but from the dark energy of the ego.

The passing shadows of the unseen fire. The crux of Plato's argument with the artists is contained in the excavation of that phrase. Whatever the artist has not explicitly copied from the world has been derived from his own ego matter, whether conscious or unconscious. Plato is so forcefully aware of the deformation of clear vision that emanates from the ego, the false source of light that he places in the cave, but behind the prisoners, so that they don't see it as the source of their own shadow world. So it is with our own ego-induced versions of the world. We stare at the versions, not realizing them to be projections fueled by our own ego, the identity with one's self that gets shaped into one's own skewed view of the world. In the creation myth of the *Timeus*, the Demiurge delegates the process of incarnation to his young subordinates, who inject us with rather too generous a supply of the "terrible and necessary" emotions necessary for human survival [69d]. Plato does not allow for the possibility of the artist doing what he says the philosopher must do: detach her truth-seeking vision from the deforming energies of the "terrible and necessary" elements of the egotistically formed point of view. Only the rigorous methods of reason, cautions Plato, can accomplish the requisite detachment. Although once, on a summer's sultry day in the city-state of Athens, uncharacteristically venturing forth from the attractions of the agora to lie in the thick grass beneath a plane tree in full bloom with an enchanting young boy, the Socrates of Plato's imagination allows for the possibility that instructed Eros can acquire a force rivaling the faculty of reason's in attempting the supernal human task: to pull us away from the ill-lit cavernous world in which nothing but our ego's own projections vividly live.

I believe that the literary imagination, too—which, of course, almost always harnesses the hot fury of Eros in its service—can also render the self permeable to influxes of large and impersonal truth. Where philosophers, as divergent as Spinoza and Hume, force us to consider the possible and strange truth of the self's fiction, the selves that we assume as writers and readers of fiction have a way of strangely finding truth.

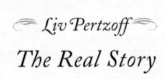

Liv Pertzoff

The Real Story

*A*N AUTHOR AT NINETY wrote that he could no longer locate the place from which stories and novels spring. I, unlike him, suspect no such place exists.

It seems to me that there is no *place*, no repository of stories and novels, but that, instead, we live inside a story writ as grand as space itself.

I was in the story just the other day. I was driving my car, crawling in a line of traffic toward a busy intersection. I noticed a disheveled man on the curb ahead holding up a handmade sign. He'd written: "Why lie? I need a beer." This caused me, the woman in the yellow car, her name is Veronica, to laugh so hard I fumbled in my wallet, opened the passenger window, and as I eased my way toward the beggar I signaled and waved some money—it was probably a c-note because I am a rich woman. I am driving a Lexus. The beggar ran to the window and gracefully, with the art of Charlie

Chaplin, tipped an imaginary cap and thanked me. He liked my laughter—and he laughed at his joke because in a previous chapter he has bought food with the money to take home to his family who are small starving children and a hollow-eyed wife with consumption, their house a hovel, their wealth but one goat and some chipped pottery jugs. This is 17th-century Shropshire and the beggar is my twelfth great-grandfather, but I digress—I'm reading back to front. I always read the last page of the story first to see if I'll like it, and generally I do with a little editing.

I don't like finding legless war-strafed refugees in the story, but if I come across any they are happy with their lot, singing together and whittling whistles from bamboo. Good times have fallen on their village and fresh fruit and meat are delivered three times a day.

I was with Castro in the jungles and recently I visited him in Havana. It was a tender reunion. He's aged since I saw him last, forty years ago, but I haven't aged which pleased and aroused him. I am still the same young, idealistic, beautiful *Revolucionaria* he remembered. We spent the night reminiscing, making secret love under the stars, drinking Cuba Libres and sharing a cigar.

In this story we inhabit we are any number of characters of all sizes and ages and genders. I inspired Tolstoy to clone Natasha—Tolstoy didn't find me in some *place* where stories "spring." We *were* the story, at least a few paragraphs in it, wherein that jealous blimp Sophie kicks Lev out of her bed and into the arms of us nubile students—I, his favorite, although but one of the many to whom he read his day's labor. We girls from fine families learned to do laundry and brush Lev's Borzois, but Lev abandoned his experiment in manual toil when he saw how the lye in the soap reddened our hands, and after he tenderly nursed Tatiana who finally choked to her death from an asthma attack set off by the dog hair in his kennels. I was myself Lev Tolstoy for several pages when he took the season in Italy and required a substitute for himself at Yasnaya Polyana.

In this story we inhabit I shop for groceries which I forget to use, and I waste enough food in a month to feed an Armenian child for a year—or is it a Chinese child I am depriving? It depends on which generation I'm in. It may be Rwanda whose annual resources I daily toss into a dumpster, but next I have led all Rwandans across the Red Sea and into the desert where manna falls, delicious manna like schmoos from Dogpatch which willingly, gratefully sacrifice themselves into any number of entrées, salads and cakes. Milk and honey flow. Rwanda flourishes again. That's on the penultimate page which you'll miss if you read the last page first.

I am a sweet, nurturing Catholic social worker named Mary, by day beloved of the souls I rescue, by night the Whore of Babylon and I never require sleep. This part of the story flies off the page, you're riveted, you can't put me down.

Jane Hirshfield

The Envoy

One day in that room, a small rat.
Two days later, a snake.

Who, seeing me enter,
whipped the long stripe of his
body under the bed,
then curled like a docile house-pet.

I don't know how either came or left.
Later, the flashlight found nothing.

For a year I watched
as something—terror? happiness? grief?—
entered and then left my body.

Not knowing how it came in,
Not knowing how it went out.

It hung where words could not reach it.
It slept where light could not go.
Its scent was neither snake nor rat,
neither sensualist nor ascetic.

There are openings in our lives
of which we know nothing.

Through them
the belled herds travel at will,
long-legged and thirsty, covered with foreign dust.

III

*Self-Deception
and the Messy Self*

Sarah Buss

The Superficial Unity of the Mind

S UPPOSE THAT TWEEDLE DUM believes that, without traversing more than half of the globe, he can get to Massachusetts from Iowa by driving due west. And suppose that, at the very same time, Tweedle Dee believes that, without traversing more than half of the globe, he can get to Massachusetts from Iowa by driving due east. Suppose, further, that each of them has the same conception of "east" and "west." It seems that, under these circumstances, Tweedle Dee and Tweedle Dum must be two different people. So, too, it seems, they must be two different people if they intend to drive in two different directions at the same time.

But what is the force of this "must"? Suppose that while wandering through Wonderland, Alice meets an odd personage (Tweedle Duo) who insists that, yes, indeed, Massachusetts is due west, about thirteen hundred miles; and yes, indeed, it is due east, about thirteen hundred miles; and yes, yes, verily, Massachusetts occupies only one spot on the globe. Once Alice has established that Tweedle Duo's protestations are sincere, she is bound to conclude that he is "out of his mind." In other words, he and his mind cannot be at one with each other. In other words, he must not be at one with *himself*. He is not "of one mind."

The moral seems to be that whether two mental states belong to a single mind depends on whether they satisfy some sort of coherence condition. According to this suggestion, our beliefs and intentions belong to us—and to no one else—because their very existence depends on whether we think they fit with everything else we believe and intend; they exist as elements in our mental life only because we bring them into existence (we "form" them) in response to our other convictions and goals.

Several philosophers have noted this connection between the coherence of our beliefs and intentions, on the one hand, and their identity and the identity of the mind to which they belong, on the other. This connection, they have argued, is the key to the force of rational requirements: we—we who do things for reasons, we "rational agents"—ought not to form contradictory beliefs or incompatible intentions because if we do, we will undermine our own integrity; our minds will fall apart; our mental states will no longer be truly *ours*. But this suggestion is problematic. For one thing, we can wonder how a person can be identified with an especially coherent set of beliefs and attitudes, given that she has the capacity to reflect on—and so, to dissociate herself from—any one of these mental states. But even if we leave this very difficult question to one side, another problem remains: if to be in the business of forming beliefs and intentions is, necessarily, to be in the business of maintaining the coherence of these mental states, then how can the requirement that we seek coherence serve as a guide or constraint on how we go about forming our beliefs and intentions? (How can it determine what we have reason to believe or intend?) If, on the other hand, we do not much care whether our beliefs or intentions are at odds with each other, then what, exactly, is the force of this requirement? (Why should we take it as a constraint on what we believe and intend?)

The answer to this second question might seem to be that, even if we do not care about coherence per se, we certainly do not want our minds to fall apart. This is, moreover, no mere contingent psychological fact: as long as we are committed to *anything*, we are necessarily committed to sustaining our capacity to make this commitment, and so as long as we are committed to anything, we are necessarily committed to our own self-preservation. Maintaining the coherence of our beliefs and intentions is, it seems, a necessary means to this end. So we seem to have good reason to ensure that our beliefs and intentions are not at odds with each other.

But do we really fall apart when our beliefs and intentions fail to cohere? Does Tweedle Duo really *lose* his mind simply by failing to be "of one mind"? If so, then how can *he* be crazy? More generally, when we say that people ought to have coherent beliefs and intentions, aren't we implying that some people are not as unified as they *ought* to be—or, at least, that nothing rules out the possibility of such disunity?

It might seem that we can respond to this challenge by calling attention to the fact that unity and coherence come in degrees. There is, we can point out, a vast middle ground between a random collection of mental states and a perfectly unified collection of mental states. People do not fall apart whenever their beliefs, intentions, etc. are not in perfect harmony. It's just that there are limits to how incoherent (how disunified) people can be. Because there are limits, we have good reason to do what we can to maintain harmony among the many disparate elements of our mental life.

But what are these limits? Indeed, if *some* incoherence is no threat to rational agency, then why should we think that there are any limits at all? If someone can tolerate even *one* contradiction, then why couldn't she tolerate countless others? Isn't she already committed to believing anything and everything? And what if she already has a pair of incompatible goals? Why couldn't she add many more goals that are incompatible with one of these original two?

The point is not that we have no good reason to avoid inner conflict. The point is that, whatever reason we have, it cannot be that inner conflict—even quite rampant inner conflict—is incompatible with our forming (and then "holding") (our own) beliefs and intentions. Indeed, when we turn our attention away from heady discussions of the nature of rational agency to the world of real rational agents, it is hard to discover any evidence for the assumption that there are principled limits to the amount of disunity a person can tolerate.

And yet there does seem to be something to the thought that we are—essentially—more than a mere bundle of mental states, or even their receptacle. And it is hard to see how we could be anything more than this if we made no attempt to ensure the coherence of our beliefs and intentions. If we were indifferent to the coherence of our beliefs and intentions, then how could our mental states be *ours* in a sense more robust than the sense in which our sensations are ours? How could they constitute our point of view?[1]

To avoid conceptual whiplash, it often helps to take a look at some data. I have just noted that real rational agents seem to survive considerable disharmony among their mental states. Perhaps if we take a closer look at how this works, we will gain insight into how a commitment to coherence can be reconciled with a tolerance of *in*coherence.

Consider, then, George Eliot's Bulstrode. At least two things are true of him. First, he has Christian beliefs and Christian values; he is committed to living the life of a devout Christian and upstanding member of the Middlemarch bourgeoisie. Second, he has egoistic desires for wealth and status, desires whose power is entirely independent of his desire to serve God. How does he reconcile these two parts of himself? According to Eliot, he "explains the gratification of his [greedy] desires into satisfactory agreement" with his more lofty aspirations. When this "agreement" is threatened, moreover, he works to preserve it.[2] He asks himself: What, exactly, does my commitment to Christian values require? Does it really preclude me from allowing a sick man with a dread secret to drink liquor, when my servant insists (contrary to the doctor's orders—but does the doctor really know best?) that liquor is just what the man needs? This, Bulstrode plausibly tells himself, is not definitively ruled out. And because it is not definitively ruled out, he can reconcile his policy of living the life of an upstanding citizen with the psychic forces that move him to defy this very policy.

This has been a lifelong pattern. The dread secret is, in effect, that his past life was not what the life of an upstanding, Christian burger should be. He has managed to hide this fact from himself by interpreting his commitment to self-promotion as a commitment to promoting God's will. By creatively interpreting the conflicts in his psyche—by "smoothing them over," as we sometimes put it—he has succeeded in holding himself together.

This case offers at least two useful lessons. First, holding oneself together—keeping one's mental life from coming apart—is compatible with preserving significant inner conflict. Indeed, one way to maintain harmony among one's mental states is simply to downplay the conflict among them. This can involve distorting the truth about oneself, as Bulstrode clearly does. But it can also involve refining one's commitments in such a way that what appeared to be a conflict no longer is. In either case—and this is the second point—what counts is how things *seem*, how they seem *to the person herself*. As long as she thinks that she is in conflict with herself, she is not "of one mind." And if she thinks that she has a way of interpreting the apparent conflict so that it is merely apparent, then she has satisfied her own implicit commitment to imposing some order on her beliefs, desires, emotions, etc. She has vindicated her guiding assumption that she has a mind, whose various elements are held together by their relationship to *her*.

Before we take a closer look at this unity-cum-appearance-of-unity, I want to say a bit more about the self-interpretation that is essential to achieving it. In a nutshell, this interpretation works by exploiting the indeterminacy of most commitments, especially those that are general enough to generate conflict in anyone with a moderately rich mental life. Almost any practical principle will serve as an example: We ought to brush our teeth. We ought not to waste time. We ought to give other people a fair hearing. We ought not to act as though we expect other people to pick up after us. These principles apply "for the most part." There are many exceptions. We discover these exceptions when we confront new situations in which applying the principles appears to conflict with our commitments to other things.

Many people believe that it is a vice to spend too much time thinking about how they look. But what, exactly, constitutes "too much time"? And does looking for grey hairs count as thinking about one's appearance? I myself have a general policy of providing for my daughter's welfare. But what counts as compliance with this policy? Among other things, I have to make an effort to ensure that she eats well. But even here, there is lots of room for interpretation. What counts as a "good (enough) diet"? And what counts as an adequate effort? At what point have I made so many exceptions to my policy that it is no longer really my policy?

This last question points to another important respect in which many of our commitments are indeterminate: we *really do* intend to do something (we have, for example, set ourselves the goal of cleaning the basement), but we don't have a very clear idea of *when* we will do it (we plan to clean it sometime, sooner rather than later, after we have taken care of various other, more pressing, matters). This indeterminacy alone permits the (apparent) reconciliation of many ends that cannot possibly be realized (or even pursued) at the same time. It may seem that one cannot really intend to write a book *and* raise children *and* be politically active *and* cook interesting meals *and* maintain a correspondence with friends *and* keep a neat house. But all of these goals can surely be met … eventually.

Given our limited control over our lives, and given our limited knowledge, we would be unwise, and indeed hubristic, to spell out most of our beliefs and intentions so precisely that they would leave little opportunity for interpretation. This arbitrary exercise of power on our part might—just might—serve to keep our various impulses in line. It is more likely to inspire rebellion.

Since Plato, philosophers have attacked the "democratic soul" as incapable of governing itself. "It is," Christine Korsgaard claims, "only an accident if [each of the impulses of a democratic soul does] not completely undercut the satisfaction of the last one.... The democratic person has no resources for shaping his will to prevent this, and so he is at the mercy of accident."[3] He is at the mercy of accident because his impulses are not subject to a law that determines whether and, if so, when they determine the will.

Even if Korsgaard were right, this would hardly count as an indictment of the democratic soul. After all, there are countless respects in which our very existence is at the mercy of accident, yet here we are. More importantly, though contingencies certainly play their part in the identity and relative power of our various impulses, the fact that these impulses are not ruled by one special part of the soul does not prevent *us* from governing ourselves. To the contrary, the democratic impulse to let every impulse have a voice is itself a "resource for shaping the will." It is what moves us to reinterpret our various commitments whenever this seems necessary to reconciling them with one another. Its power to move us is no more accidental than our rational agency itself.[4]

In short, far from being opposed to the constraints of reason, the democratic habit of accommodating as many of our heterogeneous, competing impulses as we can is itself a manifestation of reason.[5] The task of accommodation is the task of reconciliation. It is the task of (re)interpreting the impulses in such a way that they are parts of a unified whole. To be sure, the impulses themselves are not the source of this requirement: they are not themselves opposed to their opposition to one another. Nonetheless, it is they that determine how their conflict is to be resolved: how we (re)interpret one of our impulses depends on which accommodations we are willing to make; and this, in turn, depends on what our other impulses happen to be.

Because in order to unify the mind, self-interpretation need satisfy no one but the interpreter, the coherence of democratic souls is compatible with very deep internal conflict. In other words, as the metaphor of depth suggests, the mental unity required to be someone with beliefs and intentions (a "self," a "rational agent") is extremely superficial. Suppose, for example, that we believe someone has contradicted herself. And suppose that she simply denies that this is the case. (She has not, we will imagine, simply asserted "P and not-P." Rather, she has asserted something that [from what we can tell] implies this.) Or suppose that she insists that there *must* be some way to reconcile her beliefs. Or suppose that she admits that her beliefs cannot be reconciled, but she refuses to give either one up because, she insists, the cost would simply be too great. (She could not live with herself; life would lose its meaning.) In any of these cases—even the last, in which she sustains the contradiction by simply failing to notice it—she will have imposed as much unity on her mental life as is necessary for it to be her own. She will be a rational agent, with her own beliefs and desires, her own, incoherent, mental life.

Many people believe that life after death will be better than life on earth. Yet they hope that many years will pass before that happy day arrives when they and their loved ones are all in Heaven together. Many people believe that they are "in the hands" of an all-powerful, all-knowing, benevolent God. Yet they also believe that there are many evils in the world which they themselves would have prevented if they could. Do these people perceive any tension between their views? If they do not, then the tension that *others* claim to see poses no threat to their status as rational agents; it poses no threat to their having a single mind. This is not to say that their beliefs are fully intelligible. The point is that, however intelligible or rational these beliefs may be, they are sufficiently integrated into the rest of the believers' mental lives—sufficiently integrated, that is, not to pull the believers apart.

Of course, as long as, at some level, a mental conflict persists, a person is vulnerable to (re)discovering it. As Bulstrode illustrates, this is especially true when the conflict is "smoothed over" by a self-deception that serves the self at the expense of others. Very few of these others will share the self-deceiver's commitment to preserving his own self-conception. Their interpretations are thus likely to be quite different from his. And they may force him to reckon with this fact. This is just what happens to Bulstrode: under pressure from the taunts of the good citizens of Middlemarch, he is forced to see that the story he has been telling himself in order to reconcile his warring parts has been little more than a lie.

At such a juncture, one has no choice but to abandon one's previous self-interpretation. This can be as easy as being no longer disposed to believe P when one finally appreciates that one really does believe not-P. But sometimes "changing one's mind" is much more difficult. What is poor Bulstrode to do? What is he to think? What remains of his old beliefs and intentions, his old fears and dreams? He loves his wife. This, he realizes, is what matters most. Which other beliefs and intentions can be reconciled with this fundamental commitment, he doesn't yet know. He will have to figure this out slowly, painfully, one day at a time.

As he struggles to maintain his grip on himself, he may conclude that he has "a greedy streak" which he simply cannot get rid of. If he can discover no way to integrate this impulse into his self-conception, then he has only one choice: he must concede that, to this extent, he is not a unified whole; there is part of his mental life that simply cannot be integrated with the others. (In extreme cases, a person may conclude that the external mental stuff belongs to a second mind—a mind that shares the very same body.)

Paradoxically, such an admission of defeat is itself a way of reestablishing the superficial unity essential to having a mind. In designating a recalcitrant mental state as an external something that one suffers, like a pain, or like the cause of a pain, one reinterprets oneself as someone whose own mental states are *not* irreconcilable. Whether this interpretation is plausible—whether the self-denial and self-abandonment it involves is something a person can live with—will surely be due, in large part, to accidents he cannot foresee. Meanwhile, he is as unified as he needs to be, not in order to be happy or self-satisfied, but in order to be more than a jumble of mental states and more than the receptacle that registers their presence as so many random tickles and pricks.

In the movie *Bowfinger* Eddie Murphy plays a paranoid movie star who constantly repeats to himself: "Keep it together. Keep it together." Sometimes, reminding oneself that one is, indeed, the proprietor of a mind may be all one can do to preserve oneself. It may be all one can do to keep oneself together. This is clearly a stop-gap measure. It is an assertion of self meant to buy time while one struggles to come up with a credible story. How long can a person keep this sort of thing up?

Because the unity necessary for a mental life is superficial, if there ever does come a time in which we run out of resources for mental self-preservation, this will not be because we have discovered an irreconcilable tension in our mental life. As long as we stand in some relationship to our mental states, we cannot regard them all as something that just happens to us: if all of our mental states were external in this sense, then there would be no "inside" in relationship to which they were "outside," no "self" in relationship to which they were "other." This means that if any of us ever breaks up into a collection of disconnected mental states, the cause will be extra-mental. Our mental life is at the mercy of many accidents. But the existence of a mind is invulnerable to the many accidents of mental life.

It is important not to misunderstand this essential invulnerability. The fact that our minds cannot annihilate themselves is just the fact that they cannot be less than superficially coherent.[6] Clearly, this incapacity does not prevent them from hatching any number of self-destructive plots.

Once Bulstrode has left Middlemarch behind, he may reflect on his past deeds and on the unsavory impulses and habits of mind that continue to assert themselves despite his best efforts to eliminate them. Under these circumstances, his self-satisfaction may give way to self-loathing. Since he can no longer reconcile the old impulses and habits with the rest of his attitudes and beliefs, the conflict between them and him will not be strictly internal. Nonetheless, they will still have the power to make his life miserable. Like so many knocks at the door, they may continue to demand that he let them back in. Or they may keep on harassing him without protesting their exiled status—like the "voices" that originate in the dark corners of some malfunctioning brains.

Under the pressure of these assaults, there may finally come a day when Bulstrode decides he can take it no longer. He may form the intention to put an end to his suffering. How can he reconcile this intention with the fact that its very existence depends on his commitment to preserving the unity of his mental life? He will probably do what others have done under similar circumstances. He will focus on his misery. He will remind himself that this is what he is committed to annihilating: the pain, and the source of the pain—those rogue mental states that will not leave him alone. Thus does the mind preserve its superficial unity to the bitter end.

Notes

1. Two points of clarification are probably in order. First, I do not mean to imply that all mental states other than sensations are directly subject to a coherence requirement. But even if, for example, we can have conflicting wishes and hopes without being rationally impaired, the existence of these states appears to presuppose the existence of beliefs (about what is worth having; about what is possible). Second, I do not mean to imply that without beliefs, we could not possibly have a point of view. My point is simply that we have no point of view if we are indifferent to the coherence of whatever states (be they beliefs or merely belief-like) are essential to our having a point of view.

2. See George Eliot, *Middlemarch* (London: Penguin Classics, 1994), p. 619.

3. See Christine Korsgaard, *Locke Lecture V*, p. 9. See also *The Sources of Normativity* (Cambridge: Cambridge University Press, 1996), pp. 232–33.

4. Note that the philosopher's "democratic soul" is really an *anarchic* soul: it is nothing but a bunch of impulses, which take turns "ruling" according to which one happens to be strongest at the time. My point, I hope it is clear, is not that this sort of anarchy is a good thing. Rather, I am claiming that our impulses themselves can, and do, play a much bigger role in ensuring that they cohere with one another than the philosophical critiques of the "democratic soul" suggest.

5. As Richard Rorty explains (appealing to Freud), reason ("rationality") is the "mechanism that adjusts contingencies to other contingencies." *Contingency, Irony, and Solidarity* (Cambridge: Cambridge University Press, 1989), p. 33.

6. Note that, strictly speaking, the impossibility here is the impossibility of *remaining* less than superficially coherent *once one suspects that one may be less than superficially coherent*. Under these circumstances, one will necessarily find a way to conceive of one's mental states so as to preserve the superficial unity of one's mind. (As the *Bowfinger* example suggests, however, at least for a short while, this self-conception could consist of nothing more than the conviction that one's mental states are somehow part of a unified whole.)

⁓

Steven Pinker

Kidding Ourselves*

T HE IDEAL OF THE SELF as a unified rational decision-maker is under assault from many directions, and one of them is the modern science of the mind, particularly evolutionary psychology and cognitive neuroscience.

The playwright Jerome K. Jerome once said, "It is always the best policy to tell the truth, unless, of course, you are an exceptionally good liar." It's hard to lie well, even about your own intentions, which only you can verify. Intentions come from emotions, and emotions have evolved displays on the face and body. Unless you are a master of the Stanislavsky method, you will have trouble faking them; in fact, they probably evolved *because* they were hard to fake. Worse, lying is stressful, and anxiety has its own telltale markers. They are the rationale for polygraphs, the so-called lie detectors, and humans evolved to be lie detectors too. Then there is the annoying fact that some propositions logically entail others. Since *some* of the things you say will be true, you are always in danger of exposing your own lies. As the Yiddish saying goes, a liar must have a good memory.

Robert Trivers, pursuing his theory of the emotions to its logical conclusion, notes that in a world of walking lie detectors the best strategy is to believe your own lies. You can't leak your hidden intentions if you don't think that they *are* your intentions. According to his theory of self-deception, the conscious mind sometimes hides the truth from itself the better to hide it from others. But the truth is useful, so it should be registered somewhere in the mind, walled off from the parts that interact with other people. There is an obvious similarity to Freud's theory of the unconscious and the defense mechanisms of the ego (such as repression, projection, denial, and rationalization), though the explanation is completely different. George Orwell stated it in *1984*: "The secret of rulership is to combine a belief in one's own infallibility with a power to learn from past mistakes."

The neuroscientist Michael Gazzaniga has shown that the brain blithely weaves false explanations about its motives. Split-brain patients have had their cerebral hemispheres surgically disconnected as a treatment for epilepsy. Language circuitry is in the left hemisphere, and the left half of the visual field is registered in the isolated right hemisphere, so the part of the split-brain person that can talk is unaware of the left half of his world. The right hemisphere is still active, though, and can carry out simple commands presented in the left visual field, like "Walk" or "Laugh." When the patient (actually, the patient's left hemisphere) is asked why he walked out (which we know was a response to the command presented to the right hemisphere), he ingenuously replies, "To get a Coke." When asked why he is laughing, he says, "You guys come up and test us every month. What a way to make a living!"

Our confabulations, not coincidentally, present us in the best light. Literally hundreds of experiments in social psychology say so. The humorist Garrison Keillor describes the fictitious community of Lake Wobegon, "where the women are strong, the men are good-looking, and all the children are above average." Indeed, most people claim they are above average in any positive trait you name: leadership, sophistication, athletic prowess, managerial ability, even driving skill. They rationalize the boast by searching for an *aspect* of the trait that they might in fact be good at. The slow drivers say they are above average in safety, the fast ones that they are above average in reflexes.

More generally, we delude ourselves about how benevolent and how effective we are, a combination that social psychologists call beneffectance. When subjects play games that are rigged by the experimenter, they attribute their successes to their own skill and their failures to the luck of the draw. When they are fooled in a fake experiment into thinking they have delivered shocks to another subject, they derogate the victim, implying that he deserved the punishment. Everyone has heard of "reducing cognitive dissonance," in which people invent a new opinion to resolve a contradiction in their minds. For example, a person will recall enjoying a boring task if he had agreed to recommend it to others for paltry pay. (If the person had been enticed to recommend the task for generous pay, he accurately recalls that the task was boring.) As originally conceived of by the psychologist Leon Festinger, cognitive dissonance is an unsettled feeling that arises from an inconsistency in one's beliefs. But that's not right: there is no contradiction between the proposition "The task is boring" and the proposition "I was pressured into lying that the task was fun." Another social psychologist, Eliot Aronson, nailed it down: people doctor their beliefs only to eliminate a contradiction with the proposition "I am nice and in control." Cognitive dissonance is always triggered by blatant evidence that you are not as beneficent and effective as you would like people to think. The urge to reduce it is the urge to get your self-serving story straight.

Sometimes we have glimpses of our own self-deception. When does a negative remark sting, cut deep, hit a nerve? When some part of us knows it is true. If every part knew it was true, the remark would not sting; it would be old news. If no part thought it was true, the remark would roll off; we could dismiss it as false. Trivers recounts an experience that is all too familiar (at least to me). One of his papers drew a published critique, which struck him at the time as vicious and unprincipled, full of innuendo and slander. Rereading the article years later, he was surprised to find that the wording was gentler, the doubts more reasonable, the attitude less biased than he had remembered. Many others have made such discoveries; they are almost the definition of "wisdom."

> *If there were a verb meaning "to believe falsely," it would not have any significant first person, present indicative.*
> —Ludwig Wittgenstein

> *There's one way to find out if a man is honest: ask him; if he says yes, you know he's crooked.*
> —Mark Twain

> *Our enemies' opinion of us comes closer to the truth than our own.*
> —La Rochefoucauld

> *Oh wad some power the giftie gie us To see oursels as ithers see us!*
> —Robert Burns

∿

No one can examine the emotions without seeing in them the source of much human tragedy. I don't think we should blame the animals; it's clear enough how natural selection engineered our instincts to suit our needs. We shouldn't blame selfish genes, either. They endow us with selfish motives, but they just as surely endow us with the capacity for love and a sense of justice. What we should appreciate and fear is the cunning designs of the emotions themselves. Many of their specs are not for gladness and understanding: think of the happiness treadmill, the Sirens' song, the sham emotions, the doomsday machines, the caprice of romance, the pointless punishment of grief. But self-deception is perhaps the cruelest motive of all, for it makes us feel right when we are wrong and emboldens us to fight when we ought to surrender.

Trivers writes,

> Consider an argument between two closely bound people, say, husband and wife. Both parties believe that one is an altruist—of long standing, relatively pure in motive, and much abused—while the other is characterized by a pattern of selfishness spread over hundreds of incidents. They only disagree over who is altruistic and who selfish. It is noteworthy that the argument may appear to burst forth spontaneously, with little or no preview, yet as it rolls along, two whole landscapes of information processing appear to lie already organized, waiting only for the lightning of anger to show themselves.

In cartoons and movies, the villains are mustache-twirling degenerates, cackling with glee at their badness. In real life, villains are convinced of their rectitude. Many biographers of evil men start out assuming that their subjects are cynical opportunists and reluctantly discover that they are ideologues and moralists. If Hitler was an actor, concluded one, he was an actor who believed in the part.

Still, thanks to the complexity of our minds, we need not be perpetual dupes of our own chicanery. The mind has many parts, some designed for virtue, some designed for reason, some clever enough to outwit the parts that are neither. One self may deceive another, but every now and then a third self sees the truth.

Louise Bogan

Man Alone

It is yourself you seek
In a long rage,
Scanning through light and darkness
Mirrors, the page,

Where should reflected be
Those eyes and that thick hair,
That passionate look, that laughter.
You should appear

Within the book, or doubled,
Freed, in silvered glass;
Into all other bodies
Yourself should pass.

The glass does not dissolve;
Like walls the mirrors stand;
The printed page gives back
Words by another hand.

And your infatuate eye
Meets not itself below;
Strangers lie in your arms
As I lie now.

IV

Identification and the Messy Self

Ilan Stavans

The Disappearance

Honest Gentleman, I know not your breeding.
—Henry IV, Part II, Act V

For Verónica Albin

I WONDER IF STOMACH CANCER is one of the prices one might pay for gluttony, for that is what killed Maarten Soëtendrop at the age of seventy-one. It was my old friend, Yosee Strigler, who wrote informing me of the death of the corpulent, legendary actor in the heart of the Belgian *pays noir*. It was in Charleroi, the city named after a bewitched, dull Spanish king, where Soëtendrop lost his footing. And it was there that he made his final exit from the stage, too.

Yosee sent me a long, poignant letter, along with a clipping of the obituary published in *De Telegraf*, where Soëtendrop's disappearance—in Brussels it made headlines and was dubbed *De verdwijning*—is recorded in detail. I read what he sent me about the life, and the death, and the deceit. Yosee's style was succinct, affable, yet also agonizing, a reflection not only of the way his mind works but of the debates we used to have. He believed Belgian Jews were at risk. They never felt fully at home. The number of Muslims was rapidly growing. He sensed a suffocating, unstable future.

That he decided, after all these years, to mail these things to me—I've changed addresses seven times since we last saw each other—might show that friendship triumphs over passing disagreements. But it is also proof that the sparring has not ended, that, clandestinely, Yosee remains eager to prove his point. Or has he finally capitulated and accepted mine?

Yosee and I met for the first time more than two decades ago on a hike in the Sinai Desert—shortly before the Israeli army invaded Lebanon. He worked in a kibbutz near Lake Kineret; I was enrolled at Hebrew University. I believe the next time we saw each other was in Tel Aviv, at a play by Ephraim Kishon. After the show we found a cozy café on Dizengoff Street and talked for hours about the challenges of the Jewish Diaspora since Auschwitz. That he was from Charleroi (although his family moved to Brussels when he was twelve) and I from Mexico City allowed for humorous exchanges. Neither of us was fully comfortable in Hebrew, his Spanish was a path filled with puddles, and I could make myself understood in Dutch with the help of a *heymish* Yiddish, but only after a couple of beers. Our common ground was an invented language that sounded like Edmund Wilson translating *Eugene Onegin* back into Russian from Vladimir Nabokov's literal English rendition. Later Yosee and I traveled together to Masada, then went for a swim in the Dead Sea. It was during that trip that he mentioned wanting to return to Belgium, sell his belongings, and come back to Israel to make *aliyah*. "Only in Israel is the Jew safe from adversity," I remember him saying.

When I left Jerusalem after my first year as a student, Yosee happened to be on the same flight to Munich. We spent the time talking about the works of art the Nazis had stolen from collectors and shipped to Prague, which they hoped to turn into a museum of the "lost Jewish race." We parted, I backpacked around Europe on my own, and some months later I visited him and his family in Brussels, where I stayed in an apartment that belonged to a school pal of his a few blocks from Rue Royale, within walking distance from the Gare du Nord. At some point during my week-long stay Yosee took me to see a performance of *The Misanthrope* with Soëtendrop in the lead role. He told me he knew Soëtendrop, one of the best actors in Belgium, according to my friend. The two had met in Jerusalem. Tour guides fluent in Dutch, the neutral tongue of the majority of Belgian visitors, were difficult to find in those days, and Yosee not only spoke the language but was also passionate about biblical archaeology; so while still in the kibbutz he had been hired by an agency to moonlight as a guide for a group from Belgium and Holland.

Soëtendrop, Yosee said, was a powerful presence in the group, not because of his temperament—he could be at once charming and abrasive—but as a result of his fame. "Everyone has seen the movie *Doktor Travistok!* at least twice," my friend claimed, then categorically stated, "He's outstanding as the absent-minded scientist." The Old City was a natural rendezvous that brought people together, and it seemed to nurture a relationship between Yosee and Soëtendrop. Back in Brussels, the actor invited my friend to his residence in Deventer, where he met Soëtendrop's wife Natalie. That same year they celebrated Hanukah together and were served a meal Yosee described as a "bacchanal," with *latkes* the size of a salmon, Spanish cheeses, an asparagus soup, a soufflé, a salad with boysenberries. Soëtendrop's portions, Yosee believed, were nothing short of gargantuan. "Jews and food—eternal companions. At one point Maarten looked like a Rembrandt creation." As it turns out, it was the last time my friend saw the actor in person.

As Molière's Alceste, I found Soëtendrop extravagant. He played the role on mannerisms. His corpulence was stressed through hirsute clothes. Before engaging in a dialogue he oscillated his neck like a hyena devouring her prey, and he improvised a slight stutter around the letter *t*. Maybe because my friend had recounted their adventures in Jerusalem, off stage I imagined him to be loud, even obnoxious. "As I get to know him better, he appears to me to be uncomfortable with himself in *real life*, as if body and soul refused to match." Yosee underscored the two words as if for Maarten Soëtendrop the border between this world and the imaginary one had already been blurred. I remember thinking to myself: Do all actors suffer from a similar sense of unreality? In any case, the fact that my friend knew Soëtendrop in person made Molière palatable. After the performance, Yosee asked me if I was ready to greet the actor in his dressing room. I declined: unless I'm paid to represent them, I never quite know what to say to celebrities.

It seems that Soëtendrop's fading act was methodically planned over several weeks. His obesity doesn't appear to have been an obstacle. His movements were agile, even when in the hospital after his ordeal. He was a master of make-believe. Did he ever doubt his talent to conjure a parallel truth, to make people think he, the most revered of thespians in Belgium, had been mistreated by a horde of hooligans? Only if one is convinced he knew the distinction between truth and lies. "It is Maarten's sense of morality that is in need of urgent reevaluation," Yosee believes.

The basic facts are uncontestable. On the frigid Thursday evening of December 3, 1987, the police commissioner of the industrial city of Charleroi, in a hastily orchestrated press conference, announced that Soëtendrop, on tour as Sir John Falstaff in *The Merry Wives of Windsor*, had not arrived at his usual 6:30 PM call before that evening's performance. Thirty-five minutes later, the floor manager alerted the theater producer who, aware of the actor's tempestuous personality—yet conscious of his unrivaled punctuality—asked for patience. The hotel in which the actor was staying was put on alert. Repeated calls were made to his room. With the producer's permission, the room was searched. A bar and a restaurant Soëtendrop frequented were contacted. At 8:15 PM the evening performance was canceled, and, soon after, a search was announced. Since the police commissioner didn't want the media to find out *avant la lettre*, he himself let the word out: "Maarten Soëtendrop is a distinguished star. It is too early in the investigation to draw conclusions. We're hoping for the actor's safe and speedy return." A free-lance reporter dismissed the police commissioner's search as premature. "When a Muslim goes missing near a mine in Bois du Cazier, do the police bother?" Any misgivings were swiftly put to rest the following morning the minute the mailman delivered an envelope to the office of Rabbi Awraham Frydman, some fifty-five miles north of the city. A single-line, carelessly typed note claimed Maarten Soëtendrop to be under the control of the Flemish Fascist Youth Front.

News of the disappearance touched a nerve in Belgium. The Saturday newspapers offered profiles of the actor's life and career, reflected on the ideology of the previously unknown neo-Nazi group, pondered its whereabouts, and speculated about its chances of assassinating the famous Flemish actor. In the following days a series of equally muddled notes arrived at the homes of other Jewish leaders, a TV anchor, some members of the Chamber of Representatives, and Natalie Soëtendrop. (In one note a quote in French from the Constitution [Title II, Act 20] was added: "*Nul ne peut être contraint de concourir d'une manière quelconque aux actes et aux cérémonies d'un culte, ni d'en observer les jours de repos.*") After she received the note, Natalie Soëtendrop begged the kidnappers for mercy. She urged the Belgian government to act immediately yet responsibly.

"During World War II, Belgium engaged in a silence that turned us into accomplices," Yosee writes in his letter. "This time around, people were eager to shout."

In a display of solidarity, a demonstration took place in the Netherlands, at a church in Amsterdam, on Saturday, December 12, more than a week after Soëtendrop's exit in Charleroi. It attracted politicians and celebrities. The Speaker of the Belgian Parliament described the fascist group as "rats coming out of a hole." Soon after, the Justice Minister spoke about appointing a special prosecutor to investigate neo-Nazi activities.

With a voracious appetite for beef, Chilean wine, and attention, Maarten Soëtendrop had turned fifty-two on the day of his last performance in Charleroi as Falstaff. In three more days he was scheduled to travel along with the theater company to Liège, Antwerp, and Ghent. As an actor, he had an esteemed reputation as much for his thespian technique—he was a loyalist of "The Method"—as for his choice of roles. Audiences knew him not only for *Doktor Travistok!* but for films like *The Messy Self, Valpurgis,* and *The Night of the Birds.* There were reports he was under contract to be in *Amsterdamned.* Plus, Soëtendrop was the impresario behind *Aunt Julie,* a successful season of a lesser-known Pirandello play, and the musical *Anatevka,* based on Sholem Aleichem's Yiddish novel *Tevye the Dairyman.* His favorite playwright was Chekhov.

The obituary in *De Telegraf* describes Soëtendrop as the product of "a mixed background": a Jewish father, also an actor, and a Christian mother. "The embodiment of a divided spirit," Yosee states. In 1940, when Soëtendrop was five and his brother Hugo almost three, their mother abandoned the family abruptly. She had been having an affair with a married man for quite some time, a Nazi collaborator named Siegbert Himmelstrup. Soon after she filed for divorce and married her lover in 1944. The brothers were separated; Hugo stayed in Brussels where he lived with his mother, stepfather, and his three children. Maarten was sent to a farm near Leeuwarden, in northern Holland. For almost two years he was hidden from the Germans by a family. According to Yosee, the episode became a source of shame. "In his eyes, Judaism was about secrecy. His was a servant's mentality. He was hidden because he was inferior." After the war, he lived in Antwerp with a paternal uncle for two and a half years. Eventually Soëtendrop was sent to a boarding school in Bordeaux. In the sixties, he sought out his father in order to talk about his half-Jewish self. His infatuation with drama, he trusted, came from being an outsider—a foreigner—in Belgian culture. He needed his father's approval to remain on the edges, to peek in, to be aloof yet have the gravitas needed to impersonate other characters, not only himself. The father welcomed him, but chose not to answer Soëtendrop's questions about the past. "Silence... Is it right to define it as the absence of sound? Isn't it an existential condition?"

The obituary mentions a rather pallid, unforthcoming autobiographical essay Soëtendrop published in an obscure theater journal in 1991 called *Wertewelt des Judentums.* According to Yosee, in it Soëtendrop mentions that in 1979, already a promising actor in the Brussels theater scene, he underwent a religious conversion on the eve of Yom Kippur. At that time Soëtendrop was still single, for although he had expressed his love to several women, he had never proposed marriage to any of them. Later on he surveyed an existential vacuum inside himself. "I had lost touch with the inner voice," Yosee quotes him. Soëtendrop found out that the Jewish holidays were about to take place. Formally dressed, with tennis shoes appropriate for the occasion, the actor entered a synagogue in the working-class Anderlecht district, which swarmed with Muslim immigrants. Never in his life had he been exposed to prayer, and the *Kol Nidré* melody sweetened his heart. A few months later he visited Jerusalem with Yosee as his guide. A friend gave him a copy of *The Star of Redemption*, by German philosopher Franz Rosenzweig, which he read with difficulty but admiration. He started therapy with a psychoanalyst named Hermann Musaph. Unexpectedly, the sessions ratified his faith.

In 1987, in the early days of winter, Soëtendrop was in a state of stupor. In an interview, Natalie Soëtendrop portrayed him as "taciturn, under duress," yet when pressed by reporters, she refused to be more specific. The reticence turned out to be a stroke of luck. His Falstaff was universally applauded by critics all over Belgium and tickets quickly sold out. The same day he disappeared, a lengthy encomium appeared in the magazine *Dag Allemaal*.

What transpired while Soëtendrop was purportedly a hostage of the F.F.Y.F. is still the subject of conjecture and gossip. The Brussels police headquarters pushed the investigation in every geographical direction. The typed notes were painstakingly analyzed. Rumors of links of several political entities to the F.F.Y.F. circulated. Journalists looked into Soëtendrop's past for clues. Leads emerged but led nowhere.

Natalie Soëtendrop announced on TV her willingness to pay ransom, no matter the amount. It was rumored that an undisclosed sum made available by the government would be given to the captors to secure the actor's safe return. The Justice Minister quickly issued a disclaimer: "Belgium doesn't fall prey to ruffians. If the Soëtendrop family is willing to pay, it is free to act as it wishes." Soon after, another typed note arrived at Rabbi Frydman's address. It claimed the kidnappers weren't interested in ransom. Theirs was an ideological struggle "to cleanse the country of rubbish."

Then, on Wednesday, December 21, behind a curtain of snow flurries, a shivering, disheveled, ostensibly bruised Maarten Soëtendrop, noticeably thinner, his hands tied behind his back, feces on his hair, blood on his face, abdomen, and sweater, was discovered by a passerby in a dead-end street near the Groeninge Exhibition Center in the city of Bruges. "I was abducted by hatred," he was quoted as saying.

The reporter for *De Telegraf*, Erik Eddelbuettel (who authored the obituary Yosee sent along), was the first on the scene. He was followed by the police, an ambulance, and a forensic squad. It was Eddelbuettel who found a typed note stuck to Soëtendrop's sweater. It appeared to be Spanish: "*Judeos de mierda. ¡Furia!*"

"Do you recall the day?" Yosee wonders. "The news was wired all around the globe, including the United States. You sent me a comment on a piece you read in the *New York Times*."

I was indeed shocked when I read the piece. The memories of the prominent Flemish actor on stage in Brussels came back to me like a comet. His safe return pleased me, and I was angry at the publicity the neo-Nazis were receiving at Soë-tendrop's expense. I saved the clipping thinking it substantiated my friend Yosee Strigler's belief that, after the creation of the state of Israel, life in the Diaspora was no longer justifiable. I was curious as to Soëtendrop's whereabouts during his absence. What type of torture had he been subjected to? Would he be able to overcome the prolonged periods of depression associated with incidents of this nature?

Needless to say, I couldn't have envisioned the twisted knots behind the affair. A day after his reemergence, Soëtendrop, in better shape but still in the hospital, described being seized at a bar by a single man "about my size, perhaps a bit shorter, and certainly slimmer." He was pushed into a car where he was bound and blindfolded. The star of David was ripped off his neck. Later he found him-self in a sewer tunnel, daubed with feces, with a swastika dyed on his chest. He remembered being hit in the stomach, losing consciousness. The humiliation reached a climax when, aware of his surroundings, he was asked to kiss a small photograph of Adolf Hitler.

> Natalie Soëtendrop rushed to her husband's side. Actors, politicians, and religious leaders paraded through the hospital. Hermann Musaph was interviewed on TV. "Musaph is a Treblinka survivor," Yosee states. "He told viewers that, with the exception of Poland, more Jews were killed during World War II in Belgium and Holland than anywhere else."

Yosee sent Soëtendrop a greeting card the next day. He never got a response. He later found out the actor received close to three thousand just on his first day at the hospital.

On January 6, a month and three days after Soëtendrop's ordeal began, the ac-tor confessed to his own kidnapping. At two-hundred-thirty-five pounds, he was extraordinarily elastic. He had come up with the whole thing: his own injuries, the neo-Nazi commando, the typed notes, including the one in flawed Spanish. Collective sympathy soon became unimpeded animosity. The public was furious: it had trusted its actor, but the play itself turned out to be a lie. New demonstra-tions plastered the streets. There was talk of retribution. The police department sent Soëtendrop a bill. (It was dutifully paid.) There were swastikas painted in bus stops, and a cemetery was desecrated. In Brussels, the synagogue in the Anderlecht district where Soëtendrop had found his faith during a Yom Kippur service was set on fire with a Molotov cocktail. "Is it a surprise that the actor and his wife failed to respond, retreating to their Deventer residence?" Yosee wonders. "Maarten was ashamed of his deeds—but he never found the right words to articulate his emotions. It isn't surprising. When it comes to guilt, are Belgians—even Belgian Jews—capable of those words?"

To describe the rationale behind Maarten Soëtendrop's misguided self-flag-ellation is to ratify—if proof were needed—that reality invariably outdoes the most baroque of dramaturges. My alibi is that nothing in this story is invented. Eddelbuettel, in the obituary, argues that the actor had been involved in a series of Jewish efforts to block an anti-Semitic play by Rainer Werner Fassbinder, *Garbage, the City, and Death*, its debut scheduled in Brussels for 1986. It is about a prostitute, Roma, whose fortunes turn around after her encounter with a Frankfurt speculator for the municipal government called the Rich Jew. Frank, a pimp and Roma's husband, leaves her. Roma then asks her lover to kill her. As a result of his connections, the Rich Jew isn't accused of the crime; instead, Frank is. The play was originally written in 1975. Its anti-Semitism forced officials to block it in Germany. A hurricane of op-ed pieces, letters to the editor, and radio broadcasts decried the blockage as a "suspension of freedom of speech in Belgium." Political pundits talked of the tentacles of a Jewish lobby controlling the government. It was printed by the *Frankfurter Allgemeine Zeitung*. Suhrkamp Press released it in book form. The publisher withdrew it and would not release it until Fassbinder changed the name of the Rich Jew. The director steadfastly refused. In 1984, a couple of years after Fassbinder's death, the Old Opera in Frankfurt attempted to stage it once more. It was again stopped. (In the interim, the Yoram Loewenberg acting school in Israel performed it.) Another company tried to stage it in Belgium soon after without success. An anti-Fassbinder protest led by Rabbi Frydman and supported by Maarten Soëtendrop took hold. There was more censorship. A publisher in Antwerp released it in Dutch translation. In mid 1987 it was read on Belgian public radio. Still, no theater agreed to produce Fassbinder's play.

"What are the uses of hatred?" Yosee asks in his letter. "Maarten's intentions were good. His ploy might have forced a referendum in the Netherlands, the land of Baruch Spinoza and Anne Frank, but not in Belgium, where 'the mendacious amnesia'—the phrase was used by Soëtendrop—accumulated over decades remains unexposed. Instead, he ended up being confronted by a tribunal of his own device, one staged in a theater as big as the world entire. He wanted to understand the power of silence. But in this area, he was short of talent."

At the time of the confession, Soëtendrop's lawyer, Luuk Hammer, described his client as being "in a state of panic." But he wasted no time in exculpating him: "Is our illustrious theater star guiltier than the rest of us are? Maarten Soëtendrop may have lost his boundaries. He is an expert in theater but not an expert in crime."

The actor's sole response came after the Justice Minister requested an "official" apology. Soëtendrop went on camera with an epigrammatic—and, in Yosee's eyes, suspicious—statement read on Thursday, May 10, 1988. "If in any way I've offended the Belgian people in particular, and the Low Countries in general, I deeply regret it. My life has been a pandemonium since I was five."

In the obituary in *De Telegraf*, Eddelbuettel claims Soëtendrop was in the Charleroi sewer system for only three days. Disguised in a woman's clothes (wig, lavender dress, heavy winter coat), he stayed in a homeless shelter until after Christmas Day, then moved to a place on Rue Émile Vandervelde until January 2. Surreptitiously, he broke into his dressing room at the theater at midnight the next day, took make-up equipment, a curtain rope, a knife, and some paint. A night guard reported hearing odd noises but didn't spot him. Less than forty-eight hours later, he was already in his thespian apparel in Bruges.

Did Soëtendrop truly repent? Not in Yosee's eyes. "Even when he apologized to the Justice Minister, I'm convinced Maarten was still acting. In fact, he acted all the way to the grave."

In his letter, my friend offers convincing evidence. It is an indictment of journalistic practices. "Reporters only scratch the surface. They are impatient. Their next deadline is a distraction. Had they bothered to look up the actor's past meticulously," he writes, "they would have come across unsettling data. Did he really devise his own disappearance? He was an intelligent man. But he was haunted. Becoming an actor was a way to alleviate his inner doubts. It allowed him an opportunity to take a regular vacation from himself."

Yosee listed valuable information about Soëtendrop's father, mother, and brother. After a career in the regional stage, his father retired in the seventies and died of an aneurism in 1981. He and his eldest son seldom spoke to each other. The link between Soëtendrop and his mother was even more tenuous. Ostensibly, she, along with one of her grandchildren, visited him after a performance of *Platonov* in Louvain and tried to reintroduce herself. Believing she was a stalker, Soëtendrop avoided her. His mother subsequently attempted another reunion. Although by then the actor knew well who she was, he refused to see her. She died in 1994 while on a trip to Greece.

"The bond with Hugo Soëtendrop is more convoluted," Yosee adds. In *Wertewelt des Judentums*, the sections dedicated to him are called "Pandemonium." They are surveys of their tense relationship, describing Hugo as "a loving brother who learned to loathe." But they conceal more than they reveal. For instance, Soëtendrop stressed, a total of nineteen times, that since he left for the farm near Leeuwarden, he and Hugo never saw each other again. "Why over-emphasize the point?"

After Yosee read the autobiographical essay, he sent Soëtendrop a congratulatory note. In it he asked him about his brother. Again, Soëtendrop failed to respond. Yosee was intrigued, though. He looked for the name "Hugo Soëtendrop" in the national birth registry; he found it. Then he searched telephone records; this time he came up empty-handed. A reference in a school yearbook in Kortrijle led him to one François Soëten; it was a dead-end. Another one in Roeselare talked about a Sutendorp brewing company. He then searched for Soëtendrop's stepfather, Siegbert Himmelstrup. An entire dossier became available. He identified Himmelstrup as a metal worker in Antwerp, a sixty-seven-year-old devout Catholic, married with four children: Heinrich, Julian, Ute, and Elfriede. A series of archived photographs gave Yosee the certitude he wanted: Hugo Soëtendrop had been re-baptized—and reeducated—as Julian Himmelstrup. He had been a member of the Nazi Youth League. After the war, he studied engineering in Bielefeld, in Westphalia and eventually returned to Brussels. For a short while in the eighties he lived in Madrid, where he signed up for a four-week course on the Spanish Civil War. "I was rewarded with a nemesis," Yosee writes. "Hugo lived in Bruges, where he was a part-time employee at the Federal Department of the Environment. He was divorced by then and I know little about his first wife. He tried to have a child with a second wife, but it took its toll and after three miscarriages, she left him. Estranged from everyone, Hugo lived in a rented room near Rue Émile Vandervelde. Like his stepfather, whom he adored, his support for Nazism didn't diminish after the war. Indeed, until the end he believed Hitler's overall mission to racially improve Europe would one day be accomplished *in toto*."

Hugo followed his brother's career with a mix of wonder and resentment. He kept a distance: Soëtendrop's renewed faith in Judaism disgusted him. His reluctance to interact changed in the aftermath of the anti-Fassbinder protests. In Hugo's view, Belgium made an irreversible pact with the devil when *Garbage, the City, and Death* was canceled.

Knowing Soëtendrop was scheduled to be part of a rally organized by Rabbi Frydman, Hugo hid amidst the crowd. Did Soëtendrop spot him, too? Hugo heard his brother give a speech about the perils of amnesia. "It was then that he plotted Maarten's kidnapping," Yosee writes. "Or is it the other way around? I confess to be on shaky ground in this area of my search. But that doesn't make it less believable. I've discovered, for instance, that Hugo—AKA Julian Himmelstrup—gave final notice to the Federal Department of the Environment on November 27, 1987. The room he rented was vacated the day before. 'An old woman took everything with her,' the owner told me. She said Monsieur Himmelstrup was indisposed. As long as she gave me the last monthly pay, I didn't care to ask for specifics.' The Olivetti used for typing the notes purportedly written by the Flemish Fascist Youth Front was found."

That cold afternoon in Charleroi on December 3, Hugo caught up with his sibling, his tipsy older—and odder—self, at a bar on the way to the theater. "Did Maarten recognize him? There is no way to know. Julian Himmelstrup was, unlike his brother, thin, pale, and with teeth even the British would abhor. He was a nobody. That afternoon he was wearing a fedora. Probably neither of them thought the encounter would last long. I've tried to imagine the dialogue they engaged in, but it isn't easy in a generation taught not to use words. They walked a few blocks together and then they disappeared. I don't think *De verdwijning* was a *fait accompli* in the mind of either of them, as the media led us to believe. Things were improvised, the way they often are when madness sets in. But this kind of madness was more coherent, more intelligible. One of them—was it Maarten?—let his pathos run wild. Ah, the media! Is there a less trustworthy theater? Are we all fooled more often by any other device? I don't trust the interviews granted by Natalie Soëtendrop, Luuk Hammer, anyone...To me it looks as if they, I, and everyone had been fortuitously invited to a performance in the biggest theater imaginable. Harry Mulisch, who won the Prijs van de Nederlandse Letteren in 1995, published a novella-cum-play (he calls it 'a contradiction') made of a pair of monologues and an intermezzo. It is narrated at Soëtendrop's funeral. Maarten becomes Herbert Althans and Natalie Magda. But it distorts the intricacy of events. This is because literature is always a game. Why distort what has already been misrepresented?"

Yosee bluntly visualizes the scene in which the siblings have reached the Charleroi sewer system. "The city was built in 1666, the year in which the pseudo-messiah Sabbetai Zevi, who eventually became an apostate by converting to Islam, expected the world to come to an end. At the time, Spain ruled the Low Countries. The idea was to build a fortification in order to stop the imperial troops of Louis XIV. The sewer system is a macabre web made of symmetrical dungeons. Maarten and Hugo walked the maze until they found a large, dank chamber where the air was fetid. There was only a glimmer of light. The memory of the Hanukah 'bacchanal' I spent with Maarten and Natalie lies in sharp contrast in my mind. For hours they stared at each other's shadows. Had they done anything else in life?" Then Maarten probably said: "I thought I killed you inside me a long time ago. But when I saw your face in the crowd, I realized I was wrong. After we expiate the guilt we've been forced to inherit—what the Germans call *Schuld*—only one of us is likely to emerge from this darkness."

The final paragraph of Yosee's letter is the most eloquent. "So there you have it: another retelling of Cain and Abel. Before his death in a hotel in Charleroi, on Rue de la Providence, Maarten was dangerously overweight—close to three hundred pounds, according to Eddelbuettel. In the last few years the public recognized him mostly for his soap endorsements on TV. And I know little else except that on the High Holidays he and Natalie prayed at Brussels' elegant Sephardic synagogue on Rue du Pavillon and that he donated money to the Belgian Jewish Museum to buy back art stolen by the Nazis. And, of course, Maarten remained an assiduous patron of the most refined French restaurants. Did he sin through the mouth to compensate for the lack of words? These questions have no answer. When did Maarten come up with the F.F.Y.F.? Who typed the notes sent to his wife, Rabbi Frydman, and others? It doesn't matter. The fact is, Hugo was never seen again. I've checked hospices, morgues, crime logs. He seems to have vanished into smoke. In our debates, Ilan, I always took the stand that Israel would finally solve the dilemmas of the Diaspora. It would make the Jew beautiful, a bronze man, a warrior. Our ancient sense of inferiority—the metaphorical hunchback we've carried with us for generations and generations—would be disposed once and for all: no more apologies, no more inferiority complexes. As you know, I tried to live up to my opinions by making *aliyah*. It didn't work. I became a lawyer who specializes in Holocaust reparation cases. I wanted to do some good after the pervasiveness of evil. But evil is an essential component of Nature, the opposite of good. One can't exist without the other. All things considered, I'm a diasporic creature like you, one comfortable looking at things as an outsider. For centuries Jews kept the prohibition against idolatry. Among other things, this meant that acting was forbidden. To be someone else, even for a short while, is to compete with the Almighty's creation. The prohibition backfired: at heart, all Jews are actors. The art of impostures is encoded in our DNA. How else could we exist with the contradictions that inhabit us? In what other way would we pretend to live a happy life among strangers and still dwell in our unique unhappiness? Maarten's odyssey frightens me. He put a serious face in front of millions while pretending to have been kidnapped. People believed him. But who ended up losing?"

Yosee Strigler's letter was postmarked in Israel.

⸙

Richard Chess
With Solomon Ibn Gabirol

Down the aisle of dawn
a mourning run
a fast sigh along the fuse

of sadness

I look for you early,
my rock and my refuge

Off shore, a war-
ship ringed with fur, oil
lagging behind

Before your vastness
I come confused
  and afraid

At the core of prayer,
fear
  What
could the heart
compose to suit you?

Faith Adiele

Gifts

*A*GE TWO AND MY MOTHER's battle with the world continues. It is nearly Christmas, the most difficult season for the vigilant culture warrior. This year she finds herself pitted against Mona, the babysitter's three-year-old and my best friend. Mona is the olive-skinned beauty in a large family who, despite this largeness and perhaps because of this beauty, will spend her adolescence running away, and after a promising career as a restaurateur (according to her) end up in the Montana woods raising (according to her tight-lipped parents) a pack of near-feral foster kids, perhaps and perhaps not aided by an ex-con boyfriend. But for now, it is December 1965 and we want baby dolls.

Determined to raise a healthy, biracial daughter, one who will skip across fields of daisies with boys and girls of all races and creeds, colt-giddy with self-esteem, belting out "Free To Be Me" off-key, thanks to ("That Girl!") Marlo Thomas, one who will happily embrace math and science, as well as her God-given body type, my mother is thoroughly opposed to our plan. My mother does not scare easily. The apple-cheeked daughter of Nordic farm folk who threw her out for bearing an African man's child, she spends my childhood arms akimbo, all 5-foot-2 of her, at the edge of playgrounds, blue eyes glittering behind thick spectacles, just daring the white kids and their parents to say something, *anything*. You bet she's ready for Madame Alexander and Mattel.

Like Mona and I, my mother takes the hard work of childhood play seriously. She has mastered various strategies, specifically: (1) defensive shopping (in which long detours, eyes averted, are taken around toxic Barbie sites as if the dolls could teeter forward, breasts locked and loaded, on those perpetually high-heeled feet and lure us into their silicon embrace); (2) late-night revisions (where, armed with brown fingernail polish and black markers, she attacks my blond, pink-faced paper dolls and picture books with the commitment to detail of a Japanese censor scraping away pubic hair, strand by pornographic strand); and (3) the yet-to-be-proven-effective social inoculation (a.k.a., loud, protracted scoffing at marketing tie-ins and such items as lavender ponies with comb-able manes instead of practical brown plastic work horses and The Imagination God Gave You). It is exhausting.

The outside world, this time in the guise of dark-eyed three-year-old Mona, rears its seductive head. In the weeks preceding Christmas, she and I begin to beg "for babies." We are relentless. We plead our case at tea parties. We accost my mother in the foyer, direct from school, her cheeks still red from the walk up Capitol Hill. We dazzle with our reasoned arguments.

The debate goes something like this:

Mona (clutching my smaller hand possessively): "I want a baby like Faith. Tell Santa."

Faith: "Me too! Baby!"

Mother (grimacing): "How about a real dump truck?"

Faith: "No."

Mother (brightly): "A pony family?"

Faith: "No!"

Mother (still hopeful): "I know—a whole village of building blocks!"

Faith (crying): "Ahhhh!"

Mona (equally bright): "Santa's bringing me a baby doll like Faith."

Faith: "Baby!"

Mother (eyes rolling up into her head): "Oh Lord."

The carriers of my infection are the five (soon to be six) daughters, one son, and unknown number of fast-moving pets herded by my babysitter. Ever since the day Auntie Peg found us on her doorstep, wet, my mother sniffling (or was it simply allergies and the ubiquitous Seattle drizzle?) that she was "desperate for childcare" (I have never seen my mother behave desperately or claim desperation, ever), I have been raised as part of this busy Irish Catholic household. What could be better?

Unlike our government-subsidized studio and family of two, their house echoes with space and sound. It back-ends directly onto Volunteer Park—just a few steps past the garage, and Mona and I are in the largest backyard anyone could hope for, serving tea beneath a grand umbrella tree. In the evening, when my mother and Uncle Sean return from the university, where she is a junior and he a graduate student, we make a show of catching the bus in the rain. But most days, we slide into place at the rickety dinner table, me at two fitting easily between the three- and one-year-olds, before Auntie Peg cajoles Uncle Sean into putting down the paper and driving us across town to the pink housing project.

Auntie Peg reassures my mother that this baby thing is normal. All kids want to push their own strollers and boss dolls around. There's no need to worry that, at age two, I'm one Hello Kitty night light away from bleaching cream and cheerleading camp. At this age, even boys—her voice drops—want dolls.

At this my mother perks up, blue eyes sharpening. That's it—a boy doll! Provided he's anatomically correct, of course.

"Oh dear." But raising six (soon to be seven) kids has taught her to choose her battles. Auntie Peg pastes on that Catholic smile and pours another cup of tea.

The next day, taking the money Tati Rauha sent for Christmas dinner, my mother sets out in search of black, anatomically correct, male baby dolls. If anyone is up to the task, it is she. She is mistress of impossible toys, toys no one believes do or should exist, and has talked more than one clerk out of display and factory models. We may go home to peanut butter suppers and twin mattresses on the floor, but my mother routinely drags back from her hunting forays beaded teepees, miniature pinhole cameras, African drums. At times the world delivers.

1965, however, does not.

Sighing as she corrals a long strand of chestnut hair into her headband, she settles on a small, inexpensive girl doll with hard brown plastic skin and shiny black curls. Limited in repertoire, this is what the thing can do: rotate her arms at the shoulder; roll her marble eyes shut if you lay her on her back; "wet" her diapers out of a small, not particularly anatomically correct hole. My mother names her Nneka (which, though she doesn't know it, means *Mother is Supreme*—the name she nearly gave me, if not for anticipating trouble enough on American playgrounds) after my father's favorite sister (who, though this too she doesn't know, will soon be captured and hacked to pieces in the Nigerian civil war, our tribe unfortunately nicknamed—and then treated like—"West Africa's Jews").

On the way home, my mother stops by the fabric store to root through the remnant barrel. She spends the rest of the bus ride home sketching two tiny smocks.

On Christmas morning, the Irish Catholics collect us after Mass. I clamber into the noisy car (it being Sixties Seattle, I imagine a VW bus), prattling about Baby Nneka who was delivered by St. Nicholas the night before and is wearing miniature diapers cut from old ones of mine: twins. Mona's dark eyes gleam. Irish Catholic Santa doesn't come until Christmas Day, but things are looking good (despite the fact that at two, I know something three-year-old Mona doesn't, that there is no such thing as Santa Claus, being as everyone knows reindeer can't fly).

By the end of Christmas dinner, Mona and her grandparents could all use sedatives. Hearing about their granddaughter's first-ever Christmas wish, they'd begged to buy her first doll. Both parties quiver with anticipation. Auntie Peg whispers that they've gone "all out." My mother helps hand around cups of tea with a bright, almost Catholic smile pasted to her face. Nneka, with her two handmade print shifts, will certainly seem shabby compared to human hair and factory-embroidered dresses.

Finally it is Mona's turn to throw herself onto the nearly life-sized package and scratch at the gold foil wrapping paper. I clap my hands. Her sisters help her peel away the last scrap, revealing a glossy pink box with a plastic window. The grandparents lean forward. My mother and I catch our breaths.

The doll inside defies description.

Silently we all take in the crisp, white lace pinafore, the delicately blushing cheeks, the sweeping eyelashes and shiny blond curls. Exclamatory bubbles down the side of the box advertise her awesome powers and properties.

It takes a few seconds before the shrieking starts.

The room jolts awake. My mother stares at me. I stare at Mona. Mona stares at the doll. The rest of the Irish Catholics spin around and around, staring at each other. Who is shrieking and why?

Mona is shrieking, whether with delighted hysteria or hysterical disappointment isn't clear.

I am shrieking because she is.

As it seems a good idea, the one-year-old soon joins in.

Now everyone is running. Half sprint towards a hysterical Mona, who, it has been determined, is very, *very* disappointed, half towards the grandparents, who for their part, eyes as round as the doll's, certainly are too.

Auntie Peg: "Mona, what in the world is wrong?"

Mother: "Faith, what in the world is wrong?"

Faith: "I dunno."

Mother: "Then hush."

Faith: "Okay."

Auntie Peg: "Mona sweetie?"

Mona (shaking with sobs, choking, olive face crumpled, dark eyes pink): "I-I-I want a baby like Faith!"

All the parents exchange puzzled glances, palms up. The grandparents are sad shadows on the sofa, Mona's older siblings sympathetic gestures in the air around them. Auntie Peg, hardly larger than the box herself, paws at the top to extricate the doll. See how she is indeed a baby just like Faith?

Uncle Sean glances at me, quickly scanning for clues. A philosopher, he's a quiet albeit critical man, his one moment of outrage coming soon, to be directed towards the family priest when Auntie Peg becomes pregnant with their seventh child, against her doctor's strict warning, and Uncle Sean begs for some, any, dispensation to save her life. The priest shakes his head, citing Paul IV's recent encyclical forbidding all forms of birth control, even for therapeutic reasons. But, he adds brightly, if she dies, Uncle Sean and the seven children can take comfort in knowing that, in dying a good Catholic wife, she went straight to heaven.

My mother spots a tiny bottle among the doll's trousseau and snatches it up. Perhaps, she suggests hopefully, Mona can use it to feed her baby.

Auntie Peg agrees. Just like Faith! She squeezes the doll, demonstrating its soft newness, its almost-fleshy arms and legs. See how it bends, just like a real baby! She manipulates its limbs, the baby gone berserk.

I frown. Baby Nneka rotates rigidly, refusing to pander to the crowd.

Mona: "No! Like Faith!"

Now her sisters jump in, abandoning the grandparents to point out similarities between the doll and me. Fingers touch her fancy dress, those bright curls. She has so many pretty outfits! She comes with her own brush and comb! And, if Mona pulls this string, listen, listen, she talks! Just like Faith!

I upend Nneka and give a good shake. They talk?

Baby Nneka pisses her diaper and rolls her eyes up into her head.

Mona begins to hiccup, a fine sheen of snot and tears coating her face. She is glossy with grief. Her bud-pink mouth opens, but all that comes out is all she knows how to say: "I want a baby like Faith! Like Faith!"

The Irish Catholics squint at each other. Beneath lowered lashes, brother and older sisters monitor their own unopened gifts, smiling bravely. Uncle Sean fusses with the fire, poking this and that with tongs: man's work. Auntie Peg, red hair askew, sinks into the sofa, inches away from the grandparents, gray, sprawled helpless as halibut.

Baby Nneka bats her amber eyes, eyelashes like miniature black brushes, and my mother laughs. "I get it!" She pounds the ottoman, upturning her cup onto its saucer with a clatter. How could it have taken her so long? "She means a black doll. Mona wants a doll that's *black* like Faith!"

The grandparents bug their eyes, caught on the line, fighting for breath. "Oh?" the grandmother manages. Decades later I will learn that when Auntie Peg first starts caring for me, her mother accuses her of jeopardizing her own children's well-being and swears her intention not to come "within ten feet of that pickaninny." (Auntie Peg: "I was ashamed of my own mother, but I will tell you.") The story does not reveal which grandmother this is stammering on the sofa.

My mother grins.

The Irish Catholics stare at me (after all, that first time in the rain, my mother having been directed by a stranger at the bus stop to their door, Auntie Peg hadn't noticed until the second cup of tea: "Oh, she's a black baby!"). After a second they join my mother's laughter. They re-enact the scene, mimicking their own frantic actions: Like Faith, like Faith! Mona cried, and we ran this way and that! Mona knew Faith was special. She just didn't know *how*!

The story doesn't tell what happened next. How Mona was placated until Auntie Peg could obtain a black doll. How the remaining children opened their gifts, no doubt taking care to exclaim with delight. What happened to whichever grandparents these were, the expensive doll. After all, my mother and I weren't actually there. This is one of those childhood tales told so vividly and so often that we convince ourselves of having been actors, center stage. To the lingering sound of Mona's shrieks in my ears, the feel of my own tiny lungs gathering breath, my mother laughs: "Nope, Auntie Peg told me the story *days* later! But your version's effective."

There is a postscript, decades later, when the final child—another girl, the last Catholic, born as the family leaves the church, opting for life on earth—will wed an African American, much to her parents' amusement, versed as they now are in racial negotiation. Six out of seven college graduates; one black son-in-law; and only one, the prettiest, living wild in the woods. Not a bad harvest.

But for now, for now, we have 1965 and the challenges it presents pickaninnies. Seeing new potential to engender racial self-love, my mother switches strategies completely. She spends the rest of winter vacation up late sewing "African Princess-wear"—elaborate outfits from scraps of blue velvet, suede, faux leopard fur. In the coming Christmases and birthdays, a stream of new, *haute couture* African princesses arrive until I am chieftaining a small village of supermodels.

"Okay," she 'fesses up, plump lips rueful. "They were pretty. It was fun!" Indeed, prettier than the boys—Dr. Mark Luther (a.k.a., "G.I. Joe—Ethnic Model") with the creepy velveteen hair and camouflage gear; Kofi, a brown rag doll with Jackson

Five bright orange overalls and loopy yarn curls; Compromise Boy, a palm-sized baby who made up for his whiteness with a soft, peach penis. At last!

But like my mother, the story abandons gender (female body image and missing black men, be damned!), even race. Now we are seeking something even deeper, meaning shifting as we circle Christmas, peering at its gifts, crowding close enough to claim we were there.

Mona calls, forty years later still hungry for me. Now she, the one who sacrificed six siblings and two parents to feed her habit (according to her mother), before disappearing to the Montana woods with a family-sized hole in her heart (according to her), returns, married to the perhaps and perhaps not boyfriend. He hulks in the doorway, novel in hand, grin shy. The two of them wake in shifts, the sky still dark, to relieve Auntie Peg from her all-night vigil. They take turns bathing and dressing and feeding Uncle Sean with gentle hands. They switch off loading up the dogs and driving home to bathe and dress and feed the three children she found in the woods, who turned out to be his anyway.

Uncle Sean, mind sharp as ever, slurs, daily losing speech. "I sound drunk, but I'm not," he says, eyes stricken as the body wobbles and shakes. "It's this body, the Parkinson's. You believe me, don't you? I'm still me."

And as I nod, yes, vaguely aware that he's the one I don't in fact remember from before, that he's become him only now, I remember Baby Nneka in her matching diapers, my almost-namesake, my murdered aunt, my first lesson that war travels with love and that for everyone who comes to join us, someone else is apparently lost.

Meena Alexander

Song of the Red Earth

A child swings over laburnum and wisteria,
Over red earth covered in patches of grass

And frogs croaking in the gooseberry bush
And cisterns dripping water.

Torn grass makes a handkerchief,
Slow flag over a smoking abyss.

In the bone's hollows
The sparrow startles itself singing.

* * *

The child parts her lips to speak
And the sun is smeared with birthmuck.

She loiters in a theater of cruelty,
Spoils of sense, ruin of syllables,

Iconostasis jammed with broken syntax
Where a royal door should be.

* * *

Decades later the woman writes:
I have no real home

And what is left of my childhood
Is fit to be carted away

Remains of the dawn
In a spurt of circling wagons.

* * *

Gathering up bones she listens for a child,
Dark child who dreams of catastrophe,

Who hears the turtledove on the sill,
The butterfly filled

With its own insuperable dust
Hovering over springs of pure sulfur.

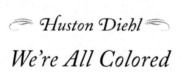

Huston Diehl

We're All Colored

BLACK AMERICANS MAKE PROGRESS," the headline of the *Weekly Reader* announced in large, bold letters. I smiled to myself as I picked up the parcel of newspapers reserved for my class in the main office. I had been teaching at Z. C. Morton Elementary School—a "Negro" school in rural Virginia—for more than a month, and I had been searching for instructional materials on African-American culture with little luck. Even though most of the major battles of the Civil Rights Movement had already been fought by the time I joined the Morton staff in the winter of 1970, the school was still segregated, its curriculum determined by a white Superintendent and an all-white school board, its rooms decorated with portraits of famous white men and images of blond, blue-eyed children. Except for a couple of paragraphs on Booker T. Washington in a Virginia state history book that celebrated the Confederate cause, none of the textbooks I was required to use taught my students anything about their own history. Now, I couldn't wait to distribute the newspapers and present my fourth-grade students with this report on the lives of black Americans like them.

As soon as they caught sight of the headlines of their *Weekly Reader*s that afternoon, however, I sensed that something was terribly, terribly wrong. Instead of the sea of waving hands that usually greeted my opening question, "Who would like to read?" I looked out over an eerily still classroom of scowling children, their bodies tense, their eyes on high alert. No one volunteered to read. Instead, my students sat warily at their desks and glared at me. A storm was brewing, but I—a twenty-one-year-old white woman who had never before lived in the South—had no idea what was wrong, no clue why they had suddenly turned angry and sullen. I called on Matilda, someone I could count on to read well and one of the class's acknowledged leaders. But she refused to read. I called on Calvin, another leader. He shook his head. I called on polite and dependable Maxine. She looked away from me. And then, much to my relief, Sheila raised her hand.

"I'll read," she volunteered. Some of the children gasped out loud at Sheila's offer, and others shot her accusatory looks, as if she had somehow betrayed them. But the tone of her voice was not conciliatory. It was defiant. Sheila smiled mysteriously at her classmates, taking the time to meet their disbelieving stares. "Watch me," her flashing eyes seemed to say. And then, in a perfectly composed voice, she began to read: "NEGRO AMERICANS MAKE PROGRESS." As she read on, she pointedly substituted the term "Negro" every time the word "black" appeared in print. At once, the tension in the room lifted. Now everyone wanted to read. Garfield and Raymond followed Sheila's lead, using "Negro" in place of the adjective "black." Debra Ann and Thomas substituted "colored" instead. Alice alternated indiscriminately between the two terms. No one uttered the word "black." Following Sheila's lead, the class collectively conspired to banish that word, refusing its power to define them, keeping at bay whatever demons it conjured up in their minds.

I didn't say anything about this communal act of censorship and revision until the class had finished reading the lead story. Then, I spoke. I told them we needed to talk about their reaction to the author's use of the term "black." I informed them that many African-Americans, including influential writers, important civil rights activists, and well-known entertainers, preferred to use the word "black" to describe themselves rather than words like "Negro" and "colored." I tried to explain the thinking behind this preference. I told them about the black power movement, the popular slogan "black is beautiful," and the efforts of prominent African-Americans to instill racial pride in their people by embracing the term "black." And I assured them that the author of the *Weekly Reader* article had in no way intended to insult them when he chose to refer to them as black. My students were unmoved. Nothing I said altered their conviction that "black" was one of the worst things you could call somebody. Eight years later these same children would pose for their senior class photographs in magnificent Afros worthy of Bobby Seale and Angela Davis, but on this February day in 1970 they adamantly refused to be identified as black, a word they understood to be a racial epithet, a threat to their integrity, a mean-spirited charge leveled at them by white people in their hometown.

"But calling someone black *is* an insult," Garfield insisted. "White people are always calling us black, just to make us feel like we're no good. They think they have the right to lord it over us, just because of the color of our skin. When someone calls me black, I want to fight him."

A chorus of emphatic "yeah"s reinforced Garfield's position.

"Colored," Debra Ann suggested, "is a better word for describing us. It's not upsetting to be called colored, 'cause that's what we are. We're all colored."

"But Negro is the best word to use," Raymond weighed in. "That's the proper name to use to describe our people. It says we're all brothers." Everyone, including the girls, nodded.

Then Sheila recounted her defiant response to a white teenager who had humiliated her by deploying the demeaning words "black girl" to enforce the customs of Jim Crow. "When I first moved back to Louisa from New York City," she told the class, "I put a penny in a gum-ball machine downtown. A real big white boy came up to me. He was wearing a varsity football jacket, and he was very tall, and his neck and shoulders were huge." She stretched out her arms to emphasize just how huge. "He was acting like I had done something terrible by putting a penny in the gum-ball machine. He walked right up to where I was standing, got in my face, and stared at me, hard. I could tell he was mad, really mad. 'Black girl,' he said to me, like I was dirt, 'Black girl, you can't use this gum-ball machine. You're black.' I was so scared I wanted to run. I was afraid he was going to hurt me. But do you know what I told him? I told him, 'You see my shoes? They're black. You see my face? It's brown. My name is Sheila, and I can buy gum from any machine I want to.' And then I got my gum and walked away. And he just stood there, staring at me."

Listening to the way my students sought to preserve their dignity by repudiating their "blackness," I began to realize how complicated and confusing—how messy—the task of defining a self was for the thirty-seven African-American children sitting in my classroom. They were only ten years old. Born in 1960, six years after the *Brown v. Board of Education* decision, they were three when Martin Luther King delivered his "I Have a Dream" speech, four when the Civil Rights

Act was signed into law, five when the Voting Rights Act was passed, six when Huey Newton and Bobby Seale founded the Black Panthers, eight when King was assassinated in Memphis. Yet they still lived in a segregated town reluctant to end its enforcement of Jim Crow laws that systematically excluded, subordinated, and disenfranchised people like them, people, that is, who had even "one drop" of "black blood" in them. How, I wondered, did they manage to sustain their fierce pride in their "Negro" and "colored" identity while recoiling in horror at the thought of being "black"? Was their response to the black power movement's defiant appropriation of the word "black" a reactionary one, evidence of their traditional rural upbringing, or was it a radical and heroic form of resistance to the racism they encountered daily? Could it be both? Had they unconsciously internalized white culture's color prejudice, tragically preferring brown skin to black (and white to brown), or had they penetrated the secret of America's "miscegenated heart"?

Sheila's story opened a floodgate, and the stories spilled out. Raymond told how, whenever he went into a store, clerks always followed him around, watching his every move, sure he was going to misbehave or shoplift because he was colored. "It makes me so mad," he confessed, "I want to steal something just to get back at them." Ramonia told how her soldier father routinely encountered discrimination at a PX store on the U.S. Army base in Vietnam where he was stationed. "Why," she asked plaintively, "can't they just treat him like all the other soldiers?" Debra Ann told how once, at a store counter, some white kids had intentionally knocked the candy she had selected onto the floor. "I just don't understand why they are so mean to us," she confided quietly. "Do you think," she asked, her eyes solemn, "there will ever be a war between colored people and white people?" Compelled to defend themselves against what they understood to be the taint of blackness, these children sought mightily to ward off the ugly, alien images of themselves they discovered in the suspicious eyes of Louisa's storekeepers, the contemptuous eyes of adolescent bullies, the mocking eyes of white children who cruelly knocked their candy on the floor.

Confiding in me about the many times they had been wounded by the hateful or demeaning actions of white people, my students seemed, for a moment, to forget that I was white. Then Rodney, who sat in the very back of the class, suddenly shot up his hand.

"What color do you think I am?" he asked. His was no curious or casual query. It was a challenge, and I could feel all eyes watching me to see if I would pick up the gauntlet. I looked carefully at Rodney before answering. I studied the color of his face, his neck, his arms. I compared the color of his skin to the children sitting near him, noting in a way I hadn't really registered before, the wide range of skin tones, the multiple shades of brown and black among the students sitting before me.

"Rodney," I said at last, "I'd say you're a very light brown—tan maybe, or beige." Rodney nodded his head in satisfaction. "Right," he declared. I could tell that he was proud of his light skin, that he wanted me to acknowledge that he was not, in any literal sense of the word, black. But my interrogation was not over.

"And what color do you think you are?" he asked, challenging me again.

I was surprised by Rodney's question, surprised and disconcerted, for it forced me to examine the set of neat racial categories I had always taken for granted. I realized that I had never really thought about being any color at all, had always simply accepted the premise that I was white. I realized, too, with a sharp stab of shame, that I had allowed the racial categories of white and black to separate me from my students by unthinkingly accepting them as valid and natural. Unconsciously, I'd based my identity on being "white." Worse, I had enjoyed the power and status my whiteness conferred upon me without ever questioning their legitimacy. I began to see that this persistent little boy questioning me from the back of the room understood far better than I how the privileges I enjoyed as a "white" person derived from an utterly absurd set of assumptions.

I held out my arm and observed it closely. Although my ancestors were German and Scots-Irish, I am not fair-skinned. During the summers of my childhood, I used to get so dark from long days in the sun that my grandfather affectionately called me his little brown bear. As a teenager, I proudly sported a fashionable, bronze suntan. Looking down at my arm that day, I realized what Rodney had obviously known all along: my skin was not much lighter than his light brown skin. Indeed, after a week or so in the summer sun, it would surely darken into a deeper shade of brown.

"I'm tan, too, Rodney," I told him. "I'm almost exactly the same color as you." Rodney smiled broadly at my admission. I hadn't fully understood how much status he derived from his light skin or considered the implications of that status for his darker-skinned classmates.

Then, noticing the veins on the underside of my forearm, I added as a playful afterthought, "And I'm even a little bit blue, too."

Rodney bolted out of his seat. Charging up to the front of the room, he grabbed my right hand and inspected it carefully, staring with a scientist's interest at the blue veins running in distinct lines from my palm to my wrist, the streaks of blue crisscrossing the back of my hand. Then he turned around to face the class and announced theatrically: "She's blue."

The class went wild.

"She's blue! She's blue!" my students shouted triumphantly. Pounding their fists on the desk, stomping their feet, they joined together in a gleeful chant: "Mrs. Hallahan's blue!"

I can't explain the giddiness of that moment. Did my students want to bring me inside their colored world, claim me as their own? Or did the prominence of my blue veins somehow mark my "white" body as aberrant, monstrous even, ridiculous and strange? Did they need some release from the seriousness of our discussion, the weight of the insults and color prejudices that the *Weekly Reader* article had dredged up from their past? Or did they seek to express the absurdity of their society's racial classifications by embracing an upside-down world—the teacher is not white but blue and her "black" students have the power to make her so? I joined in their giddy laughter. I did not mind at all being colored blue that Friday afternoon. Released from the tidy binary of white and black, I reveled in my messy, multicolored, mongrel self.

Unlike my African-American students, who daily grappled with the indignities of Jim Crow, I had had little reason to question the dominant social and racial hierarchy when I was a child, growing up white and affluent in a small, predominantly white Pennsylvania town in the 1950's. I was, after all, a direct beneficiary of that hierarchy. It bestowed on me a unified sense of self, assuring me of my inherent worth, protecting me from external threats to my integrity, conferring on me an enviable status in the world. But it also blinded me to the racial inequalities all around me.

The only African-American I knew intimately when I was a child was my family's live-in housekeeper. Tall and reed-thin, with flawless coffee-colored skin, an elegant beauty, and a fierce intelligence, Alberta Sherwood supported herself and her invalid father by washing, ironing, scrubbing, dusting, and vacuuming my family house and caring for my two sisters and me. Despite my strong attachment to her, I never questioned why she was the servant, I the served. I devoured the rich chocolate cakes Alberta baked especially for me—the quick "one egg" cake sometimes deployed to coax me out of a sulk and the more elaborate "ultra cake," made with sour cream and butter, layered with chocolate custard, topped with a dark chocolate glaze, and offered up for my birthday celebrations. But, though our mutual love of chocolate was a bond that connected us, I never once questioned why Alberta ate alone in the kitchen while the family gathered around the dining room table. I was grateful for the way her affectionate nickname for me—Messy Bessy—legitimized and even honored my natural propensity to spill milk on the counter, dribble spaghetti sauce over the tablecloth, cover the floor in glue and glitter, and splatter my clothes with mud and finger paint. But, although I had been taught to address all adults in a formal manner, I was oblivious to the way my affectionate name for her (I—we all—called her Alberta) demeaned her, denying to her the dignity and status I automatically accorded all white adults. I admired this young, African-American woman who loved books even more than I did, retreating on her breaks with a cup of coffee and a hefty novel to the family room where she became completely absorbed in her reading. But I never asked why someone of her intellect and curiosity was ironing my clothes and making my bed.

Yet I could not always suppress the troubling contradictions that threatened my tidy and smug sense of self, contradictions that Alberta's presence in my family home made visible. I will never forget arriving at my grandparents' place one sunny summer day and discovering, to my dismay, that my grandmother had painted the black face of the hitching post white. I have no idea how long this hitching post—a stock figure of a slave jockey—had stood there or who had installed it, an improbable icon on this fifty-five acres of fallow land (a child's paradise) in northwestern Pennsylvania, far from the imposing plantations of the American South and the wealth that slavery had made possible. I can only guess at what symbolic import it was originally meant to carry, standing as it did by the stone steps to my grandmother's garden, greeting visitors as they drove down the long gravel driveway to the modest, clapboard house. But in my childish ignorance it had delighted me, especially when my grandfather Sporty tied up his horse, Lady Grey, to the jockey's ring in order to boost me into the saddle. Until that morning, I had never questioned why the face of the little jockey we called "Mo" was coal black, never thought about why a statue of a Negro jockey stood on my white grandparents' property. It had never occurred to me that this figure, with its jaunty cap, white breeches, and bright red coat, helpfully holding out its arm to receive the reins of a horse, might be offensive.

I was shocked that day to discover the statue with its freshly painted white face. It looked completely ridiculous, bizarrely defaced, and I found its newly assigned racial identity strangely upsetting. Why, oh why, had my grandmother done something so odd? I could only gather from a brief exchange among the grownups that something Alberta had said about the hitching post when she accompanied the family on a previous visit had so mortified Gram that she had dug out an old can of white paint from the basement and set about earnestly attempting to turn Mo into a white man. The little figure that had always delighted me, I vaguely understood, had fallen into disgrace. By whitening its face, my grandmother sought to remove some deep shame she felt at its presence in her garden. Her gesture was my first inkling that an insidious serpent haunted my Eden.

My grandmother's impulse to tidy things up after the sting of Alberta's remark may have been born of repentance, but it was also an act of erasure, distancing my family from America's long history of racism, denying our complicity. It didn't so much engage issues of race as protect me from them, driving all the difficult and troubling questions underground. What was I to make of a bigoted remark, spoken by a family friend, at a party my parents hosted? How was I to reconcile my town's widely embraced civic ethos of fairness and tolerance with the fact that the few black citizens in my community lived in a single neighborhood in the poorer section of town and were primarily employed as janitors, cooks, bartenders, handymen, and domestics, never as teachers, doctors, lawyers, or businessmen? How was I to make sense of the fact that the first genuine intellectual I had ever known was my family's black housekeeper? For all my grandmother's good intentions, Mo's white face kept all these questions at bay.

But, if Gram's gesture helped to preserve my tidy sense of self by assuring me that my family and I could not possibly be racists, that tidiness, like the thin layer of white paint covering Mo's blackness, was a veneer. Underneath was muddle and confusion. The messiness of my childish efforts to make sense of racial—and class—identity is evident in my complicated response to Alberta's departure. When her father died, Alberta was finally free to pursue her ambitions. She quit her job with my family, moved to Washington, D.C., and began a life-long job at a city bookstore. Stubbornly loyal to her, I was not about to accept the new cleaning lady, a white woman named Thelma Howsare. The woman I was instructed to call Mrs. Howsare had grown up in the Appalachian mountains, the child of barely literate parents, and she had been forced to quit school after the eighth grade to help care for her younger siblings during the Depression. She spoke in a thick, colorful, and to my child's ears, comical, Appalachian dialect, nothing like any kind of dialect I'd heard before, and I was immediately suspicious of her. Never mind that Mrs. Howsare would go on to work for my parents for more than thirty years, timing her home-made bread to come out of the oven when I arrived home from school, bringing us fruit and vegetables and flowers from her abundant garden, and teaching me with her mental astuteness that intelligence is not the sole possession of the formally educated. When she was newly hired, I was dead set against her. And, improbable as it now sounds, I disapproved of her on the grounds that she was white.

Race became a crucial factor in my resistance to Mrs. Howsare the night I learned about the theft at Mamie Snyder's house. Mamie was a good friend of my older sister Debbie who, whispering conspiratorially in our bedroom late one night, after the lights were out, told me about the theft: how the Snyders' new cleaning lady—the *white* cleaning lady—had been caught with valuables she had stolen from Mamie's mother. The story shocked us, not only because a crime like this was almost unheard of in our small town, but because it involved, in some deeply personal way, a violation of family and home. In the dark that night, the crime seemed bigger and scarier than it was, the threat more general and pervasive. Surely, we thought, it was significant that the thief was white. Nothing had ever been stolen from the Snyders when they had employed a black housekeeper. Were we, then, vulnerable, now that our beloved Alberta had been replaced by a white cleaning woman? We moved swiftly, relentlessly, from the particular to the general. Maybe white cleaning ladies were inherently untrustworthy; maybe they were all potential thieves: sneaky, cunning, dishonest, unreliable, disloyal, and greedy. Spinning our paranoid theory in the dark, we frightened ourselves, for soon we were projecting our evil stereotype onto the innocent Mrs. Howsare, fanning our childish fears by imagining her a sinister intruder in our home.

The next morning I acted out my fear. Attempting to befriend me, Mrs. Howsare asked me to demonstrate my little sister's new, plastic toy cash register. I set the register up on the kitchen counter and banged fiercely on its keys. The cash drawer shot open with a forceful ping, and I scooped up twenty dollars in play money. Slapping the cash into her hand, I looked Mrs. Howsare directly in the eyes and declared, coldly, mercilessly, "Here's your week's pay; you're fired." I knew immediately that I had made a mistake, for she winced, an emotional reaction that shattered the demonic image of her I had foolishly concocted in the night. I could tell that my cruel remark had hurt her, and I was sorry. Recalling this story now, I see that I had as a young child already internalized my family's class position, already imagined myself the boss with power over the hardworking adult hired to care for me.

I still wonder, though, why my sister and I—white children living in a largely white community—were so quick to mistrust a cleaning woman because she was white. Did we fear something dangerous or unreliable buried in our own white bodies? Or, more likely, did we need to distance ourselves, as privileged, middle-class white children, from white women who scrubbed floors, cleaned toilets, and addressed people as "you'uns"? And why did we draw such a sharp distinction between black and white domestic workers? Did we assume African-American housekeepers were more trustworthy simply because that was all we had ever known or because, in our grief over Alberta's departure, we idealized what we had lost? Or did we prefer our black caretaker because we intuitively recognized that she, like us, was of a higher class than the Appalachian white woman? Or, even more troubling, had we fully internalized the racist assumption that blacks are inferior to whites and belong in the kind of menial jobs white people shun? Is it possible that we suspected our white cleaning lady because we thought a respectable white person would not take such a menial job, a black person's job?

Back in 1970 my African-American students taught me just how complex, unstable, contradictory, and uncertain—how messy—the formation of a racial identity can be. Until I realized how profoundly they needed to trouble the tidy categories of Jim Crow, I had been reluctant to address the messy kinds of questions I have been raising in this essay. I had been afraid of offending. And, as a white person, I had much invested in believing I was innocent of all racial prejudice. The ten-year-old children in my class forced me to confront my prejudices, but they also showed me how productive, if painful, it can be to acknowledge and grapple with the contradictory, confusing, and irrational assumptions about race we all secretly harbor.

They attended a segregated school with approximately 450 other African-American students and a nearly all-black staff; yet when they drew pictures, they almost always copied images of white children from their course materials. Intent on disrupting this puzzling phenomenon, I instructed them one day to draw a friend in the room. But many drew pictures of me, often exaggerating the length of my hair and lightening its brown color to a bright, bright yellow. I was well aware that the girls, especially, were fascinated by my hair, for, during my first weeks in the classroom, they crowded around my desk every morning to inspect it, stroking it in wonder, discussing like expert beauticians its texture, its length, its lack of curl. I tried in vain to convince them that their hair—braided into multiple strands, fastened by brightly colored barrettes, tied back in unruly pony tails, decorated with ribbons, artfully separated into neat cornrows—was every bit as beautiful, but in their hearts they believed that my hair (white women's hair) was the gold standard, against which theirs would always be deficient. For them, in those initial weeks, I was an exotic other. When they looked at me, they focused on what made me different. I was therefore not prepared for the note Denise slipped me one rainy morning. On it she had drawn a striking picture of an African-American woman, her hair short and black, her brown face framed by dangling earrings, a brown coat over her bright red dress, black boots pulled up over her checked stockings. Underneath the picture, Denise had carefully penned a message: "This is you Miss

Hallahan." The red dress, the brown coat, the black boots and checked stockings were, indeed, faithful renderings of the clothes I wore that day. But my long, brown hair—the object of all that adoration—had been blackened and cropped short, my light skin darkened to a rich, chocolate brown. I viewed Denise's picture as an enormous compliment, a precious communication from the quiet little girl with the knowing, observant eyes. But what, I wonder, was she telling me?

V

Well-Being and the Messy Self

Martha C. Nussbaum

Winnicott on the
Surprises of the Self

I

N O INVESTIGATION OF THE "MESSY SELF" would be complete without consideration of psychoanalytic thought, which has done so much to turn our attention to our surprising, complicated, largely hidden insides. All the great psychoanalytic thinkers have their own contributions to make to the study of the self, but there is one who, I believe, has more to contribute than any other: Donald Winnicott, the British pediatrician and analyst who made psychoanalysis more flexible than it had been in the hands of Freud and Klein, a humanistic art of personal interpretation rather than a would-be science, and who invented key concepts such as that of the "transitional object" and the "facilitating environment" that are at the heart of analytic practice today.

Unlike Freud, Donald Winnicott is not a cultural icon, read in Great Books courses, revered and reviled.[1] Unlike Jacques Lacan, he is not an intellectual cult figure, with a band of zealous disciples and an impenetrable jargon. There is no school of Winnicott, there are no courses in his methods. All this is as he wished it. Nobody was more skeptical of cults and the rigidity they induced. All his life he was obsessed with the freedom of the individual self to exist defiantly, resisting parental and cultural demands, to be there without saying a word if silence was its choice. In his own writings he spoke with a voice that was determinedly his own, surprisingly personal, idiosyncratic, playful and at the same time ordinary. One could not extract a jargon from it if one tried, and one cannot talk about his theoretical ideas without confronting live complex human beings. That, perhaps, is why he has never had a secure home in the academy, so enamored of beautiful scientific or pseudo-scientific structures, so fearful, often, of real people and the demands their complexity imposes. At the same time, for these same reasons he has had an enormous influence on the practice of psychoanalysis, particularly in America.

Because Winnicott has influenced practitioners more than academics, he has had little attention from philosophers. Freud is by now a staple of the philosophy curriculum, controversial though his ideas are in some quarters. Klein had the good fortune to have Richard Wollheim as her philosophical exponent. Wollheim's rich and passionate books have left us with a keen sense of what Kleinian ideas (such as projection and introjection) can contribute to an account of the self.[2] Winnicott's insights, however, have at least as much to offer as those of Freud and Klein to people thinking about the self in society—above all, perhaps, to philosophers, fond as we typically are of order, system, and simplicity. Winnicott knew how messy and complex people are when they were allowed to be themselves. He also knew how endangered human complexity always is, in the face of society's constant demand for conformity and order. In Winnicott's view, such demands typically stifle creativity, forcing people to hide rather than unfolding themselves. "We are poor indeed," he once remarked, "if we are only sane." Philosophy, a profession that usually demands not only sanity but also a high degree of order and rationality, is always at risk of allying itself with society's repression of the true self. Perhaps it can avoid this risk, if it learns to listen more than it usually does to the voices of disorder and play, to the childlike within the adult. So philosophy, perhaps more than other professions, needs Donald Winnicott.

Winnicott was always a rebel, even within a profession whose very existence constituted a rebellion against standing social norms. When he burst on the London psychoanalytic scene, an odd rumpled man exploding with ideas (like a "Catherine wheel" shooting off sparks, said a fellow analyst), analysts still saw human emotions mainly in terms of Freud's account of primitive instinctual drives, with sexual gratification as their goal. Melanie Klein was already making her important contribution to Freudian theory by insisting on the crucial importance of the earliest stages of life. But Klein held on to Freud's hedonic theory, seeing the infant's search as aimed at pleasure, which she, apparently along with Freud, understood to be a single undifferentiated experience. (Winnicott's great contemporary, Scottish analyst W. R. D. Fairbairn, once wrote that she would have avoided this error had she studied the works of John Stuart Mill.) And she insisted that the infant's psychic drama was played out inside its own subjective space, with figures that were the demonic projections of its own inchoate sense of parts of reality. The actual environment and its people were of no interest to her.

Winnicott learned much from Klein, with whom he had a close if uneven friendship. He absorbed from her the importance of the young child's fantasy life, to which, as a practitioner, he had remarkable empathetic access. (The analysis of a little girl published under the title of *The Piggle* is one of the great examples in English literature of an adult entering the wild conflict-ridden world of a young child.) He insisted, however, that the infant seeks from the start complex forms of relationship and reciprocity, not simply its own pleasure. And the infant's development cannot be understood without looking at its real surroundings, at the objects, responsive or non-responsive, that either create a "facilitating environment" for emotional growth or cause the self to hide, its place taken by a rigid mechanical surrogate. Thus, he famously said, "there is no such thing as a baby" on its own: we are always dealing with a "nursing couple." If psychoanalysis in America has largely become a theory of emotional nurture and exchange rather than one of hedonic satisfaction, it is thanks to Winnicott.

Winnicott also situated psychoanalysis far more accurately than had many of its other practitioners, seeing it as an imaginative humanistic endeavor, akin both to poetry and to love, rather than as an exact science with unvarying rules. To fellow analyst Harry Guntrip, who was his patient, he remarked, "We differ from Freud who was for curing symptoms. We're concerned with living persons, whole living and loving." (This somewhat unfair treatment of Freud shows the aggressive side of the gentle analyst's personality.) As for the goal of the process, it was not simply the removal of symptoms; it was the ability to play, to be creative. Mere sanity, as Winnicott insisted, would be a very impoverished goal.

II

If we want to appreciate what motivated Winnicott's radical reworking of psycho-analytic ideas of the self, we should know something about his life. His struggle on behalf of the freedom to play in a world marred, as he saw it, by oppressive demands for conformity was not just intellectual; it was the story of his entire life.[3] Born in 1896 in the West of England, to a prosperous middle-class Methodist family, he had a superficially happy childhood. The inner reality was, however, far more complicated. Winnicott's father, Frederick, a rigid man who never appears in photos without perfectly waxed moustaches, evidently imposed rigid standards of behavior. The young Donald loved to play with a beautiful female wax doll, and his father so teased him about this non-male behavior that the little boy smashed his beloved toy. Shortly thereafter (Winnicott reports in a fragmentary memoir written near the end of his life), he decided, looking at himself in the mirror, that he was "too nice," and started to behave aggressively. One day his father heard him saying "Drat!" and immediately sent him off to boarding school. If much of his life and thought was devoted to nonconformity and protection of the "true self" from invasion by the forces of conformity (including gender-conformity, a topic that fascinated him), this preoccupation is surely the outgrowth of his father's intrusiveness and the pain it inflicted. In a late essay on the self, which he describes as "a protest from the core of me," he remarks that "[r]ape, and being eaten by cannibals, these are mere bagatelles as compared with the violation of the self's core.... For me this would be the sin against the self." The fact that his father's rigidity targeted aggressive behavior above all may in part explain why, in later life, Winnicott associated both creativity and sexuality with the release of aggression.

By contrast to Frederick, Winnicott's mother, Bessie, is a shadowy figure. People who recall the family say little about her. Winnicott's biographer F. Robert Rod-man, however, pieces the fragments together convincingly, arguing that Bessie was both depressed and frightened of her sexuality. Winnicott once told a close friend that his mother weaned him early because she disliked the pleasurable feelings that nursing caused. Late in life Donald described the pain of having to keep his depressed mother alive in a poem called "The Tree" (partly about Christ's suffering):

> Thus I knew her
> Once, stretched out on her lap
> as now on dead tree
> I learned to make her smile
> to stem her tears
> to undo her guilt
> to cure her inward death
>
> To enliven her was my living

The implicit demands of Bessie's depression were yet another invasion of the self, which clearly involved forbidding both aggressive and sexual feelings. Not surprisingly, no member of that family had a healthy sexual life. Winnicott's two sisters, very attractive women, never married. Donald chose as his first wife a mentally disturbed woman, Alice Taylor, who rarely bathed and who used to commune with the spirit of T. E. Lawrence through her parrot. The marriage lasted for twenty-six years but was never consummated. Sexual impotence was a major theme in Donald's early life; he later connected the ability to enjoy sex fully with the idea of giving oneself permission to be aggressive. Several close associates link the strain of caring for the increasingly dotty Alice with a series of heart attacks that made Donald's health increasingly fragile.

Meanwhile, after service on a destroyer during World War I (he spent much of his time reading the novels of Henry James), Donald took a medical degree at Cambridge and went into pediatrics. His interest in children had been strong for years. In a letter home from Cambridge he describes his delight in arranging theatrical games for the local Boy Scouts: it was "such a revelation of the powers of the imagination of the boys that I shall never forget that day.... Each one was absolutely different from the others, and half the charm lay there." From the first, then, what delighted him was the messiness of individuality—even in the Boy Scouts, an organization that often attracts by its promise of conformity and purity. Donald once estimated that during his career he had treated 60,000 children. His rich experience gave psychoanalysis a new empirical dimension.

At the same time, no doubt owing to his own personal problems, his interest in psychoanalysis was already strong. While seeing pediatric patients, he went into training analysis with James Strachey (who wrote inappropriately gossipy letters about Donald's sexual problems). He graduated from the British Institute for Psychoanalysis in 1935; at that point he began analysis with the Kleinian analyst Joan Riviere. Here begins Winnicott's lifelong involvement with Klein's ideas and with Melanie Klein herself. Chosen by Klein in 1935 to analyze her son Eric, Winnicott was drawn deeply into the Kleinian circle, where he never felt completely at home. Rodman depicts well the conflict between the Kleinians, so intent on theoretical purity, so insistent on orthodoxy, and Winnicott, who had a deep need to rebel and to go his own way. His friendship with Klein continued strong until her death, but increasingly, in letters to her, he urges her to watch out for her cultlike school and to realize that theoretical closure and perfection are inappropriate goals.

Meanwhile, in a series of papers that won increasing attention, he was challenging the foundations of Klein's theoretical approach, insisting on the importance of the real-life mother's actual behavior and of living human interaction. After Klein's death, and to some extent before it, her school treated Winnicott coldly. (Here, I believe, blame may be placed on both parties. Certainly they were a rigid lot, too enamored of theoretical perfection, and certainly Winnicott, with his idiosyncratic ideas and his subversive humor, was not their "type." But it is also clear that Winnicott needed to feel that he was in rebellion against conformity-demanding enemies. It seems unclear how much of the persecution he felt was genuine and how much his own construction.)

Working with evacuated children during the Second World War, Donald met social worker Clare Britton; in 1944 the two began an affair that led, in 1949, to the dissolution of the marriage to Alice (Donald had to wait until his father died before he would take this step) and to a long and extremely happy marriage that lasted until his death in 1971. Plainly they did have a successful sexual relationship, and they shared a love of humor, music, and poetry. Clare was utterly different from Alice, "beefsteak," as one friend said, rather than "elderflour fritters." The couple indulged in elaborate jokes and wrote silly poems to one another during boring moments in conferences (including a lovely scatological putdown of racist politician Enoch Powell). Another friend called them "two crazy people who delighted each other and delighted their friends." Asked by Rodman whether they ever quarreled, the elderly Clare recalled, "In fact the question of hurting each other did not arise because we were operating in the play area where everything is permitted." Sometimes, she added, Donald would wake up in the night and say, "'I'm potty about you, do you know that?'"

Clare, a tough woman and a very successful worker with needy children (who eventually received the Order of the British Empire for her work), seems also to have had a remarkable capacity for unanxiously "holding" Donald's mercurial temper, his vicissitudes, his health difficulties. She recalls that once, after an especially serious cardio-pulmonary illness, she found him up in a tree outside their home, sawing off a limb. Her first impulse was to get him down, to make him rest. But then "I thought, 'No, it's his life and he's got to live it. If he *dies* after this, he dies.' But that was him. He wanted to *live*." At the opening of an autobiography that he was just beginning at the time of his death, he writes, "Prayer: Oh, God, may I be alive when I die." "And he was, really," Clare concludes.

As Donald's success increased, so did his confidence in his own judgment. At times, this confidence led to increasingly serious errors of judgment. In these relatively early days psychoanalysis lacked the clear code of ethics that it has today;

nonetheless, Donald's errors look bad, even against this more flexible background. We can already see ethical lapses in his collusion with Melanie Klein to conceal from her son Eric the fact that his mother and his analyst are corresponding. It seems just common sense that the analyst should not reveal a patient's confidences to his mother, even if she is a great analyst. Many such lapses followed. Winnicott analyzed Marion Milner, a close friend who was probably in love with him. He analyzed a patient who was a tenant in the house he and Alice shared. He encouraged Clare to take up analysis with Klein while he himself was in close contact with her. He socialized with patients. His long analysis of and friendship with Pakistani analyst Masud Khan involved numerous ethical lapses, as well as great credulity toward one of the most unprincipled and destructive analysts who ever practiced.[4] Khan was a mendacious charmer who may have attracted Winnicott erotically or may have stood in for the son Winnicott never had. At any rate, despite the mounting evidence of Khan's compulsive mendacity and his ethical lapses with patients, Winnicott continued to support him. In general, Winnicott seems to have had little awareness of appropriate boundaries and little regard for the evolving ethical norms of the profession.

On a trip to New York in 1969, Donald suffered a particularly serious cardiac crisis after the flu. Identifying himself with Cathy in *Wuthering Heights*, he wrote that he longed to come home before dying. He lived for another year, but in a weakened condition. During this period, amazingly, Winnicott continued to see patients; he wrote and delivered new papers, broaching significant new areas. He was particularly emphatic about the importance of recognizing the social rigidity of gender norms and the mixture of genders in all human beings. (This part of his work, which would have anticipated and illuminated the current vogue for talking of the "social construction" of gender, was, sadly, undeveloped at his death.) Most impressively, he continued to correspond generously with strangers. Winnicott's biographer Rodman, then a young analyst just out of the army, received a four-page commentary on his first article. A troubled man from Oklahoma, writing to Winnicott out of the blue, got a helpful three-page letter about the roots of aggression. Analyst Alan Stone, who met him at this time (and found Winnicott unable to walk without stopping), reports:

> he held me in the center of his attention (or so it seemed to me) in a way that I have never experienced with any other human being. It was not that he made constant eye contact, or that he interjected the traditional psychoanalytic hum of empathy, or that he was selflessly accepting. As we walked he spoke of his own ideas, he reacted and responded with dignity and originality, yet all the time I felt recognized and encouraged—I was in a "facilitating environment."

Not all of his correspondence was good-natured. Ill-argued dismissals of complexity always made him angry. To an analyst enamored of simplistic biological explanations of human phenomena, he writes, "There seems to be no playing in what you write, and therefore a lack of creativity. Perhaps you reserve your creativity for some other area of your life, in friendships for instance, or in painting, I don't know."

He died in January 1971, after watching an old movie comedy on TV.

III

Winnicott's main ideas emerge gradually over time, in a series of papers rich in clinical content. He never wrote a tidy summary of them, and it belies the nature of his thought to attempt such a summary. One can, however, at least sketch the narrative of infancy and childhood as he saw it, being careful to remember that, for Winnicott, particularity is everything and that he is the heir as much of Wordsworth and Emily Brontë as of Freud and Klein.

While Freud saw human beings as driven by powerful instincts that need to be tamed if morality and culture are to be possible, Winnicott had confidence in the unfolding of the developmental process, which would produce ethical concern as an outgrowth of early struggles if things went well enough. He felt that development usually goes well and that mothers are usually good enough. Mothers are usually preoccupied with their infants right from birth. Usually they attend to their needs well, enabling the self to develop gradually and eventually to express itself.

At first, the infant cannot grasp the mother as a definite object and thus cannot have full-fledged emotions. Its world is symbiotic and basically narcissistic. Gradually, however, the infant develops the capacity to be alone—aided by its "transitional objects," a famous phrase invented by Winnicott to refer to the blankets and stuffed animals that enable children to comfort themselves when the mother is absent. (He loved Charles Schulz and wondered whether Linus's blanket showed the influence of his ideas.) Eventually the child usually develops the ability to "play alone in the presence of its mother," a key sign of growing confidence in the developing self. At this point, the child begins to be able to relate to the mother as a whole person rather than as an extension of its own needs.

Winnicott always spoke of mothers. He seems to have had a blind spot for the role of the father, until close to the end of his life. At the same time, he did increasingly stress that "mother" was a role rather than a biological category, that real mothers had aspects of both genders, and that analysts, biologically male and female, typically play a quasi-maternal role. Perhaps one reason for his neglect of the father was that he conceived of his own identity, often, in female terms: as Cathy in *Wuthering Heights*, as a nurturing mother "holding" his troubled patients.

When the child becomes able to perceive its mother as a whole person, a painful emotional crisis ensues: for the child now understands that the very same person whom it loves and embraces is the person against whom it has directed aggressive and angry wishes (when needs are not met automatically). Here Winnicott is following Klein's lead. But instead of Klein's somewhat forbidding and philosophically obscure concept of "the depressive position," Winnicott articulates his insight in terms of the concept of the developing "capacity for concern," giving the psychoanalytic category a distinctively ethical heart, or rather showing that the relationship between infant and mother is ethical as well as erotic. In his important papers on concern, he describes the way in which genuinely moral feeling bootstraps itself into existence out of the child's very love of its mother and the awareness that its aggression has projected harm. He thus was able to see morality as operating in tandem with love, rather than as merely a forbidding set of quasi-paternal demands. (He stressed the crucial role of the imagination in coming to grips with this crisis: only through developing the capacity to imagine its mother's feelings does the child become capable of generous and reparative acts.)

If imagination and concern are sufficiently developed at this stage, they may prove the beginnings of an adult moral life. Winnicott believed, however, that the adult moral life stood in continual need of nourishment of the playful and imaginative capacities, so easily suppressed by the demands of "the real world." He attached particular importance to the arts, which help people under social pressure (as all people ultimately are) to keep on enriching their sense of the "potential space" between individuals. In this way, the arts enrich the moral life—not by being didactic, which would lose the whole value of art, but precisely by being wild and not fully "sane." He believed that it was precisely the unreality or craziness in art that was its reality; conformist or didactic art would be unreal, an ally of the False Self that accedes to society's demands. (The recent film about J. M. Barrie, *Finding Neverland*, is very Winnicottian in spirit, and there were obviously deep similarities in belief and personal style between these two enemies of British respectability. When the grief-stricken little boy Peter calls artistic play "silly rubbish," we know that exactly the reverse is true: it is the absence of art in the life around the boy that is "silly rubbish," the crazy play a road to reality.)

Throughout the child's development, it is crucial that the mother should provide the child with a "facilitating environment" that allows it to express itself, expressing even its destructiveness and hate, without getting the message that the mother will thereby be destroyed. Remarkably, mothers usually accept their children's hate and are not destroyed. (This ability was also an essential part of the good analyst's equipment as he saw it. After Harry Guntrip talked at him aggressively for half an hour in an analytic session, Winnicott says, "You see, you talked very hard at me and I am not destroyed.") Most of the time this process goes reasonably well. It will go awry if the mother is too fearful or depressed (like Winnicott's own mother) or if she too rigidly demands conformity and perfection in herself and in her child (like Winnicott's father).

One marvelous document concerning the latter sort of failure is Winnicott's analysis of a young male medical student, known as B, published in the volume *Holding and Interpretation*. Married to a husband whom she saw as demanding perfection in everything, B's mother wanted to be a perfect mother and, hence, to have a perfect baby. This meant that she did not want her baby to be a real baby—needy, messy, crying. Already in infancy, B got the message that his own needs were inappropriate and that the only way to achieve anything was by being quiet and "good." So stifling was her demand that he could not, like most young children, gradually develop a capacity to release his mother from her need to be perfect. This capacity would have required attending to her as a live imperfect human being, but that would have meant accepting his own incompleteness and imperfection, something that her demand made impossible.

B's suppression of himself led to rigidity and emotional paralysis in later life. A competent intellectual "False Self" (a favorite Winnicottian way of referring to the self we present to a world desirous of conformity) had developed the capacity to cope with the world, but the needy childlike "True Self" had gone underground and remained at an infantile level—rather than gradually developing capacities to relate emotionally and to express itself in the world. B could have sex, but only with a woman he saw as an undifferentiated object, predictable as a masturbatory fantasy. He could not even remember people's individuating features. During sessions he was unable to recall his wife's Christian name. All of these flights from the individuality of the other were ultimately, the analysis shows, flights from his own partiality and neediness: to the self bent on invulnerability, others exist only as looming threats to one's own projects. "I feel that you are introducing a big problem," B says to Winnicott. "I never became human. I have missed it."

In the analysis itself, the patient repeatedly expects perfection from Winnicott and is terrified by the space created by the analyst's own evident human imperfection. "The alarming thing about equality," he remarkably states, "is that we are then both children and the question is, where is father? We know where we are if one of us is the father." Winnicott points out, in response, that in a good personal relationship there is an element of "subtle interplay" that presupposes an acceptance of human imperfection. Love means many things, "but it has to include this experience of subtle interplay, and we could say that you are experiencing love and loving in this situation."

We might say (if oversimply) that for Freud, our cultural and personal problem is how to transcend the human. For Winnicott, it is how to bear the exposure of being imperfectly human. Play, art, and love come powerfully to our aid, but there remains what he called "the inherent difficulty in regard to human contact with external reality."

IV

Winnicott's theoretical writings emphasize empathy, imagination, and the highly particular transactions that constitute love between two imperfect people. One might have had these insights without being able to translate them into analytic practice. According to Harry Guntrip, Fairbairn (who analyzed him before his analysis with Winnicott) had this problem.[5] His theories spoke of the importance of a "personal relationship of genuine understanding" between therapist and patient, and when he discussed his ideas outside of the office the two men communicated well. In the analytic setting, however, Fairbairn became rigid and formal, imposing theory-based interpretations rather than seeking out the core of the person. Winnicott was entirely different. First of all, he quickly attained a more satisfactory insight into Guntrip's idiosyncratic emotional history, because he did not insist on seeing everything in terms of a pre-established theoretical construct. And he was able to create for the sixty-year-old analyst, a man of personal courage and powerful intellect, a "holding environment" so that Guntrip's need for constant activity and talk ceased, and he could enjoy simply being himself. "I could let my tension go and develop and relax because you were present in my inner world," he wrote in his journal. Here we see the extent to which Winnicott cast himself in the role that he had dubbed maternal, opening up his own later investigations into the social rigidity of gender distinctions.

Pediatrician first and always, whether with adults or with children, Winnicott was always willing to play, to respond to the moment, to surprise, to adopt unconventional methods if they seemed right. (All too often, he wrote, the patient brings his False Self into analysis and the analyst addresses himself to that, because it is easy to talk to a False Self; a False Self usually has well-developed skills of social self-expression and interrelationship, whereas the True Self may be stuck at an infantile level and be quite inarticulate. But if analysis addresses itself to the False Self, it never gets anywhere.) Sometimes he sat on the floor; sometimes he offered a cup of tea; sometimes he held a hand. Sometimes sessions were daily, and sometimes months apart.

Winnicott's unconventional methods are nowhere clearer than in the case of "the Piggle," a little girl named Gabrielle who was two and a half when she began to see Winnicott and five when she finished. We have Winnicott's own detailed notes of every session. Sessions were held on demand by the child, often months apart. Sometimes they included participation by the parents (sophisticated and analytically aware) as well as letters and phone calls from them. In one particularly memorable session, held on a very hot summer day, Gabrielle, casting Winnicott in the role of herself, plays at being a new baby coming out through the birth canal by repeatedly sliding down from her father's lap onto the floor, "and I had to be very cross wanting to be the only baby. 'You're not to be the only baby,' said the Piggle. And then another baby was born and then another...." After many repetitions (one of Winnicott's great points as an analyst of children is that he never loses patience with repetition), Gabrielle gets the idea that it would be fun to try a different way of being born, this time from the top of her father's head. "It was funny. I felt sorry for father, and I asked him if he could stand it. He replied: 'O.K., but I would like to take my coat off.'"

This remarkable analysis shows us many things about Winnicott as therapist, but nothing more than his utter respect for the child's world of objects. Almost his first remark, in notes of the first session, is, "Already I had made friends with the teddy-bear who was sitting on the floor by the desk." Throughout the long analysis, we sense that Winnicott's poetic capacity, his willingness not to be "only sane," enables a degree of entry rare for any adult into the unhappy child's world, with its black mommy, its Sush baby, and the terrifying babacar. "To say that he understood children would to me sound false and vaguely patronizing," said one obituarist. "It was rather that children understood him." Such was his respect for his young patient that he refused to get ahead of her. "Importance of my not *understanding* what she had not yet been able to give me clues for," he writes. Understanding, however, was not the whole of it. As both the Guntrip analysis and the treatment of Gabrielle show, he made both children and adults feel the presence of a good mother, in whose presence they were free to emerge and be.

Perhaps these great empathic and creative gifts were connected to Winnicott's ethical failures. Because he had such insight, he sometimes felt, apparently, that he had moved beyond the need to consider normal ethical rules. Because he could on occasion defy convention with brilliant success, he trusted his own idiosyncratic judgment too far. His hatred for the types of social rules that imprison the self concealed from him the fact that ethical rules have great worth in human life, permitting people to live together on terms of mutual trust and even mutual creativity. It may be, as Clare observed, that when people have an intimate relationship of trust they do not need to *think* about ethical rules. That does not mean, however, that they can violate them without harming the relationship. Nor does the fact that analyst and patient have (at best) a relationship of mutual trust and holding imply that the ethical norms of the profession can be flouted at will. Especially in the relationship with Khan, whose disgraceful conduct (having affairs with some patients, using others to advance his social standing) Winnicott first ignored and then denied, we see that his distrust of rules had gone much too far. From such ethical failures we can see the extent to which good ethical judgment needs to be a dialogue between rules and concrete particular perceptions, rather than the rejection of the former in favor of the latter.

V

One can find much to criticize in Winnicott's ideas, as well as in his practical judgment. His account of the role of the father, as I have mentioned, is deficient, perhaps as a result of the fact that he never completely worked out his intuitive ideas about the malleability of gender and relationship between rigid gender norms and the False Self. I am also unconvinced by his constant connection between self-assertion and "hate," a word he used too loosely. A person who has been repressed by demands for conformity might indeed hate those demands and might feel the assertion of the self as a form of aggression; such, clearly, was Winnicott's personal situation. But in the more benign case in which the capacity for concern and social interaction develops in partnership with love, self-assertion (and the sexuality he linked to it) may take a wider range of forms, involving an aggression that is playful and has nothing to do with hate. We see this clearly in his relationship with Clare, and we see it in his relationship with patients such as Guntrip and Gabrielle. Winnicott implicitly acknowledges the fact that erotic self-assertion takes many forms, in his insightful remarks about art, culture, and play. But these insights remain inconsistently integrated into his writings.

More serious is the problem that Winnicott's ideas about the True Self sometimes verge on an excessive romanticism—as when he suggests that any communication with the outside world involves a deformation of a True Self that is fundamentally incommunicado.[6] At other times, he more plausibly suggests that the True Self will, if all goes well, develop capacities for communication and reciprocity. But the mark of his childhood remained, and he repeatedly stressed (excessively to my mind) the artificiality of the social, the radically asocial nature of all that is authentic. (Here he really is the heir of Emily Brontë.)

This Brontëesque disdain for the social, one strand in some of his analytic papers, is impossible to square with his growing interest in social and educational reform—with the construction of a society that is not death to the self but, instead, a holding environment that allows children to mature in a loving atmosphere and permits adults to express their individuality without penalty. Winnicott's ideas about society have rich implications for primary education, for the role of the arts in civic culture, and for many other aspects of our common life. Indeed, I believe that one may get many valuable insights about contemporary political life by posing systematically the question, "What would it be like for society to become, in Winnicott's sense, a 'facilitating environment' for its citizens?" In thinking this idea through, one would come upon an enriched conception of the meaning of liberal "individualism": not selfishness but the ability to grow and to express oneself; not solitary self-sufficiency but "subtle interplay"; not the transcendence of human passions but the secure "holding" of human need and imperfection.

John Stuart Mill had many of these insights. Mill's work is deeply Winnicottian in spirit, in its emphasis on the unfolding of individuality and the badness of social pressures to conform, in its interest in the role of political arrangements in supporting human needs, in its questioning of rigid gender distinctions, and above all, perhaps, in its emphasis on the importance of poetry and the emotions for a decent personal and also public life. Mill, however, was a proper Victorian, who never would have wanted to talk about the Sush baby and the babacar—much though at some level his *Autobiography* alludes to such matters.[7] He never (one imagines) would have allowed his head to be used as a birth canal, and, though he might have made friends with the teddy bear who was sitting on the floor, he never would have admitted as much in print. Winnicott's greater willingness to investigate the messy forbidden underpinnings of adult love and compassion makes his work a source of rich insights for the Millean liberal. If such aspects of the self are not accepted, but are hidden and even hated, it is unlikely that societies will stably attain the recognition of human equality.

In the end, for Winnicott the theorist, the really important thing was the genuine flourishing (not mere satisfaction) of each person, and the same was true of Winnicott the doctor. At the end of his analysis of Gabrielle, as the five-year-old prepares to leave him, he remarks, "So the Winnicott you invented was all yours and he's now finished with, and no one else can ever have him." The two sit together, reading an animal book. Then he says, "I know when you are really shy, and that is when you want to tell me that you love me." "She was very positive in her gesture of assent."

As B says, alarmed by the prospect of equality, "We know where we are if one of us is the father." Not to know where we are—and to take delight in the not-knowing: this is Winnicott's great gift to political philosophy, as also to the philosophy of human love.

Winnicott was indeed a poet among theoreticians, as he was a compassionate doctor among analysts. If one can derive many related insights from the reading of his favorite authors, such as Henry James, Shakespeare, and Wordsworth, it was Winnicott who was able to formulate these insights into guidelines for the therapeutic treatment of unhappy people, giving psychoanalysis a hopeful and also a liberal face, one that emphasized people's capacities for love and society's capacity for "holding" diversity, play, and freedom.

Notes

1. In this article I refer to the following works of Donald Winnicott: *The Maturational Processes and the Facilitating Environment* (Madison: International Universities Press, 1965) (a collection of his most important papers); *Playing and Reality* (London and New York: Routledge, 1971) (another important collection of analytic papers); *Home Is Where We Start From* (New York: Norton, 1986) (a posthumously published collection of essays and speeches); *The Piggle* (Madison: International Universities Press, 1977) (an edited version of Winnicott's journals of an analysis of a little girl); *Holding and Interpretation* (New York: Grove Press, 1972) (a fragmentary record of an analysis of a young man).

2. Richard Wollheim, *The Thread of Life* (New Haven and London: Yale University Press, 1984); *On the Emotions* (New Haven and London: Yale University Press, 1999); see also his autobiographical *Germs: A Memoir of Childhood* (McClelland & Stewart, 2005).

3. See F. Robert Rodman, *Winnicott: Life and Work* (Cambridge, MA: Perseus Publishing, 2003), from which all the biographical information in this article derives. Rodman also edited Winnicott's correspondence and had a close working relationship with Clare, Donald's widow. He interviewed her extensively, and the citations from her in this article derive from those interviews (reported in the biography). See my related review of the biography in *New Republic*, October 27, 2003, pp. 34–39.

4. For a fuller account of this relationship, see Rodman, and for a summary see my review.

5. See Jeremy Hazell's illuminating biography of Guntrip, *H. J. S. Guntrip: A Psychoanalytical Biography* (London and New York: Free Association Books, 1996), with extensive citations from Guntrip's journals of these two analyses.

6. Here Winnicott has close affinities with Samuel Beckett, particularly his *The Unnamable*.

7. See my "Mill Between Bentham and Aristotle," *Daedalus,* Spring 2004: 60–68, which presents what might be called a Winnicottian interpretation of Mill's famous mental crisis and the text of Marmontel that played a role in resolving it.

Carol Edelstein

Buried

Under this mountain of tires,
this baby buggy's rusting frame, buried
under the cage of a bird whose plaintive phrase
once occupied the narrow canal just below music;
under rotted shingles, tangled springs, mattresses
soaked with the juices of love, of illness,
with the sweat of the overworked
and the simply tired; buried under chipped
cups, stained rugs, bundled printed matter
and loaves of upswept leaves; all soaked with rain,
stewed by sun, under all this there lies
another perfect moon—similar, I was told, to the one
simmering now up there, above our easy laughter,
lake with moored canoe, our future
fattening like a strawberry.
And I said I would dig for this moon,
dig until I could find it, dig until I could
put its terrible light out.

Robin West

Legal Selves

*A*s Thomas Hobbes famously opined, law exists in large part to reduce the violence of our unregulated lives and thereby improve our well-being. Life in a state of nature—life outside law—is brutal, nasty, and short, Hobbes taught. Life under law, by contrast, is less violent and much safer, and for that reason, more pleasurable: with the order given by law, we are freed to enjoy not just longevity, but also commerce, transportation, culture, education, gentility, family ties, and the pleasures and affections of intimacy. Without legal order, we have no time or energy for any of that; our waking lives are fully absorbed with the fearful project of defending ourselves against the lethal aggressions of others.[1]

Both the larger and the legal worlds have reached some measure of consensus that Hobbes was right on this point. Whether they be from Zaire, Kosovo, Bosnia, Iraq; underpoliced U.S. large city neighborhoods; or the private recesses of a violent home, there are few survivors of unregulated violence ready to doubt that life with a responsible state ready to deploy a noncorrupt police force that will in turn protect us against the homicidal urges of others is preferable to life lived in perpetual fear of the unchecked private violence of a master, a drug lord, a husband, a mother, a lynch mob, a street gang, or a rival clan. The peace of mind and the enrichments we gain by ceding the authority to use legitimate monopolized violence to a central sovereign, so as to protect us against the multiple threats of violence from others, are a good bargain: we gain not just safety but the pleasures of life that are otherwise displaced by fear. It's a bargain we willingly make, or would willingly make if put to us, in a second. For lawyers, perhaps worldwide, it may be this conviction—the conviction that a sovereign that can successfully deter private, physical violence is a desirable improvement over nature—this "Hobbesian thesis," as Rawls called it in his famous work on justice in liberal societies[2]—that unites the profession. Law exists to deter violence; that is its *raison d'etre*. If it doesn't succeed, something is badly amiss. But if it does, life is better for it. Legal selves—selves under law—are happier than the violent and violated selves that have such brutal and short lives in the unregulated state of nature Hobbes so cleanly and so chillingly depicted.

Of course, life in an unregulated, lawless, Hobbesian state of nature, presumably, is also *messy*. Does law also exist to do something about the mess? Although Hobbes did not see it, or if he did he didn't much worry over it, it is clear now even to his most ardent followers that eradicating messiness through legal regulation is no part of any sensible social compact. Here too we find widespread consensus among lawyers, at least in constitutional liberal societies: the benefits of tidiness are just not worth the cost of policing against messiness, all things considered. First, messiness does no harm, really, to anyone, other than causing aesthetic offense to some. Messiness may render life unattractive—*may* do so—but like it or loathe it, messiness, unlike violence, does not make life brutal, nasty, or short. Tidiness alone, unlike safety, is not a condition of the blessings of civilization—the culture, the arts, the transport, the commerce—Hobbes extolled. Furthermore, one man's messiness may be another's loveliness—there's no accounting for taste in this stuff. On the other side of the ledger, the costs are formidable. Such an all-embracing understanding of the legal compact, so as to include messiness as the evil to be eradicated through law, raises a very real danger (present in any event) that an overly intrusive Leviathan, rather than the mess it seeks to conquer, may become the greater evil, itself rendering life brutal, nasty, and short. Lastly, perhaps most importantly, we all, including even the most hide-bound rule-loving lawyers, sense that messiness itself is a kind of freedom, or at least a manifestation of it, and perhaps should not only be unregulated but somehow protected against unwise regulation, if possible, for its own sake.

For all of these reasons and perhaps others, lawyers in constitutional legal orders typically hold both the straightforward conviction that law should not overregulate against messiness and the somewhat more complicated legalist hope that if at all possible, a higher constitutional law should protect our messes against unwise attempts by the state to use ordinary "lower" law in such a counterproductive, foolish, and even dangerous way. Combining these two insights, we might sensibly conclude that central to contemporary legalism[3]—lawyers' legalist faith, so to speak—at least in constitutional societies, is a *modified* version of the "Hobbesian thesis" summarized above. In constitutional liberal democracies, we protect against the harms to safety, self, pleasure, and life occasioned by and threatened by private violence, by invoking law so as to police against the violence, deterring its occurrence and punishing offenders. We protect our harmlessly messy selves, in turn, by invoking constitutions and constitutional authority, particularly the rights of privacy those constitutions often (not invariably) promise, so as to police against the law that might needlessly threaten them. If we can use law to deter violence, and harness it from the useless or worse inclination to clean up our mess, law will indeed be a boost to well-being, virtually no matter how we define it, and much as Hobbes envisioned. I will call this faith—the faith, that is, that law will improve well-being, precisely because it can deter violence while respecting the mess of our private lives, the "modified legalist contract."

Of course, and as lawyers acknowledge, our political lives are not quite as tidy as all this might suggest, even in theory, much less in practice. Rather, in theory, the mess that the law must leave alone and the violence it must deter are the endpoints on a "mess-to-violence" harm spectrum, and there is a widely acknowledged vast gray area in the middle. These days, most of the harms that we regulate through law are worse than messes, yet not the sort of violence—homicide, attempted homicide, battery—the deterrence of which is at the core of the state's *raison d'etre*. Pollution caused by industry is more than just a mess, but it is not really violence, although the injuries it causes to asthmatic children may be lethal. Likewise, the economic losses sustained by stockholders because of corporate fraud, or the physical injuries sustained by workers on the job because of workplace negligence, or the thousands of mangled limbs brought on by automobile accidents—these are harms, some intentional and some not, that are all worse than messiness, but are not really violence, and are all in various ways deterred or regulated by law. The law violates no rights of freedom or privacy by regulating any of them. But they are not, like the injuries and fears occasioned by violence, at the core of the justification of state authority. So, regarding *these* sorts of harms in the middle of the mess-to-violence spectrum—harms that are more than messes but less than violence—it is by no means clear whether law's intrusion increases or threatens well-being, and so citizens rightly argue: how great is the harm, how costly the legal regulation, where does the balance lie? That argument is the stuff of our politics, and those arguments are messy indeed. It is no part of legalism to deny any of this.

On the poles, however, one finds, among lawyers, a tidy, crystal-clear, legal agreement: an agreement in effect about the limits of our messy politics rather than the content of it. That agreement is central to the profession's defining faith in law, a faith that for the last half century legal scholars have come to call "liberal legalism." Where harms are trivial, the law *must not intrude*, whatever the politics that might counsel otherwise: for an example, consider the U.S. Supreme Court's recent pronouncement in *Lawrence v. Texas* that moralistic laws criminalizing homosexual sodomy violate our constitutional guarantees of freedom and privacy. On the other side of the spectrum, where the harm is caused by violence, the law *must intrude*, whatever the prevailing political sentiment of the moment: for a vivid example, consider the Fourteenth Amendment to the U.S. Constitution, which states that no state may deny the "equal protection of the law"—intended, in part, to guarantee the state's protection of newly freed slaves against the violence of vengeful lynch mobs[4]—the political will of dominant whites to the contrary notwithstanding. It is this agreement regarding the endpoints of the spectrum—a purportedly legalistic and apolitical agreement regarding what the law *must* and *must not* do—that I am calling the "modified legalist contract." The contract may be only implicitly or imperfectly held by citizens in many liberal democracies. But whatever its status worldwide, there is no question that it is widely, openly, and explicitly held in U.S. legal culture—as evidenced not only by the theorizing of scores of legal philosophers and the briefs and arguments of hundreds of constitutional lawyers but also by the many Supreme Court opinions that in some way or other invoke its basic logic.

The thesis of this essay is that this tidy legalist consensus hides a mess of its own, too often swept under the rug. Perhaps lawyers can and do agree that messes are trivial and that a messy life is one the law must leave untouched, that violence by contrast is serious indeed and that a violently victimized life, unlike a messy life, is a life the law must seek to recompense. The problem is that from time to time, and I think we are now in such a time, many of us inside as well as outside the legal profession seemingly can't tell the difference between a mess that is trivial and an act of violence that oppresses or kills. To put the point in terms congenial to this collection, sometimes the line—normally quite thick and pretty clear—between a "messy self" that the law not just should, but constitutionally must, leave alone and a violent or "violated self" that the law not just should, but politically must, address disappears. To refer back to the clichéd point made in passing above, one man's mess may be another man's loveliness, but that same mess may be another man's—or woman's—violence. When that happens—when the lines we must draw, cultur-ally and socially, between a mess and an act of violence, between a messy self and a violated self, are blurred—the modified Hobbesian thesis, and the liberal legalist faith it grounds, in effect fall apart. When *that* happens, in turn, then the question of whether the ambiguously messy life is one the law must, constitutionally, leave alone, or whether it is a violated life the law must, politically, address, becomes very much a function of whose perspective counts as authoritative. At such times and whatever other social costs we may incur because of this confusion, our legal responses to the messes in our lives become profoundly ambivalent. The law itself becomes a mess.

In this essay, I only want to illustrate this dilemma, not solve it, by presenting (or re-presenting) depictions of these ambiguous lives—perhaps messy, perhaps violated—and the law that is left in their wake. The first example is taken from an early twentieth-century play about a domestic murder, the second from contempo-rary legal scholarship on sexually harassed workers. In both the dramatic depiction of domestic violence in the early twentieth century and the scholarly debate over sexual harassment on the job in the early twenty-first century, we see a state and a community that cannot clearly discern the line, so essential to the modified legal-ist contract, between the violence the law must deter and the mess it must leave untouched. When that happens, familiar legal categories—such as the meaning of "murder" or "self-defense" or "justified homicide," or "assault" or "battery," or "con-sent" or "de minimus," or "unwanted" or "discriminatory" or "unwelcome"—lose their points of reference. The categories themselves then become worse than useless: they obfuscate and distort reality. Law becomes unhinged from the modified legal contract that underlies it; law loses its self-confidence. That was true of the "law" (or lack of it) governing domestic violence a hundred years ago, and it is true of the law of sexual harassment in the workplace now. Whenever that line is lost, we lose the confident inference that either the intrusion of law or the staying of law's hand is a boon to our overall well-being.

Lastly, I will draw a very limited moral about how the law might best respond, when the messy life the Constitution must insulate and protect from the law's peering eye, looks, to some but not all of us, like the "violence" that the law ab-solutely must deter, compensate, or at least very seriously regard. At that point, I will suggest, law itself must forego the categories and return to basics. We are right to believe so fervently that the law should intervene to deter violence and must stay its own hand and leave the messes alone—but it does both, just as Hobbes saw, to improve well-being. Whenever we truly can't categorize an act or a life as "violent" or "messy" we must forego the categories, and attend to the narratives that underlie them. To get past the impasse, we need to hear the stories of the people whose lives are affected by the law's overreach into our messy freedom or its passivity in the face of our victimization. The law must, from time to time, make room for the narrative voice. With respect to the status, nature, and well-being of our sexual lives at work, we are now in such a time.

Domestic Trifles

Consider first the "trifles" in Susan Glaspell's near-canonical, deeply feminist, early-twentieth century one-act play of that name.[5] The play's opening scene is of a very messy kitchen: the audience sees a half-made loaf of bread; flour spewed on the counter; a dirty hand towel; an unwieldy, oversized, slightly grotesque stove; an unfinished quilt with (the audience later learns) erratic sloppy stitching; jars of badly stored jam ready to explode in an opened cabinet; and, ominously, a half-hidden strangled songbird in a mangled birdcage. The messy kitchen, the audience immediately learns, is the workplace of a farmwife, who is suspected of and being investigated for the murder—by strangulation—of her cold, "hard," emotionally and perhaps physically abusive husband. In the eyes of the prosecutor and the police chief sent to investigate the murder, the mess in the kitchen is a domestic "trifle," not worthy of their investigative time or talents. At the play's outset, the men leave the trifling kitchen to investigate the rest of the house, presumably in search of the hard evidence that might inculpate the dead farmer's wife.

The prosecutor's wife and a neighboring farmwife, both of whom have accompanied the men out to the farmhouse, sit together in the kitchen, waiting for the men to finish their inspection. The audience eventually sees the kitchen—and the suspect's messy domestic life—through these two women's eyes. Over the hour, the women first, and quite efficiently, expose the mess in the kitchen, and particularly the strangled songbird, for what it is: not a trifle, but very hard evidence indeed, and evidence not only of a motive for the murder of the farmer by his wife but also of that wife's messy, flattened, violated, snuffed, emotionally deadened *self*. The farmwife's true and melodious self, the self these neighboring women recall from when all three were girls, the women surmise as they sit in the kitchen, had been at least metaphorically strangled by the tedium and loneliness of her adult life and by the coldness of her adult companion, just as her beloved songbird had been literally strangled, and apparently by the same hands. The murdered farmer's renowned "hardness," the women eventually reason, had caused in his wife a soul-numbing loneliness, had left her emotionally battered, and had inflicted upon her an inhuman prison of silence in which she had lived out her adult life: without the joy, companionship, human conversation, or the company of other women, children, or friends, or even the music that had once given her life its pleasures. Sitting in the farmer's wife's kitchen, waiting for the men to complete their police work, these two women see the farmwife's adult self reflected in the kitchen's mess and the nature of her marriage reflected in the strangled songbird. The joyful and musical girl they once knew, by becoming a farmer's wife, had become not just a messy self, but a deeply violated and silenced one.

Through the course of the play, the two women effectively assume the role of jurors: a role denied them, of course, on account of their gender by the law at that time. (Thus, the novella Glaspell wrote that followed the performance of *Trifles* was retitled *A Jury of Her Peers*.) As de facto jurors, the wives eventually decide that the farmer's violation of his wife's true self was sufficiently grievous as to justify, as self-defense, her killing of the man who violated her. On the basis of that unstated judgment, in the play's climactic moment, the women resolve, in an act of first-wave feminist solidarity, to hide from their husbands—to hide from the law—the strangled songbird. They do so knowing full well that the dead bird, if found, would have provided, even to the otherwise clueless men investigating the crime, a motive for the woman's crime. In this story (loosely based on the facts of a real case, which Glaspell, a journalist as well as playwright, had reported),[6] in the eyes of these characters, the mess in the kitchen was not a trifle but evidence, and evidence not only of a killing but also of the emotional battery that mitigated it. That battery, again in the eyes of these characters, was also not a trifle—not just messiness—but rather a violation of self so profound as to be a form of violence, violence that, in their eyes, rendered the eventual homicide justified self-defense. In this story, *all* of the lines necessary to maintain the legalist's modified Hobbesian thesis—the line between a "messy self" and a "violated" self, between a trifle and something of life-and-death importance, between emotional coldness and the sort of physical violence that justifies lethal self-defense, between the killing of a bird—a trifle—and the killing of a human being—a capital crime—were not just blurred; they were erased.

So the *law's* response, still within the play's alternative domestic world—meaning the law, here, as decreed by two women sitting in a kitchen—became more than just a bit of a mess. Emotional coldness typically, then as now, is not the sort of violence that justifies lethal self-defense. "Loneliness" is not the fear for one's life that, by black-letter law, might render a homicide against one's aggressor justified self-defense. Even the strangling of a beloved pet songbird does not justify the killing of a man. The housewives, acting as the jurors they could not be in the polity, blurred the distinction between a messy and a violated life, between trivia and profundity, and eventually, as a legal matter, between murder and justified self-defense. By the end of the play, furthermore, the audience fully sympathizes.

Why? Why all this blurring? Why do the women acquit, and why does the audience go along with it? The "law on the books" at the time covering justified self-defense—the definitions of murder, self-defense, provocation, justification, and so forth—was seemingly crystal clear: neither a strangled songbird nor the infliction of emotional pain is the sort of provocation that justifies killing in self-defense. The "official" law's response on these sorts of facts, noncontextualized so to speak, was not messy at all. The women know this. One of them, in fact, as one of the men offhandedly remarks, after all, was "married to the law." By resolving to conceal the evidence that would have facilitated a finding of guilt, the juror-wives basically acquit, from their perspective. From the official law's perspective, though, they abet a homicide and defraud the court. Glaspell makes the audience complicit: the wives' eventual decision to hide evidence, at the end of the play, is a moment of triumph. The play even ends on a comic note. So, one way to put the question, in late twentieth-century terms, is just this: what made this dramatized act of legalist disobedience—the blurring of the lines necessary to make the modified Hobbesian contract coherent—in this bit of social realist theater so appealing?

One compelling answer—suggested by groundbreaking scholarship on the background of *Trifles* by law professor Marina Angel—is that these were not ordinary times, legalistically, either inside the theater or in the very real trials on which Susan Glaspell, a legal journalist with a crime beat, routinely reported.[7] Rather it was a time during which the line between violence in the home and domestic messiness was, for many, imperceptible. In a series of articles on the play and the novella that followed it, Angel describes the play as being about the early twentieth-century version of that subclass of murder trials we *now* call "battered spouse" cases. The farmer's wife was a battered spouse; she killed her husband in an act of self-defense the law would not recognize, but her peers did. The wives in the kitchen acquitted the defendant, presciently, on the basis of a battered spouse defense. Now the mind-boggling irony that Angel's important work on the legal background of this play so effectively reveals is this: these days, when a woman we now call a "battered wife" is accused of the murder of her violent husband, such a defendant will typically try to introduce evidence of her husband's violence against her in the expectation that evidence of such violence might mitigate or fully justify her crime. *Back then,* however, Angel shows, precisely the opposite dynamic was at work: female family members of such an accused would conspire to conceal evidence of discord in the marriage so as to obfuscate the wife's possible motive for the killing, while the prosecutor would seek to introduce such evidence. Thus, in a complete reversal of current litigation strategy in such cases, the *prosecutor* (not the defense) would seek to put in evidence of the husband's violence, or ill temper, or drunkenness, while the *defense* (not the prosecutor) would seek to keep such evidence out. The defense, in fact, would typically seek to depict, sometimes dishonestly and perjuriously, a serene, content, unmessy, blissful domestic or marital life.

What should we make of this incredible irony uncovered by Angel's scholarship? Minimally, we need to modify, considerably, the claim made above regarding the clarity of the early twentieth century's law of self-defense as it pertained to domestic killings. Obviously, if we look at this large legal picture of the "law on the streets" and the "law in the courthouse," so to speak—a violent marriage, a battered wife who kills, a defense that consists of perjured testimony aiming to paint a false depiction of domestic tranquillity, all so as to thwart or corrupt the proceedings—rather than the law on the books, what's clear is that whatever might have been the case with respect to the "law on the books," the "law" on the street and in the courthouse was not clear at all. The law—as enforced by jury verdicts, and as used by defense counsel and their perjurious witnesses—was deeply ambivalent about these women who killed their husbands over trifles; self-defense law as practiced was a mess.

The law's ambivalence, however, went deeper, as Angel's historical reconstruction of the background of Glaspell's play reveals. Clearly, it was not only the law of self-defense as interpreted in the courthouse and on the street that was a mess, and it was not only the law of self-defense that was the object of Glaspell's critical gaze. What must be remembered, when reading Glaspell a hundred years later, is that *for centuries,* the "violent battery" of a wife by her husband was *itself* not regarded, even by the law on the books, as a crime at all. Early twentieth-century law at the time of *Trifles* was in a state of flux, but early nineteenth-century law—on the books and in the courthouse both—defining and regulating battery basically read like this: a violent battery *outside* the home is violence, the occurrence of which the law exists to deter, in well-understood Hobbesian fashion. Violence *in the home,* by contrast—when exerted "reasonably" by a husband upon his wife—was a trifle. It wasn't even called "battery," it was called "chastisement." It was messiness at worst and legitimate discipline at best. The "law," quite explicitly, left it alone.[8] Through the course of the nineteenth century this status quo began to change in piecemeal fashion as various jurisdictions took up various reforms, eventually criminalizing, at least on the books, a man's physical assault and battery of his wife. But reform was slow—no breathtaking *Brown v. Board*-like constitutional pronouncement from a high court, no ennobling act of Congress. By the time of Glaspell's writing, the distinction central to the Hobbesian thesis—the distinction, that is, between the violence between private citizens that the law must deter and the "messes" left by the legitimate discipline by a political superior—a husband—of his political inferior—his wife—in a domestic home—was still "blurred." It was still, though, in many jurisdictions, there. What would be violence outside the home was often something different inside: it was legitimate discipline at best, and a mess at worst.

So look again at the real cases on which the playwright-journalist Glaspell reported: early twentieth-century cases in which a wife killed a possibly violent, possibly abusive husband, this time keeping in mind the problematic law of "chastisement." In such cases, the killing of the husband by the battered, chastised wife would be clearly homicide and clearly criminal. There could be no "abused spouse" defense, at the time Glaspell wrote her play, however, because there could be no clearly "abused spouse." The idea of a "battered wife" was still, for many, pretty much oxymoronic. Wives were not "battered," they were chastised.[9] They were not crime victims when beaten; they were political subjects—of their husbands. They lived, for practical purposes, in a Hobbesian state of nature. When they killed their husband, they could not claim justified self-defense any more than could a slave in the antebellum South who defended himself with lethal force against a violent master. The wife, like the slave, was not a victim of criminal violence, she was the subject of discipline. *By fiat*, her life was a mess. The law could view her as an aggressor worthy of punishment but not as a victim worthy of protection against her husband's abuse.

There is, though, a problem with all of this, an elephant in the room. The audience doesn't know definitively, in Glaspell's play *Trifles*, whether the wife was physically abused or not. The gap is more than a little troubling. It leaves the play's message—if Angel has the message right—a bit of a mess, legalistically speaking. Clearly, if the wife was beaten up by her husband's fists, that violence, at least today, might exculpate—if various conditions were met—or at least mitigate the crime. In contrast, if she was "merely" beaten down by a loveless marriage to a "hard" man, that only metaphorical "violence" surely would not count, dead songbird or no. We're given no direct evidence in the play itself that such violence either did or did not occur. The facts are maddeningly ambiguous. Why might Glaspell have done this, particularly if she was concerned, as a journalist and feminist, with domestic violence?

Angel does not address this—she simply assumes that the farmwife was physically abused. One possible explanation for Glaspell's lack of "clarity" on the point, I suggest, and one that is consistent with Angel's interpretation, is that, as Glaspell well knew, the *law* at the time, at this point of mid-reform, still did not clearly "see" the difference between physical violence in the home and the messiness of political chastisement: the former was the latter. If the law did not "see" it, why should we, the readers? The fictional wives in *Trifles* did indeed blur the distinction between a messy life and violated life, between the strangling of a bird and the strangling of a man, between the physical fear that would justify lethal self-defense and the emotional scarring that would not. But in this, they ironically mirrored the law; they did not pervert it. The law at the time, although in a state of flux, nevertheless continued to erase the difference between the domestic intimacy it should rightly leave alone and violence: the act that leads directly to the very state of selfhood, nasty and brutal and short, that the law is charged to prevent. It called the former tranquillity, and it called the latter chastisement, meaning discipline. The discipline no less than the tranquillity was to be protected, not prevented, by the Hobbesian legal order.

So in *Trifles*, the fictional representation of this toxic brew—the law's denial of the criminality of domestic violence and the corruption of the legal process by those sympathetic to wives who were charged with domestic murders of their chastisers—all of the lines relevant to our modified Hobbesian thesis—were blurred, erased, or reversed: the line between a domestic mess and domestic violence, between discipline and criminality, between justified self-defense and murder, between a trifle and a life-threatening attack. As little more than exclamation point, Glaspell also reversed, or erased, the line separating those who could and could not sit as jurors, implicitly in the play, explicitly in the title—*A Jury of Her Peers*—of the novella based on the play. Glaspell was clearly a committed suffragist and accomplished crime-beat journalist, fully cognizant that in her real world, there was no jury of peers for battered women who killed. Thus the title of the novella. The title of the original play—*Trifles*—however, is the more potent political metaphor. The wife killed her husband over a trifle—a dead songbird—while the law trifled with women's lives by failing to protect them against oftentimes lethal domestic violence. Putting these insights together, we might sum it up this way: the law governing self-defense—the "law," according to which the strangling of a songbird or coldness toward one's wife does not constitute the sort of provocation that might in turn render a homicide-justified self-defense—was indeed unambiguous, but it was unambiguous only by silencing the women whose perspective, if authoritative, might uncover the violent patriarch within domesticity—violence the law regarded as nothing but a trifle. Given a jury of her peers, chastisement is domestic violence; given a jury of her peers, the law that should protect the woman subjected to it is revealed as the law that protects instead our subjugation.

Within that context, given a jury of her peers, a woman's awkward, ugly, dysfunctional stove looks like an instrument of violence; a messy kitchen and sloppy stitching are evidence of a profoundly violated self; and the murder of a songbird is a sufficient provocation for lethal self-defense. Glaspell's *Trifles,* just for a moment, but for a sizable number of early feminists, suffragists, and fellow travelers, swept this entire legal and domestic mess out from under the rug.

Sexual Hassles: A Call for Narrative

Now let me look at a distinctly contemporary legalist confusion: the behaviors now labeled by law as "sexual harassment" at work and the harms caused by those behaviors. The sorts of behaviors we now call sexual harassment are neither clearly "consensual" (and therefore clearly legal—something the law *must* leave alone) nor cleanly "nonconsensual" (and therefore something the law *must* address). Rather the legal definition of sexual harassment is that the sexual advance be *unwanted,* or *unwelcome,* not that it be nonconsensual.[10] To take an example, Paula Jones (assuming the truth of her allegations) did not suffer a *nonconsensual* sexual encounter with Bill Clinton—she quite literally did not have *time* to withhold "consent" before he accosted her in a hotel room, pulled down his pants, and demanded a blow job. Nor did she "consent" in the ordinary use of that term. Yet the encounter, if it occurred as she reported, was obviously harassing (if that's not harassment, what is?). Paula Jones lost her case on a pretrial motion not because what she alleged was not sufficiently egregious to constitute an act of harassment, but because the trial court found she had no evidence that she had suffered any damage.[11] Likewise, women pressured to give sex for job security or advancements do not withhold consent—if they did, and the sex happened over their refusal, the sex would be *rape* and criminal, not just unwanted harassment. Similarly, women who tolerate a hostile, sexualized work environment that interferes with their job performance do so for economic reasons, not because they have been literally forced to do so against their will. The quid pro quo sex-at-work exchanges and the hostile sexualized work environments that are targeted by sex harassment law are unwanted but tolerated; they are offensive and injurious. They are not, however, nonconsensual.

The endurance of all of that unwanted sex at work, according to the logic of sex harassment law, is that not only is such sex harmful, but it is also, if left unregulated, politically subordinating. Thus the idea behind the law is that sufferance of unwanted sex at work is a violation of the equality that is the goal of equal employment law—not just a violation of the personal integrity that is the goal, for example, of tort law, or a breach of the public peace that is the goal of criminal law. By deterring those aggressions and compensating for them when they occur, we equalize the victims with the perpetrators: rather than labor under the thumb of the aggressor in the next cubicle, rather than submit to unwanted sex with a superior for no reason other than survival on the job, rather than tolerate, because one's economic survival requires it, sexual leers, pats on the ass, whispered dehumanizing and humiliating sexualized torments from coworkers, a woman on the job can stand on her rights to be free of all of this. The behavior is harassment, or so the law surmises, and she is legally entitled to a workplace that is rid of it.

But is it really harmful? Over the last half decade, a number of influential feminist and libertarian legal scholars have put forward the argument that what the law now regards as actionable "sexual harassment" is in fact harmless, or even desirable, sexual flirtation, expression, and horseplay—just the sort of messiness that the law quintessentially must leave be.[12] In the view of these critics, the authors of our current sexual harassment law have badly mistaken the merely messy for the violent and violated: the law, in effect, calls what is in fact nothing more than messiness legally actionable violations of personal and physical integrity. Thus behavior that is now roundly denounced not only by the law itself but also by most employers as being hostile, assaultive, aggressive, oppressive, and for all of those reasons clearly illegal (or actionable) sexualized behavior on the job is claimed by the new critics as quintessentially harmless: if harmful, only trivially so, but often not harmful at all, and rather both desirable and desired. What the law calls harassment is actually the soft, emotional, affective, or playful edge to an otherwise harsh, tedious, oppressive work environment. Sexualized banter and play at work are the kind of behavior that humane work policies should protect or even promote. Sexual harassment law, in short, mistakes the messes that manifest freedom, which the law must leave alone, for the acts of private violence the law quintessentially must stop.

Furthermore, our current sexual harassment law, according to its new critics, not only wrongly deters (and wrongly compensates for) relatively harmless flirtation, it also carries not insignificant costs, weighty enough to suggest the need to at least rethink, and perhaps scuttle, the law itself. First, because the law is almost unavoidably overbroad, it chills nonharassing speech at work that ought to enjoy First Amendment protection. Second, employers have used, or misused the law to create a "sanitized workplace," in Professor Vicki Shultz's provocative phrase, stripping workers of their humanizing sexual impulses, leaving in their stead robotic drones, further entrenching the powers of managerial capitalists bent on wringing the last drop of excess labor value from our workday. Third, the law itself constitutes, according to Professor Janet Halley, a bizarre, whether or not intended, form of "sexuality harassment": the very presence of the law is a threat to sexual minorities, particularly gay men and lesbians, whose embattled presence on job sites is now further undermined by the ever-present danger of frivolous lawsuits implicitly or even explicitly theoretically grounded in the utter unacceptability of their sexual being. The law raises the experience of a "homophobic panic attack" to the status of a "cause of action" premised on a violation of one's precious civil rights: a self-loathing homophobic worker experiences a remark, horseplay, or a double entendre from a member of his own gender as in some sense sexual and perhaps enticing, and in a frantic attempt to reassert his own heterosexual identity, labels the remark "harassment," thus signaling, to himself and the world, his unequivocal understanding that it was unwanted—and hence assaultive. He then sues—publicly underscoring his status as victimized heterosexual rather than closeted queer. More generally, sex harassment law might invite the same sexphobic reaction even in cross-sex cases: a woman desperate to deny even her own heterosexual desires tries to ward off all sexual interactions at work, and above all else, to deny her own complicity with them or enjoyment of them, but if unsuccessful, she brings the federal courts to the rescue, labels the sex assaultive, hence unwanted, hence actionable, all the better to reassert her own orderly self as unsullied and pure. "Civil rights," in the eyes of the law's critics, have ironically—if also just a bit comically—become the handmaiden of a foolish and prudish Victorianism.

The specifically legal (and constitutional) questions raised by this newly critical anti–sexual harassment scholarship are complex and beyond the scope of this chapter. The cultural question it raises, however, goes to the heart of the question posed by this chapter: is what we now call "sexual harassment" truly harmful or not? Did the law overshoot the mark? Is "sex-at-work," when neither consensual nor nonconsensual but clearly unwanted, when experienced by the sexual self at work, messy or violent? Is it the sort of harm we rightly demand that law deter, or is it the messy residue of freedom we rightly demand that law leave be? Is the "sexually harassed self" at work a messy self the law must leave alone or a violated self the law must recompense? Is sexual harassment an act of violence, or at least something close to it, or is it just a sloppy mess? Again, if the former, the law must or at least may respond; if the latter, the law should and perhaps must leave it alone.

In a moment, I will suggest a way to rephrase the question this critical scholarship raises, and then suggest an answer to it, but first let me put the debate itself in some historical context. It is well worth noting that this debate—a debate among feminists as well as between feminists and nonfeminists—over the distinction between harmful and oppressive aggression and the playful or only trivially harmful flirtation that may be at its core—is not without precedent. Twenty years ago, a related ambiguity animated the so-called sex wars within feminism, triggered by the attempts of some radical feminists to render the sufferance of pornography compensable through law. So-called antipornography ordinances, written by legal feminists and then proposed to a handful of city councils around the country,[13] eventually generated not only a major judicial pronouncement from the Seventh Circuit Court of Appeals that the ordinances were unconstitutional infringements on free speech[14] but also a robust and critical backlash among feminists.

Common to much of that debate, as well as to the now ongoing debate between the sex harassment law and its defenders and its feminist critics, was the manifest ambiguity regarding the status, content, and meaning as well as the aesthetic and hedonistic valence of the aggressive sexuality, which, whatever else it is, sexual harassment at work often is, and at least some pornography often expresses. If we value, or overvalue, the eroticism that sometimes accompanies violent aggression and its depictions, then we run the serious risk of trivializing, or not seeing *at all*, the violence that is too much a part of our sexual lives. Both the antipornography movement and the campaigns against sexual harassment raise this clearly Hobbesian question—whether we have become so inured to sexualized violence that we don't even know it when we see it. On the other hand, the risk also raised by both is that we have become overvigilant in our aversion to sexual aggression: we might so distrust the erotic that when we see eroticism we tend to see violence and violation everywhere, even where there is none of that. We see violence and danger in sadomasochistic pornography where there is at most only ill-understood erotic pleasure. We see harassment at work where there is only harmless, even if unwanted, flirtation. This confusion is at once both broad and deep and has far-ranging legalist consequences. If we can't distinguish violence from messiness wherever eroticism is present, then all of our law touching on sexual violence and sexual privacy is badly compromised. Indeed it is. Cultural confusion over the erotic has upended not only our sexual negotiations; it has unsettled the perimeters of justified liberal legalism.

So how to proceed when the lines are blurred? To resolve legal ambiguities in the face of cultural confusions, I think, requires us—lawyers—to look and listen closely and without preconception to depictions of selfhood: it requires, in short, a willingness to suspend our legalist confidence and defer to narrative over rule. We now know, more or less, that domestic violence is and feels like the violence that moved Hobbes to urge the creation of a sovereign, and needs to be treated by law as such. We know that, in large part, because of our attentiveness over the past couple of centuries to stories like *Trifles*. We know it more concretely because of our willingness, during the second wave of legal feminism in the 1960s and 1970s, to hear and produce *stories* of such violence, unadorned so to speak, and respond accordingly—meaning legally. As a result we're pretty clear now on the status of violence in domestic life—it's violence, not chastisement; it's criminality, not legitimate sovereignty. We're much less sure of the status of violence in eroticism, and this has spilled over into our understanding and misunderstanding of sexual harassment on the job.

Uncoincidentally, it is *there*—where we are least sure—that the need for narrative—for multiple conflicting recountings of the subjectivity of sex at work—is most strikingly unmet. We don't have, in popular consciousness, a chronicler of the subjective feel of sexually harassed workers' injuries. That lack has real consequences. We don't know, in law or culture, how to even *speak* of these harms. A worker who receives, endures, or is targeted by the sexual joke, or innuendo, or leer, or advance, or touch, and who does not want any of that, is literally "sexualized"—that person becomes "for sex" in the eyes of the harasser rather than "for work." She is being used for sex rather than used for her labor. She is valued, to put it more positively, for her sexuality rather than the quality of her work. But is that really so bad? If it is bad, is it bad enough that it's worth ceding a part of one's humanity—the engagement in fully wanted sexual play—all for the sake of a boring, monotonous job that might yield great productivity to employers and stockholders but promises no intrinsic rewards or feelings of subjective self-worth for workers in any event? Again, is the self, sexualized at work, just a messy self? Or is she a violated one?

There is, in my view, no way to answer these questions definitionally, or analytically, or analogically. Clearly there's no absolute, intrinsic harm in being "sexualized" or "objectified"; we are sexual creatures and we are objects of the sexual desires of others, and there aren't too many of us who complain of those natural facts. The "sexualized self" in bed or elsewhere with a partner she desires is hardly thereby injured even when sexualized. Likewise, surely no one objects, across the board and absolutely and all the time, to being "objectified." Again, when wanted, sexual objectification is a pleasure not an injury. The sexualized, objectified self is not injured by virtue of being sexualized and objectified.

Rather, I believe, the sexualized self at work, sustaining unwanted sexual advances, is "objectified" differently—perhaps so differently that the word choice here is unfortunate. The aspect of selfhood projected at work—the working, productive self, valued for her work, her productivity, and the skill required to produce it—is ignored, and an aspect of selfhood that is not being offered—the sexual—is appropriated. It is in this sense that the sexual self at work becomes an object, taken at will by another. The worker as worker, by virtue of the assault, loses the pleasures and rewards of work, as the citizen of the state of nature vulnerable to unregulated assault loses the pleasures and rewards of civilization. *That too* is injurious, as Hobbes saw, albeit in another context: it is the loss, in effect, of the working self, and the rewards of that self, no less than the chill and fear of assault that we suffer when this peculiar form of aggression goes unchecked by the state.

At least in my experience, my sexually harassed self at work was violated, not messy, and stripped of whatever nonmonetary rewards are to be had from even demeaning work: that fleeting but real sense of competency, productivity, and contribution to the collective adult project of remaking the world for communal cohabitation. No doubt in part because of that experience, I believe that unwanted sex at work is assaultive and usually accompanied by an intent to harm; to my mind, that such assaults are motivated by sexual desire does not make it less so (although as a matter of law it used to). My conclusion: unwanted harassing sex at work is harassment, and both is and ought to be actionable precisely because it carries the whiff, or more, of the violence so pungently captured by Hobbes's famous plea for a pacific order and precludes the pleasures that freedom from fear facilitates. But why should anyone inclined to disagree believe this? To make the case sustainable requires, at this point in our history and at this stage of development of our consciousness of each other's sexual and violated selves, more than the bald, if courageous and paradigm-shifting, assertion that sexual harassment at work is a form of "discrimination," or a violation of equality norms, or an instance of treating one group differently from another on the basis of an impermissible immutable characteristic. Before it will be broadly perceived as any of those, it must first be perceived as *harmful*—sometimes violent, but always violative, rather than messy and free.

Finally, to make the case sustainable that harassment is a harm will ultimately require more than the neat legal categories, syllogistic arguments, and pat analogies from past precedent to present case that so permeate, and even characterize, legal discourse. To resettle the law, when the ground underneath it has moved, requires a messier and more explicitly narrative mode of communication. To understand sexual harassment at work as a violation of self, and a form of violence the law must correct, rather than a mess the law must leave alone, requires recognition of injury where none had been, until the late 1970s or early 1980s, either asserted or heard. That recognition, in turn, will not happen without narrative recounting—and recounting, and recounting. For sexual harassment to be understood as injurious and hence actionable requires the lawmaker—meaning the legislator, the judge, the juror, and the citizen—to both understand and then empathize with the subjective feel not only of the messy self reveling in sexual play at work but also of the violated self hurt by it: the self at work who is threatened by whispered and hidden and secretive sexual violations; invaded by uninvited fingers, hands, swats, and pats; chilled and assaulted by suggestive and hostile banter from coworkers and superiors about pubic hairs on coke cans, foot fetishes, blow jobs, penis size, cunts, and beavers. To understand the seriousness of these injuries, I believe, requires narrative accounts of the myriad ways by which, because of all of that, a worker—any worker—whether well paid or underpaid, challenged by her work or deadened by its monotony, respected or demeaned, can be barred from the pleasures and rewards *otherwise* obtainable from productive work: barred, that is, by violence and the fear of it, from the liberating order otherwise promised by a decent law that respects us all.

Notes

1. Thomas Hobbes, *The Leviathan,* ed. Richard Tuck (Cambridge, UK: Cambridge University Press, 1996 [1651]), p. 89.

2. John Rawls, *Theory of Justice,* rev. ed. (Cambridge, MA: Harvard University Press, 1999 [1971]), p. 211.

3. I am using the term in the sense introduced by Judith Shklar in her classic work *Legalism: Law, Morals, and Political Trials* (Cambridge, MA: Harvard University Press, 1964).

4. The Supreme Court has somewhat notoriously refused to read the Fourteenth Amendment in this way. According to the Court, there is no constitutional right to a police force; the Fourteenth Amendment's guarantee of equal protection of the law guarantees only a degree of rationality in our law, not that the law protects against violence. Under the Court's interpretation, only half of the legalist agreement summarized above is a part of our constitutional pact: while case law and constitutional text support the right of privacy that protects messiness, only political consensus, not constitutional authority, guarantees that the state does indeed have a positive duty to protect against private violence. *DeShaney v. Winnebago County,* 489 U.S. 189 (1989), pp. 201–203.

5. Susan Glaspell, *Trifles,* in "Plays by Susan Glaspell: Trifles, *The Outside, The Verge, Inheritors*" in *British and American Playwrights 1750–1920,* ed. C. W. E. Bigsby (1987). Glaspell later rewrote the play as a novella under the title *A Jury of Her Peers,* which was reprinted in *American Short Stories,* 7th ed. (2001).

6. Marina Angel, "Teaching Susan Glaspell's *A Jury of Her Peers* and *Trifles,*" *Journal of Legal Education* 53 (2003); "Susan Glaspell's *Trifles* and *A Jury of Her Peers:* Woman Abuse in a Literary and Legal Context," *Buffalo Law Review* 45 (1997).

7. Angel, *supra* note 6.

8. For example, *Bradley v. State,* 1 Miss. 156 (1824) held that husbands were "permitted to exercise the right of moderate chastisement, in cases of great emergency, and use salutary restraints in every case of misbehavior, without being subjected to vexatious prosecutions, resulting in the mutual discredit and shame of all parties concerned."

9. For a good review of the legal history of chastisement, see Elizabeth Schneider, "The Law and Violence against Women in the Family at Century's End: The American Experience," in *Cross Currents: Family Law and Policy in the United States and England,* ed. Stanford Katz et al. (2000); Schneider, "Battered Women, Feminist Lawmaking, Privacy, and Equality," in *Women and the United States Constitution: History, Interpretation, and Practice,* ed. Sibyl A. Schwarzenback and Patricia Smith (2003); Deborah Epstein, "Effective Intervention in Domestic Violence Cases: Rethinking the Roles of Prosecutors, Judges, and the Court System," *Yale Law Journal* 11 (1999).

10. For example, *Meritor Savings Bank v. Vinson,* 477 U.S. 57 (1986), p. 68: "The gravaman of any sexual harassment claim is that the sexual advances were 'unwelcome'"; *Canutillo Independent School District v. Leija,* 101 F.3d 393 (5th Cir. 1996), p. 409: the plaintiff must generally "prove that the sexual harassment is unwelcome in order to state an actionable claim"; *Knox v. State of Indiana,* 93 F.3d 1327 (7th Cir. 1996), p. 1336: jury instruction requiring finding that "requests" or "advances" had been "unwelcome" was proper; and West, Sanger, and Larson on sexual harassment in *Directions in Sexual Harassment Law,* ed. Catharine A. MacKinnon and Reva B. Siegal, eds. (2004).

11. Beverly I. Moran, "The Political Is Personal," and Robin West, "Sex, Harm, and Impeachment," in *Aftermath: The Clinton Impeachment and the Presidency in the Age of Political Spectacle,* ed. Leonard V. Kaplan and Beverly I. Moran (2001).

12. Janet E. Halley, "Sexuality Harassment," in *Directions in Sexual Harassment Law,* ed. Catharine A. MacKinnon and Reva B. Siegal (2004); Vicki Schultz, "The Sanitized Workplace," *Yale Law Journal* 112 (2003): 2061; Vicki Schultz, "Reconceptualizing Sexual Harassment," *Yale Law Journal* 107 (1998): 1683.

13. For a legal history of the ordinances, see Paul Brest and Ann Vandenberg, "Politics, Feminism, and the Constitution: The Anti-Pornography Movement in Minneapolis," *Stanford Law Review* 39 (1987): 607. For a discussion of the ambiguities and confusion in the debate generally, see West, "The Feminist-Conservative Anti-Pornography Alliance and the 1986 Attorney General's Commission on Pornography Report," *American B. Found. Res. J.* 4 (1987): 681.

14. *American Booksellers v. Hudnut,* 771 F.2d 323 (7th Cir. 1985).

VI

Creativity and the Messy Self

෨

Corwin Ericson
Unimaginative

But oh! each visitation / Suspends what nature gave me at my birth ...
—Samuel Taylor Coleridge, "Dejection: An Ode"

*I*WAS ONCE ASKED TO SPEAK ON A PANEL called "Keeping the Imagination Alive" at a university event; the other topics included words like "work" and "budget," so I figured I had it easy. Thinking I was on intimate, friendly terms with my imagination, I thought it and I might orate a bit and then field questions from the audience in a collegial fireside manner. However, as I often find with creative collaborations, my partner was hardly up to the task, despite its legendary reputation.

The imagination gets defined as "the formation of a mental image of something that is neither perceived as real nor present to the senses." Furthermore, the *American Heritage Dictionary* tells us that the imagination has the ability to "confront and deal with reality using the creative powers of the mind." The implication is that the imagination is capable of rolling up its sleeves and working off the cuff; that it's there to help, no matter how unusual the situation. I thought I would be a natural, that I'd be just a hammock and a butterfly away from lucidity and insight. I rolled my eyes inward to observe the clever elves as they cobbled together a work of genius but found instead a rat king, a mare's nest, a sketchpad of harebrained doodles, eels escaping through the grass.

I looked at my Coleridge, Emerson, and Stevens books that were to serve as fetishistic goads for the creation of this work. They remained disapprovingly silent. I looked out the window and spied my imagination in the yard, eating grass and exposing itself to the neighbors. I looked on the World Wide Web. There, I found its spoor; a search on "'Corwin Ericson,' imagination" registers one hit, a vestige of a magazine's table of contents. Mostly, though, imagination seems to be dressed up to go to work on the Web. It's most often paired with "solutions," as in "We offer imaginative solutions to your data storage needs with a variety of redundant array packages." I am dubious. Maybe my imagination could hold down a job like this, but more likely, it would get something else to punch the clock for it.

On the Web, imagination is also found frequently to be shacked up with cheap children's arts-and-crafts projects. Toilet paper tubes, Popsicle sticks, Styrofoam balls, poster paint, mucilage. Children are often told to "use your imagination." Adults know this really means "fuck off," but we grown-ups want to phrase this sentiment in helpful, instructive terms. If children are sick, they can use their imaginations in bed, staging Robert Louis Stevensonian battles on knee-summits and blanket-crevasses. Usually though, a child is told to take his imagination outside, where he can find a stick, which he could pretend is a Game Boy or a cell phone or a gun. If a child uses a stick for any of its natural purposes, like whacking, poking, or burning, parents would be remiss if they did not discipline the child by imprisoning him in his room with only his imagination to keep him company.

Boredom and isolation are the real known associates of imagination, not the upright alibis of problem-solving and artistry. I imagine that if I were to be locked away, the first items on my agenda would be to be tortured, raped, and then killed. If, by some lucky chance, I were to be given the opportunity to be my own worst enemy in an isolation cell, then it would be my imagination that would save my bacon. I'd relive the carefree days of my youth spent traipsing the great outdoors, stick in hand, whacking and poking all I wanted. But wait, this is not imagination finally helping me, this is memory; the idylls of my stick-wielding youth are kept in my memory and I am staying sane in my cell by remembering, not imagining. In fact, it was my imagination that put me in this horrid cell in the first place. Before it had its perverted way with me, I was sitting in my comfortable study—my imagination has punished me, abandoned me in an oubliette, even, for just thinking about it.

My imagination, when I look at it coldly, is shiftless, idle, leering, annoying, impolite, poundingly dull, hopelessly vague. It offers me little relief from the lumber of living because it comes up with worse. For instance, my imagination regularly fails to offer me sumptuous dining when I'm eating ramen noodles. It would be nothing to imagine myself eating in some ideal hand-drawn noodle shop of the mind, but no, it's busy distracting me with what I should have said to Zoran Zubic, a hostile technical writing student I failed a decade ago. And I overboil the ramen and have to eat cereal for dinner. And the milk's sour and I can't even manage to imagine that it tastes better, since the sour milk is making me imagine pink hairy cow udders and that squirt-squirt sound and then I'm nauseated.

It likes to entertain itself by making me think I'm clever—I find myself thinking, what if there were animals that one could eat, and they had a hide one could wear or even build tents with, and it produced secretions that one could drink, and its very shit would help one grow food? Oh yeah, cows. Thanks a lot, imagination.

My imagination seems to be at its busiest when it's trying to see through clothing, or convincing me that there is indeed SOMETHING AWFUL OUT THERE. What my imagination needs is a job, frankly. As it loafs around my mental house, it makes a mess of things that need to be kept tidy so I can perform all of those rent-check-generating tasks that it scorns. When it delivers me something pleasant, like erotic stimulation, it's almost always in the form of an inappropriate surprise, and it seems to want congratulations for it. My imagination is the only part of me that has no concern for the preservation of my health or even my life. It seems to believe that it would be better off without me. I suspect I'd be a well-adjusted, better socialized person without my imagination.

Perhaps we have art to save ourselves from our imaginations. It could be that only art drags us away from our petty solipsisms, lends us the impression that there are higher purposes. That could be the job that imagination could work at, keeping itself busy making art to save ourselves from ourselves. But can it be trusted to work without heavy supervision? Is imagination divisible from thinking, sensing, and emoting? Sometimes it seems autonomic; I have to check in with it to see what it's been up to all day while I was at work. Its response is typically a churlish "Nothing." And it's dead right. It spent the workday making mental images of me not working—not images of famous sex partners, not a sculpture I want to make, not even a more comfortable chair, just unhelpfully not working.

The thing is, though, its power lies in contradictions, in associative leaps that ignore reason. Its cooperation seems invisible but its complaints are deafening. I chafe against reality and all the miseries of corporeality, but I find myself grateful for the phenomenal world to save me from my peevish imagination. One goes outside to play, while one's imagination slips back inside to watch TV. One sits down to write a paean to one's imagination, and it responds by throwing one in a dungeon. Whacking and poking with a stick is an entirely satisfying and real experience—why does the stick need to be confronted and dealt with by my imagination? As an adult, I have found even more visceral and fundamentally satisfying ways of whacking and poking with my stick. There is nothing more real than sexuality, nothing that makes us more blatant, no more real a way to connect with another person. Even when alone, one's power of creation is made plainly obvious. With my stick in hand, or elsewhere, I have the ability to experience genuine *unimagined* euphoria, so who invited my imagination? Where did these closets full of chaps and thongs come from? Why is my high-school French teacher here? Why does she have a saddle? Why are we in the shoe department of Kmart? Is that your mother? What I know for certain is painful or humiliating or impossible seems fun, worthy of intense speculation, according to my imagination. Something so simple, so pleasant, so utilitarian that any animal on earth can do it, I and my imagination make complicated, fearful, metaphorical—contradictory. That's how my imagination confronts and deals with reality. That's how art is made; without imagination, we'd just make more babies, more copies of ourselves, thinking we couldn't do any worse.

Oliver Sacks

The Man Who Mistook His Wife for a Hat

D R. P. WAS A MUSICIAN OF DISTINCTION, well known for many years as a singer, and then, at the local school of music, as a teacher. It was here, in relation to his students, that certain strange problems were first observed. Sometimes a student would present himself, and Dr. P. would not recognize him; or, specifically, would not recognize his face. The moment the student spoke, he would be recognized by his voice. Such incidents multiplied, causing embarrassment, perplexity, fear—and, sometimes, comedy. For not only did Dr. P. increasingly fail to see faces, but he saw faces when there were no faces to see; genially, Magoo-like, when in the street, he might pat the heads of water hydrants and parking meters, taking these to be the heads of children; he would amiably address carved knobs on the furniture and be astounded when they did not reply. At first these odd mistakes were laughed off as jokes, not least by Dr. P. himself. Had he not always had a quirky sense of humor and been given to Zen-like paradoxes and jests? His musical powers were as dazzling as ever; he did not feel ill—he had never felt better; and the mistakes were so ludicrous—and so ingenious—that they could hardly be serious or betoken anything serious. The notion of there being "something the matter" did not emerge until some three years later, when diabetes developed. Well aware that diabetes could affect his eyes, Dr. P. consulted an ophthalmologist, who took a careful history and examined his eyes closely. "There's nothing the matter with your eyes," the doctor concluded. "But there is trouble with the visual parts of your brain. You don't need my help, you must see a neurologist." And so, as a result of this referral, Dr. P. came to me.

It was obvious within a few seconds of meeting him that there was no trace of dementia in the ordinary sense. He was a man of great cultivation and charm who talked well and fluently, with imagination and humor. I couldn't think why he had been referred to our clinic.

And yet there was something a bit odd. He faced me as he spoke, was oriented toward me, and yet there was something the matter—it was difficult to formulate. He faced me with his *ears,* I came to think, but not with his eyes. These, instead of looking, gazing, at me, "taking me in," in the normal way, made sudden strange fixations—on my nose, on my right ear, down to my chin, up to my right eye—as if noting (even studying) these individual features, but not seeing my whole face, its changing expressions, "me," as a whole. I am not sure that I fully realized this at the time—there was just a teasing strangeness, some failure in the normal interplay of gaze and expression. He saw me, he scanned me, and yet ...

"What seems to be the matter?" I asked him at length. "Nothing that I know of," he replied with a smile, "but people seem to think there's something wrong with my eyes." "But you don't recognize any visual problems?"

"No, not directly, but I occasionally make mistakes."

I left the room briefly to talk to his wife. When I came back, Dr. P. was sitting placidly by the window, attentive, listening rather than looking out. "Traffic," he said, "street sounds, distant trains—they make a sort of symphony, do they not? You know Honegger's *Pacific 234*?"

What a lovely man, I thought to myself. How can there be anything seriously the matter? Would he permit me to examine him?

"Yes, of course, Dr. Sacks."

I stilled my disquiet, his perhaps, too, in the soothing routine of a neurological exam—muscle strength, coordination, reflexes, tone.... It was while examining his reflexes—a trifle abnormal on the left side—that the first bizarre experience occurred. I had taken off his left shoe and scratched the sole of his foot with a key—a frivolous-seeming but essential test of a reflex—and then, excusing myself to screw my ophthalmoscope together, left him to put on the shoe himself. To my surprise, a minute later, he had not done this.

"Can I help?" I asked.

"Help what? Help whom?"

"Help you put on your shoe."

"Ach," he said, "I had forgotten the shoe," adding, sotto voce, "The shoe? The shoe?" He seemed baffled.

"Your shoe," I repeated. "Perhaps you'd put it on."

He continued to look downward, though not at the shoe, with an intense but misplaced concentration. Finally his gaze settled on his foot: "That is my shoe, yes?"

Did I mis-hear? Did he mis-see?

"My eyes," he explained, and put a hand to his foot. "*This* is my shoe, no?"

"No, it is not. That is your foot. *There* is your shoe."

"Ah! I thought that was my foot."

Was he joking? Was he mad? Was he blind? If this was one of his "strange mistakes," it was the strangest mistake I had ever come across.

I helped him on with his shoe (his foot), to avoid further complication. Dr. P. himself seemed untroubled, indifferent, maybe amused. I resumed my examination. His visual acuity was good: he had no difficulty seeing a pin on the floor, though sometimes he missed it if it was placed to his left.

He saw all right, but what did he see? I opened out a copy of the *National Geographic Magazine* and asked him to describe some pictures in it.

His responses here were very curious. His eyes would dart from one thing to another, picking up tiny features, individual features, as they had done with my face. A striking brightness, a color, a shape would arrest his attention and elicit comment—but in no case did he get the scene as a whole. He failed to see the whole, seeing only details, which he spotted like blips on a radar screen. He never entered into relation with the picture as a whole—never faced, so to speak, its physiognomy. He had no sense whatever of a landscape or scene.

I showed him the cover, an unbroken expanse of Sahara dunes. "What do you see here?" I asked.

"I see a river," he said. "And a little guest house with its terrace on the water. People are dining out on the terrace. I see colored parasols here and there." He was looking, if it was "looking," right off the cover into midair and confabulating nonexistent features, as if the absence of features in the actual picture had driven him to imagine the river and the terrace and the colored parasols.

I must have looked aghast, but he seemed to think he had done rather well. There was a hint of a smile on his face. He also appeared to have decided that the examination was over and started to look around for his hat. He reached out his hand and took hold of his wife's head, tried to lift it off, to put it on. He had apparently mistaken his wife for a hat! His wife looked as if she was used to such things.

I could make no sense of what had occurred in terms of conventional neurology (or neuropsychology). In some ways he seemed perfectly preserved, and in others absolutely, incomprehensibly devastated. How could he, on the one hand, mistake his wife for a hat and, on the other, function, as apparently he still did, as a teacher at the music school?

I had to think, to see him again—and to see him in his own familiar habitat, at home.

A few days later I called on Dr. P. and his wife at home, with the score of the *Dichterliebe* in my briefcase (I knew he liked Schumann), and a variety of odd objects for the testing of perception. Mrs. P. showed me into a lofty apartment, which recalled fin-de-siècle Berlin. A magnificent old Bösendorfer stood in state in the center of the room, and all around it were music stands, instruments, scores.... There were books, there were paintings, but the music was central. Dr. P. came in, a little bowed, and, distracted, advanced with outstretched hand to the grandfather clock, but, hearing my voice, corrected himself, and shook hands with me. We exchanged greetings and chatted a little of current concerts and performances. Diffidently, I asked him if he would sing.

"The *Dichterliebe!*" he exclaimed. "But I can no longer read music. You will play them, yes?"

I said I would try. On that wonderful old piano even my playing sounded right, and Dr. P. was an aged but infinitely mellow Fischer-Dieskau, combining a perfect ear and voice with the most incisive musical intelligence. It was clear that the music school was not keeping him on out of charity.

Dr. P.'s temporal lobes were obviously intact: he had a wonderful musical cortex. What, I wondered, was going on in his parietal and occipital lobes, especially in those areas where visual processing occurred? I carry the Platonic solids in my neurological kit and decided to start with these.

"What is this?" I asked, drawing out the first one.

"A cube, of course."

"Now this?" I asked, brandishing another.

He asked if he might examine it, which he did swiftly and systematically: "A dodecahedron, of course. And don't bother with the others—I'll get the icosahedron, too."

Abstract shapes clearly presented no problems. What about faces? I took out a pack of cards. All of these he identified instantly, including the jacks, queens, kings, and the joker. But these, after all, are stylized designs, and it was impossible to tell whether he saw faces or merely patterns. I decided I would show him a volume of cartoons which I had in my briefcase. Here, again, for the most part, he did well. Churchill's cigar, Schnozzle's nose: as soon as he had picked out a key feature he could identify the face. But cartoons, again, are formal and schematic. It remained to be seen how he would do with real faces, realistically represented.

I turned on the television, keeping the sound off, and found an early Bette Davis film. A love scene was in progress. Dr. P. failed to identify the actress—but this could have been because she had never entered his world. What was more striking was that he failed to identify the expressions on her face or her partner's, though in the course of a single torrid scene these passed from sultry yearning through passion, surprise, disgust, and fury to a melting reconciliation. Dr. P. could make nothing of any of this. He was very unclear as to what was going on, or who was who or even what sex they were. His comments on the scene were positively Martian.

It was just possible that some of his difficulties were associated with the unreality of a celluloid, Hollywood world; and it occurred to me that he might be more successful in identifying faces from his own life. On the walls of the apartment there were photographs of his family, his colleagues, his pupils, himself. I gathered a pile of these together and, with some misgivings, presented them to him. What had been funny, or farcical, in relation to the movie, was tragic in relation to real life. By and large, he recognized nobody: neither his family, nor his colleagues, nor his pupils, nor himself. He recognized a portrait of Einstein because he picked up the characteristic hair and moustache; and the same thing happened with one or two other people. "Ach, Paul!" he said, when shown a portrait of his brother. "That square jaw, those big teeth—I would know Paul anywhere!" But was it Paul he recognized, or one or two of his features, on the basis of which he could make a reasonable guess as to the subject's identity? In the absence of obvious "markers," he was utterly lost. But it was not merely the cognition, the gnosis, at fault; there was something radically wrong with the whole way he proceeded. For he approached these faces—even of those near and dear—as if they were abstract puzzles or tests. He did not relate to them, he did not behold. No face was familiar to him, seen as a "thou," being just identified as a set of features, an "it." Thus, there was formal, but no trace of personal, gnosis. And with this went his indifference, or blindness, to expression. A face, to us, is a person looking out—we see, as it were, the person through his persona, his face. But for Dr. P. there was no persona in this sense—no outward persona, and no person within.

I had stopped at a florist on my way to his apartment and bought myself an extravagant red rose for my buttonhole. Now I removed this and handed it to him. He took it like a botanist or morphologist given a specimen, not like a person given a flower.

"About six inches in length," he commented. "A convoluted red form with a linear green attachment."

"Yes," I said encouragingly, "and what do you think it is, Dr. P.?"

"Not easy to say." He seemed perplexed. "It lacks the simple symmetry of the Platonic solids, although it may have a higher symmetry of its own.... I think this could be an inflorescence or flower."

"Could be?" I queried.

"Could be," he confirmed.

"Smell it," I suggested, and he again looked somewhat puzzled, as if I had asked him to smell a higher symmetry. But he complied courteously, and took it to his nose. Now, suddenly, he came to life.

"Beautiful!" he exclaimed. "An early rose. What a heavenly smell!" He started to hum *"Die Rose, die Lilli."* Reality, it seemed, might be conveyed by smell, not by sight.

I tried one final test. It was still a cold day, in early spring, and I had thrown my coat and gloves on the sofa.

"What is this?" I asked, holding up a glove.

"May I examine it?" he asked, and, taking it from me, he proceeded to examine it as he had examined the geometrical shapes.

"A continuous surface," he announced at last, "infolded on itself. It appears to have"—he hesitated—"five outpouchings, if this is the word."

"Yes," I said cautiously. "You have given me a description. Now tell me what it is."

"A container of some sort?"

"Yes," I said, "and what would it contain?"

"It would contain its contents!" said Dr. P., with a laugh. "There are many possibilities. It could be a change purse, for example, for coins of five sizes. It could ..."

I interrupted the barmy flow. "Does it not look familiar? Do you think it might contain, might fit, a part of your body?" No light of recognition dawned on his face.[1]

No child would have the power to see and speak of "a continuous surface ... infolded on itself," but any child, any infant, would immediately know a glove as a glove, see it as familiar, as going with a hand. Dr. P. didn't. He saw nothing as familiar. Visually, he was lost in a world of lifeless abstractions. Indeed, he did not have a real visual world, as he did not have a real visual self. He could speak about things, but did not see them face-to-face. Hughlings Jackson, discussing patients with aphasia and left-hemisphere lesions, says they have lost "abstract" and "propositional" thought—and compares them with dogs (or, rather, he compares dogs to patients with aphasia). Dr. P., on the other hand, functioned precisely as a machine functions. It wasn't merely that he displayed the same indifference to the visual world as a computer but—even more strikingly—he construed the world as a computer construes it, by means of key features and schematic relationships. The scheme might be identified—in an "identi-kit" way—without the reality being grasped at all.

The testing I had done so far told me nothing about Dr. P.'s inner world. Was it possible that his visual memory and imagination were still intact? I asked him to imagine entering one of our local squares from the north side, to walk through it, in imagination or in memory, and tell me the buildings he might pass as he walked. He listed the buildings on his right side, but none of those on his left. I then asked him to imagine entering the square from the south. Again he mentioned only those buildings that were on the right side, although these were the very buildings he had omitted before. Those he had "seen" internally before were not mentioned now; presumably, they were no longer "seen." It was evident that his difficulties with leftness, his visual field deficits, were as much internal as external, bisecting his visual memory and imagination.

What, at a higher level, of his internal visualization? Thinking of the almost hallucinatory intensity with which Tolstoy visualizes and animates his characters, I questioned Dr. P. about *Anna Karenina*. He could remember incidents without difficulty, had an undiminished grasp of the plot, but completely omitted visual characteristics, visual narrative, and scenes. He remembered the words of the characters but not their faces; and though, when asked, he could quote, with his remarkable and almost verbatim memory, the original visual descriptions, these were, it became apparent, quite empty for him and lacked sensorial, imaginal, or emotional reality. Thus, there was an internal agnosia as well.[2]

But this was only the case, it became clear, with certain sorts of visualization. The visualization of faces and scenes, of visual narrative and drama—this was profoundly impaired, almost absent. But the visualization of schemata was preserved, perhaps enhanced. Thus, when I engaged him in a game of mental chess, he had no difficulty visualizing the chessboard or the moves—indeed, no difficulty in beating me soundly.

Luria said of Zazetsky that he had entirely lost his capacity to play games but that his "vivid imagination" was unimpaired. Zazetsky and Dr. P. lived in worlds which were mirror images of each other. But the saddest difference between them was that Zazetsky, as Luria said, "fought to regain his lost faculties with the indomitable tenacity of the damned," whereas Dr. P. was not fighting, did not know what was lost, did not indeed know that anything was lost. But who was more tragic, or who was more damned—the man who knew it, or the man who did not?

When the examination was over, Mrs. P. called us to the table, where there was coffee and a delicious spread of little cakes. Hungrily, hummingly, Dr. P. started on the cakes. Swiftly, fluently, unthinkingly, melodiously, he pulled the plates toward him and took this and that in a great gurgling stream, an edible song of food, until, suddenly, there came an interruption: a loud, peremptory rat-a-tat-tat at the door. Startled, taken aback, arrested by the interruption, Dr. P. stopped eating and sat frozen, motionless, at the table, with an indifferent, blind bewilderment on his face. He saw, but no longer saw, the table; no longer perceived it as a table laden with cakes. His wife poured him some coffee: the smell titillated his nose and brought him back to reality. The melody of eating resumed.

How does he do anything? I wondered to myself. What happens when he's dressing, goes to the lavatory, has a bath? I followed his wife into the kitchen and asked her how, for instance, he managed to dress himself. "It's just like the eating," she explained. "I put his usual clothes out, in all the usual places, and he dresses without difficulty, singing to himself. He does everything singing to himself. But if he is interrupted and loses the thread, he comes to a complete stop, doesn't know his clothes—or his own body. He sings all the time—eating songs, dressing songs, bathing songs, everything. He can't do anything unless he makes it a song."

While we were talking my attention was caught by the pictures on the walls.

"Yes," Mrs. P. said, "he was a gifted painter as well as a singer. The school exhibited his pictures every year."

I strolled past them curiously—they were in chronological order. All his earlier work was naturalistic and realistic, with vivid mood and atmosphere, but finely detailed and concrete. Then, years later, they became less vivid, less concrete, less realistic and naturalistic, but far more abstract, even geometrical and cubist. Finally, in the last paintings, the canvasses became nonsense, or nonsense to me—mere chaotic lines and blotches of paint. I commented on this to Mrs. P.

"Ach, you doctors, you're such Philistines!" she exclaimed. "Can you not see *artistic development*—how he renounced the realism of his earlier years, and advanced into abstract, nonrepresentational art?"

"No, that's not it," I said to myself (but forbore to say it to poor Mrs. P.). He had indeed moved from realism to nonrepresentation to the abstract, yet this was not the artist but the pathology, advancing—advancing toward a profound visual agnosia in which all powers of representation and imagery, all sense of the concrete, all sense of reality, were being destroyed. This wall of paintings was a tragic pathological exhibit, which belonged to neurology, not art.

And yet, I wondered, was she not partly right? For there is often a struggle, and sometimes, even more interestingly, a collusion between the powers of pathology and creation. Perhaps, in his cubist period, there might have been both artistic and pathological development, colluding to engender an original form; for as he lost the concrete, so he might have gained in the abstract, developing a greater sensitivity to all the structural elements of line, boundary, contour—an almost Picasso-like power to see, and equally depict, those abstract organizations embedded in, and normally lost in, the concrete.... Though in the final pictures, I feared, there was only chaos and agnosia.

We returned to the great music room, with the Bösendorfer in the centre, and Dr. P. humming the last torte.

"Well, Dr. Sacks," he said to me. "You find me an interesting case, I perceive. Can you tell me what you find wrong, make recommendations?"

"I can't tell you what I find wrong," I replied, "but I'll say what I find right. You are a wonderful musician, and music is your life. What I would prescribe, in a case such as yours, is a life which consists entirely of music. Music has been the center, now make it the whole, of your life."

This was four years ago—I never saw him again, but I often wondered about how he apprehended the world, given his strange loss of image, visuality, and the perfect preservation of a great musicality. I think that music, for him, had taken the place of image. He had no body-image, he had body-music: this is why he could move and act as fluently as he did, but came to a total confused stop if the "inner music" stopped. And equally with the outside, the world ...[3]

In *The World as Representation and Will*, Schopenhauer speaks of music as "pure will." How fascinated he would have been by Dr. P., a man who had wholly lost the world as representation, but wholly preserved it as music or will.

And this, mercifully, held to the end—for despite the gradual advance of his disease (a massive tumor or degenerative process in the visual parts of his brain), Dr. P. lived and taught music to the last days of his life.

Notes

1. Later, by accident, he got it on, and exclaimed, "My God, it's a glove!" This was reminiscent of Kurt Goldstein's patient "Lanuti," who could only recognize objects by trying to use them in action.

2. I have often wondered about Helen Keller's visual descriptions: whether these, for all their eloquence, are somehow empty as well? Or whether, by the transference of images from the tactile to the visual, or, yet more extraordinarily, from the verbal and the metaphorical to the sensorial and the visual, she did achieve a power of visual imagery, even though her visual cortex had never been stimulated, directly, by the eyes? But in Dr. P.'s case it is precisely the cortex that was damaged, the organic prerequisite of all pictorial imagery. Interestingly and typically he no longer dreamed pictorially—the "message" of the dream being conveyed in nonvisual terms.

3. Thus, as I learned later from his wife, though he could not recognize his students if they sat still, if they were merely "images," he might suddenly recognize them if they moved. "That's Karl," he would cry. "I know his movements, his body-music."

Donald Morrill

(You . . ., there . . ., listening . . .)

You, there, listening
for the poem to speak a truth
useful for the nights when one, surprised by a diagnosis,
lies planning his funeral through vengeful tears—
forgive it if it speaks of the gold dust of spring
seeding the laces of boots.
Poems are as impolite
as they are perceptive, as beside the point
as the actual. Their gold sticks to unsuspecting hands
tying and untying two ordinary knots
then grasping other hands and objects.
What else can we offer
but our secrets and their failed understanding?
The surprised one lies alone with his vision—forever.
He craves comfort, while the poem strives to imagine him
laboring to realize those knots will outlast him.
A poem's wilderness can make you mad that way.
So that, stuck with it,
you go to him, maybe,
and try to give what no poem can.

About the Contributors

Diane Ackerman is the author of twenty works of poetry and nonfiction, including most recently *An Alchemy of Mind* (prose) and *Origami Bridges: Poems of Psychoanalysis and Fire.*

Faith Adiele's memoir, *Meeting Faith,* won the PEN Beyond Margins Award for Best Biography/Memoir of 2005. Her work has appeared in *O, Essence, Ploughshares, Transition: An International Journal, Ms., Tricycle: The Buddhist Review,* and numerous anthologies. Adiele resides in Pittsburgh, where she is Assistant Professor of English at the University of Pittsburgh. She is finishing a memoir about growing up Nigerian/Nordic/American, which inspired the PBS documentary *My Journey Home.*

Meena Alexander's volumes of poetry include *Illiterate Heart* (winner of a 2002 PEN Open Book Award) and *Raw Silk* (2004). Her memoir, *Fault Lines* (Publishers Weekly Choice, Best Books of 1993), was reissued in 2003 with a chapter called "Lyric in a Time of Violence." She is the editor of the anthology *Indian Love Poems* (2005). She is Distinguished Professor of English at the Graduate Center at Hunter College, City University of New York.

Louise Bogan's volumes of poetry include *Body of This Death* (1923), *Poems and New Poems* (1941), *Collected Poems* (1954), and *The Blue Estuaries: Poems 1923–1968* (1968). Her other works include a literary history, *Achievement in American Poetry, 1900–1950* (1950); and collections of criticism, *Selected Criticism* (1958) and *A Poet's Alphabet* (1970).

Sarah Buss is Associate Professor of Philosophy at the University of Iowa. She is coeditor of *Contours of Agency* and has published numerous articles on autonomy, happiness, moral responsibility, practical rationality, and respect for persons.

Richard Chess has published two books of poetry, *Tekiah* and *Chair in the Desert.* His poems have appeared in several anthologies, including *Telling and Remembering: A Century of American Jewish Poetry* as well as many journals. In 2002, he received the North Carolina Board of Governors Award for Teaching Excellence. He has also been the recipient of the University of North Carolina Association Ruth and Leon Feldman Professor Award in 1999/2000 and the Distinguished Teacher in the Humanities Award in the same year. He directs the Center for Jewish Studies at UNCA and UNCA's Creative Writing Program. He is also on the MFA faculty of the Program for Writers at Warren Wilson College.

Jane F. Crosthwaite is a member of the Mount Holyoke College Religion Department. Although her earliest work was on Emily Dickinson and the interface of religion and literature, her most recent work has focused on a range of Shaker studies. She has published articles and given numerous presentations on Shaker women, theology, and spirit drawings, and is currently completing a book with Christian Goodwillie on the theology and music of the first Shaker hymnal.

Arthur C. Danto is Johnsonian Professor Emeritus of Philosophy at Columbia University and an art critic for *The Nation*. He is the author of numerous books, including *Nietzsche as Philosopher, Mysticism and Morality, The Transfiguration of the Commonplace, Narration and Knowledge, Connections to the World: The Basic Concepts of Philosophy,* and *Encounters and Reflections: Art in the Historical Present,* which won the National Book Critics Circle Prize for Criticism in 1990. *The Madonna of the Future* won the Prix Philosophie in 2004.

Huston Diehl is Professor of English and Collegiate Fellow at the University of Iowa. She has published extensively on Renaissance drama and the religious and visual cultures of early modern England. Her book *Staging Reform, Reforming the Stage: Protestantism and Popular Theater in Early Modern England,* was named an "Outstanding Book" by *Choice* magazine. Her teaching memoir, *Dream Not of Other Worlds: Teaching in a Segregated Elementary School, 1970,* will appear in spring 2007.

Carol Edelstein is a poet, fiction writer, and essayist whose work has appeared in numerous literary magazines and anthologies. Her second book of poems, *The Disappearing Letters,* won the 2005 Perugia Press Award.

Corwin Ericson's essay "Unimaginative" was originally presented as a lecture at the University of Massachusetts at Amherst's MFA in English fortieth anniversary celebration in 2003. It was subsequently published in *Redactions: Poetry and Poetics* 2 (Fall 2003). Ericson is managing editor of the *Massachusetts Review* and an occasional college instructor. His work has been published in *Harper's, Volt, Fence, Conduit,* and elsewhere.

Beth Ann Fennelly is the recipient of a 2003 National Endowment for the Arts Award. Her poems have been anthologized in *The Pushcart Prize 2001, Penguin Book of Sonnets, Poets of the New Century,* and *Best American Poetry* (1996 and 2005). Her first book, *Open House,* won the 2001 *Kenyon Review* prize and the GLCA New Writers Award. Her second book of poetry, *Tender Hooks,* was published in 2004, and a book of nonfiction, *Great with Child,* was published in 2006.

Patricia Foster is the author of *All the Lost Girls* (memoir) and *Just Beneath My Skin* (essays), editor of *Minding the Body* and *Sister to Sister,* and coeditor of *The Healing Circle.* She is Professor in the MFA Program in Nonfiction at the University of Iowa.

Rebecca Goldstein is the author of five novels, including *The Late Summer Passion of a Woman of Mind, The Mind-Body Problem, The Dark Sister, Mazel,* and *Properties of Light* as well as a collection of short stories, *Strange Attractors.* She is also the author of *Incompleteness: The Proof and Paradox of Kurt Gödel* and the forthcoming *Betraying Spinoza: The Renegade Jew Who Gave Us Modernity.* The recipient of numerous prizes for fiction and scholarship, she became a MacArthur Fellow in 1995.

Jane Hirshfield's sixth poetry collection, *After,* appeared in 2006. Previous books include *Given Sugar, Given Salt* (a National Book Critics Circle finalist); a collection of essays, *Nine Gates: Entering the Mind of Poetry* (1997); and three books collecting the work of women poets from the past. Her awards include fellowships from the Guggenheim and Rockefeller Foundations, the Academy of American Poets, and the National Endowment for the Arts, and her work appears in *The New Yorker, Atlantic, Best American Poetry,* and many literary publications.

Mary Kinzie is the author of *Drift* (poems) and *A Poet's Guide to Poetry.* "Facing North" is part of a verse meditation to be called *The Poems I Am Not Writing.* She is the literary executor of the American poet Louise Bogan.

Donald Morrill is the author of three books of nonfiction, *The Untouched Minutes* (winner of the River Teeth Literary Nonfiction Award), *Sounding for Cool,* and *A Stranger's Neighborhood,* as well as two volumes of poetry, *At the Bottom of the Sky* and *With Your Back to the Half the Day.* Currently he is Visiting Professor in the Nonfiction Writing Program at the University of Iowa and poetry editor of the *Tampa Review.*

Martha C. Nussbaum is Ernst Freund Distinguished Service Professor of Law and Ethics at the University of Chicago, appointed in the Philosophy Department, Law School, and Divinity School. Her most recent books are *Hiding from Humanity: Disgust, Shame, and the Law* (2004) and *Frontiers of Justice: Disability, Nationality, Species Membership* (2006).

John O'Donohue is an Irish poet and philosopher who lives in the solitude of a cottage in the West of Ireland and speaks Gaelic as his native language. He has degrees in philosophy and English literature and was awarded a doctoral degree in philosophical theology from the University of Tübingen in 1990. His books include *Anam Cara, Eternal Echoes, and Beauty.*

Gayle Pemberton is the author of *The Hottest Water in Chicago: Notes of a Native Daughter* and *The Road to Gravure: Black Women and American Cinema.* She is the author of a number of creative nonfiction essays on American culture and African American life. She is Professor of English, African American Studies, and American Studies at Wesleyan University.

Liv Pertzoff writes short fiction and essays. She lives in Williamsburg, Massachusetts.

Steven Pinker is Johnstone Professor of Psychology at Harvard University and author of *The Language Instinct, How the Mind Works, Words and Rules,* and *The Blank Slate.*

Oliver Sacks is Clinical Professor of Neurology at the Albert Einstein College of Medicine, Adjunct Professor of Neurology at the NYU School of Medicine, and consultant neurologist to the Little Sisters of the Poor. His writings include *Awakenings, An Anthropologist from Mars, The Island of the Colorblind, A Leg to Stand On, The Man Who Mistook His Wife for a Hat,* and *Seeing Voices.*

Debra Spark is the author of the novels *Coconuts for the Saint* and *The Ghost of Bridgetown* and editor of the anthology *Twenty under Thirty: Best Stories by America's New Young Writers.* Her most recent book is *Curious Attractions: Essays on Fiction Writing.*

Ilan Stavans is Lewis-Sebring Professor of Latin American and Latino Culture and Five College–Fortieth Anniversary Professor at Amherst College. His most recent books are *Dictionary Days* and *Lengua Fresca.* The story in this book is included in *The Disappearance: A Novella and Stories.* A feature movie based on the novella was released in 2006.

Wendy Wasserstein, who died in January 2006, Pulitzer Prize–winning playwright, was the author of *The Heidi Chronicles, The Sisters Rosensweig, Bachelor Girls, An American Daughter, Seven One-Act Plays, Uncommon Women and Others,* and *Shiksa Goddess.*

Robin West is Professor of Law at Georgetown University Law Center. She teaches and writes in the fields of constitutional law and theory, jurisprudence, law and humanities, and feminist and gender studies. Her latest books are *Re-Imagining Justice* (2003), and *Gender, Sexuality, and Marriage* (2007).

C. K. Williams is the author of nine books of poetry, the most recent of which, *The Singing,* won the National Book Award for 2003. His book of essays, *Poetry and Consciousness,* appeared in 1998, and a memoir, *Misgivings,* in 2000. His book *Repair* was awarded the 2000 Pulitzer Prize, and his collection *Flesh and Blood* received the National Book Critics Circle Award. He has published translations of Sophocles' *Women of Trachis,* Euripides' *Bacchae,* and poems of Francis Ponge, among others. His *Collected Poems* appeared in 2006. He teaches in the Writing Program at Princeton University.

About the Editor

Jennifer Rosner holds a doctoral degree in philosophy from Stanford University. She is author of several articles on the nature of the self and human agency. Currently, she is writing a memoir about deafness in her family, which she traces back to the 1800s.